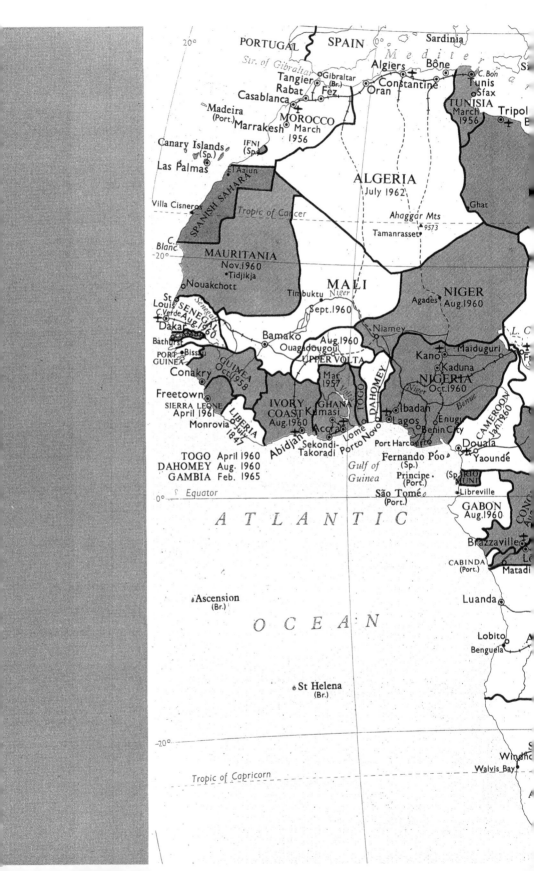

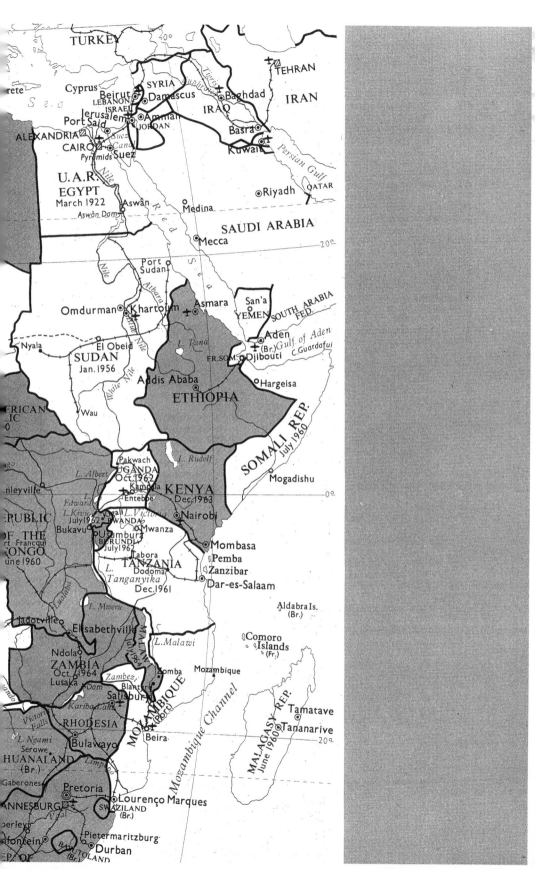

NEO-COLONIALISM
The Last Stage of Imperialism

By the same Author

Africa Must Unite
Axioms of Kwame Nkrumah
Class Struggle in Africa
Consciencism
Dark Days in Ghana
Ghana (Autobiography)
Handbook of Revolutionary Warfare
I Speak of Freedom
Neo-Colonialism
*Revolutionary Path**
*Rhodesia File**
*The Struggle Continues**
Voice from Conakry
What I Mean by Positive Action

Pamphlets

The Big Lie
Ghana; The Way Out
The Spectre of Black Power
Two Myths: *The Myth of the "Third World"*
            "African Socialism" Revisited
What I Mean by Positive Action

* Published Posthumously

NEO-COLONIALISM
The Last Stage of Imperialism

KWAME NKRUMAH

PANAF
London

NEO-COLONIALISM

ISBN   0 901787 23 X

Panaf Books
75 Weston Street
London SE1 3RS

*This book is dedicated to
the Freedom Fighters of Africa
living and dead*

'The enormous dimensions of finance-capital concentrated in a few hands and creating an extremely extensive network of close ties and relationships which involves not only the small and medium capitalists, but also even the very small; this, on the one hand, and on the other the bitter struggle against other national State groups of financiers for the partition of the world and the right to rule over other countries—these two factors taken together cause the complete conversion of all the possessing classes to the side of imperialism. The signs of the times are a "general" enthusiasm regarding its prospects, a passionate defence of imperialism, and every possible camouflage of its real nature.'—LENIN, *Imperialism.*

Contents

Introduction

THE neo-colonialism of today represents imperialism in its final and perhaps its most dangerous stage. In the past it was possible to convert a country upon which a neo-colonial regime had been imposed—Egypt in the nineteenth century is an example —into a colonial territory. Today this process is no longer feasible. Old-fashioned colonialism is by no means entirely abolished. It still constitutes an African problem, but it is everywhere on the retreat. Once a territory has become nominally independent it is no longer possible, as it was in the last century, to reverse the process. Existing colonies may linger on, but no new colonies will be created. In place of colonialism as the main instrument of imperialism we have today neo-colonialism.

The essence of neo-colonialism is that the State which is subject to it is, in theory, independent and has all the outward trappings of international sovereignty. In reality its economic system and thus its political policy is directed from outside.

The methods and form of this direction can take various shapes. For example, in an extreme case the troops of the imperial power may garrison the territory of the neo-colonial State and control the government of it. More often, however, neo-colonialist control is exercised through economic or monetary means. The neo-colonial State may be obliged to take the manufactured products of the imperialist power to the exclusion of competing products from elsewhere. Control over government policy in the neo-colonial State may be secured by payments towards the cost of running the State, by the provision of civil servants in positions where they can dictate policy, and by monetary control over foreign exchange through the imposition of a banking system controlled by the imperial power.

Where neo-colonialism exists the power exercising control is often the State which formerly ruled the territory in question, but this is not necessarily so. For example, in the case of South Vietnam the former imperial power was France, but neo-colonial control of the State has now gone to the United States. It is possible that neo-colonial control may be exercised by a consortium of financial interests which are not specifically identifiable with any particular State. The control of the Congo by great international financial concerns is a case in point.

The result of neo-colonialism is that foreign capital is used for the exploitation rather than for the development of the less developed parts of the world. Investment under neo-colonialism increases rather than decreases the gap between the rich and the poor countries of the world.

The struggle against neo-colonialism is not aimed at excluding the capital of the developed world from operating in less developed countries. It is aimed at preventing the financial power of the developed countries being used in such a way as to impoverish the less developed.

Non-alignment, as practised by Ghana and many other countries, is based on co-operation with all States whether they be capitalist, socialist or have a mixed economy. Such a policy, therefore, involves foreign investment from capitalist countries, but it must be invested in accordance with a national plan drawn up by the government of the non-aligned State with its own interests in mind. The issue is not what return the foreign investor receives on his investments. He may, in fact, do better for himself if he invests in a non-aligned country than if he invests in a neo-colonial one. The question is one of power. A State in the grip of neo-colonialism is not master of its own destiny. It is this factor which makes neo-colonialism such a serious threat to world peace. The growth of nuclear weapons has made out of date the old-fashioned balance of power which rested upon the ultimate sanction of a major war. Certainty of mutual mass destruction effectively prevents either of the great power blocs from threatening the other with the possibility of a world-wide war, and military conflict has thus become confined to 'limited wars'. For these neo-colonialism is the breeding ground.

Such wars can, of course, take place in countries which are not neo-colonialist controlled. Indeed their object may be to establish in a small but independent country a neo-colonialist regime. The evil of neo-colonialism is that it prevents the formation of those large units which would make impossible 'limited war'. To give one example: if Africa was united, no major power bloc would attempt to subdue it by limited war because from the very nature of limited war, what can be achieved by it is itself limited. It is only where small States exist that it is possible, by landing a few thousand marines or by financing a mercenary force, to secure a decisive result.

The restriction of military action of 'limited wars' is, however, no guarantee of world peace and is likely to be the factor which will ultimately involve the great power blocs in a world war, however much both are determined to avoid it.

Limited war, once embarked upon, achieves a momentum of its own. Of this, the war in South Vietnam is only one example. It escalates despite the desire of the great power blocs to keep it limited. While this particular war may be prevented from leading to a world conflict, the multiplication of similar limited wars can only have one end—world war and the terrible consequences of nuclear conflict.

Neo-colonialism is also the worst form of imperialism. For those who practise it, it means power without responsibility and for those who suffer from it, it means exploitation without redress. In the days of old-fashioned colonialism, the imperial power had at least to explain and justify at home the actions it was taking abroad. In the colony those who served the ruling imperial power could at least look to its protection against any violent move by their opponents. With neo-colonialism neither is the case.

Above all, neo-colonialism, like colonialism before it, postpones the facing of the social issues which will have to be faced by the fully developed sector of the world before the danger of world war can be eliminated or the problem of world poverty resolved.

Neo-colonialism, like colonialism, is an attempt to export the social conflicts of the capitalist countries. The temporary success of this policy can be seen in the ever widening gap between the richer and the poorer nations of the world. But the internal contradictions and conflicts of neo-colonialism make it certain that it cannot endure as a permanent world policy. How it should be brought to an end is a problem that should be studied, above all, by the developed nations of the world, because it is they who will feel the full impact of the ultimate failure. The longer it continues the more certain it is that its inevitable collapse will destroy the social system of which they have made it a foundation.

The reason for its development in the post-war period can be briefly summarised. The problem which faced the wealthy nations of the world at the end of the second world war was the impossibility of returning to the pre-war situation in which there was a great gulf between the few rich and the many poor. Irrespective of what particular political party was in power, the internal pressures in the rich countries of the world were such that no post-war capitalist country could survive unless it became a 'Welfare State'. There might be differences in degree in the extent of the social benefits given to the industrial and agricultural workers, but what was everywhere impossible was a return to the mass unemployment and to the low level of living of the pre-war years.

From the end of the nineteenth century onwards, colonies had been regarded as a source of wealth which could be used to mitigate the class conflicts in the capitalist States and, as will be explained later, this policy had some success. But it failed in its ultimate object because the pre-war capitalist States were so organised internally that the bulk of the profit made from colonial possessions found its way into the pockets of the capitalist class and not into those of the workers. Far from achieving the object intended, the working-class parties at times tended to identify their interests with those of the colonial peoples and the imperialist powers found themselves engaged upon a conflict on two fronts, at home with their own workers and abroad against the growing forces of colonial liberation.

The post-war period inaugurated a very different colonial policy. A deliberate attempt was made to divert colonial earnings from the wealthy class and use them instead generally to finance the 'Welfare State'. As will be seen from the examples given later, this was the method consciously adopted even by those working-class leaders who had before the war regarded the colonial peoples as their natural allies against their capitalist enemies at home.

At first it was presumed that this object could be achieved by maintaining the pre-war colonial system. Experience soon proved that attempts to do so would be disastrous and would only provoke colonial wars, thus dissipating the anticipated gains from the continuance of the colonial regime. Britain, in particular, realised this at an early stage and the correctness of the British judgement at the time has subsequently been demonstrated by the defeat of French colonialism in the Far East and Algeria and the failure of the Dutch to retain any of their former colonial empire.

The system of neo-colonialism was therefore instituted and in the short run it has served the developed powers admirably. It is in the long run that its consequences are likely to be catastrophic for them.

Neo-colonialism is based upon the principle of breaking up former large united colonial territories into a number of small non-viable States which are incapable of independent development and must rely upon the former imperial power for defence and even internal security. Their economic and financial systems are linked, as in colonial days, with those of the former colonial ruler.

At first sight the scheme would appear to have many advantages for the developed countries of the world. All the profits of neo-colonialism can be secured if, in any given area, a reasonable proportion of the States have a neo-colonialist system. It is not necessary that they *all* should have one. Unless small States can combine they must be compelled to sell their primary products at prices dictated by the developed nations and buy their manufactured goods at the prices fixed by them. So long as neo-colonialism can prevent political and economic conditions for optimum development, the developing countries, whether they are under neo-colonialist control or not, will be unable to create a large enough market to support industrialisation. In the same way they will lack the financial strength to force the developed countries to accept their primary products at a fair price.

In the neo-colonialist territories, since the former colonial power has in theory relinquished political control, if the social conditions occasioned by neo-colonialism cause a revolt the local neo-colonialist government can be sacrificed and another equally subservient one substituted in its place. On the other hand, in any continent where neo-colonialism exists on a wide scale the same social pressures which can produce revolts in neo-colonial territories will also affect those States which have refused to accept the system and therefore neo-colonialist nations have a ready-made weapon with which they can threaten their opponents if they appear successfully to be challenging the system.

These advantages, which seem at first sight so obvious, are, however, on examination, illusory because they fail to take into consideration the facts of the world today.

The introduction of neo-colonialism increases the rivalry between the great powers which was provoked by the old-style colonialism. However little real power the government of a neo-colonialist State may possess, it must have, from the very fact of its nominal independence, a certain area of manoeuvre. It may not be able to exist without a neo-colonialist master but it may still have the ability to change masters.

The ideal neo-colonialist State would be one which was wholly subservient to neo-colonialist interests but the existence of the socialist nations makes it impossible to enforce the full rigour of the neo-colonialist system. The existence of an alternative system is itself a challenge to the neo-colonialist regime. Warnings about 'the dangers of Communist subversion' are likely to be two-edged since they bring to the notice of those living under a neo-colonialist system the possibility of a change of regime. In fact neo-colonialism is the victim of its own contradictions. In order to make it attractive to those upon whom it is practised it must be shown as capable of raising their living standards, but the economic object of neo-colonialism is to keep those standards depressed in the interest of the developed countries. It is only when this contradiction is understood that the failure of innumerable 'aid' programmes, many of them well intentioned, can be explained.

In the first place, the rulers of neo-colonial States derive their authority to govern, not from the will of the people, but from the support which they obtain from their neo-colonialist masters. They have therefore little interest in developing education, strengthening the bargaining power of their workers employed by expatriate firms, or indeed of taking any step which would challenge the colonial pattern of commerce and industry, which it is the object of neo-colonialism to preserve. 'Aid', therefore, to a neo-colonial State is merely a revolving credit, paid by the neo-colonial master, passing through the neo-colonial State and returning to the neo-colonial master in the form of increased profits.

Secondly, it is in the field of 'aid' that the rivalry of individual developed States first manifests itself. So long as neo-colonialism persists so long will spheres of interest persist, and this makes multilateral aid—which is in fact the only effective form of aid—impossible.

Once multilateral aid begins the neo-colonialist masters are faced by the hostility of the vested interests in their own country. Their manufacturers naturally object to any attempt to raise the price of the raw materials which they obtain from the neo-colonialist territory in question, or to the establishment there of manufacturing industries which might compete directly or indirectly with their own exports to the territory. Even education is suspect as likely to produce a student movement and it is, of course, true that in many less developed countries the students have been in the vanguard of the fight against neo-colonialism.

In the end the situation arises that the only type of aid which the neo-colonialist masters consider as safe is 'military aid'.

Once a neo-colonialist territory is brought to such a state of economic chaos and misery that revolt actually breaks out then, and only then, is there no limit to the generosity of the neo-colonial overlord, provided, of course, that the funds supplied are utilised exclusively for military purposes.

Military aid in fact marks the last stage of neo-colonialism and its effect is self-destructive. Sooner or later the weapons supplied pass into the hands of the opponents of the neo-colonialist regime and the war itself increases the social misery which originally provoked it.

Neo-colonialism is a mill-stone around the necks of the developed countries which practise it. Unless they can rid themselves of it, it will drown them. Previously the developed powers could escape from the contradictions of neo-colonialism by substituting for it direct colonialism. Such a solution is no longer possible and the reasons for it have been well explained by Mr Owen Lattimore, the United States Far Eastern expert and adviser to Chiang Kai-shek in the immediate post-war period. He wrote:

'Asia, which was so easily and swiftly subjugated by conquerors in the eighteenth and nineteenth centuries, displayed an amazing ability stubbornly to resist modern armies equipped with aeroplanes, tanks, motor vehicles and mobile artillery.

Formerly big territories were conquered in Asia with small forces. Income, first of all from plunder, then from direct taxes and lastly from trade, capital investments and long-term exploitation, covered with incredible speed the expenditure for military operations. This arithmetic represented a great temptation to strong countries. Now they have run up against another arithmetic, and it discourages them.'

The same arithmetic is likely to apply throughout the less developed world.

This book is therefore an attempt to examine neo-colonialism not only in its African context and its relation to African unity, but in world perspective. Neo-colonialism is by no means exclusively an African question. Long before it was practised on any large scale in Africa it was an established system in other parts of the world. Nowhere has it proved successful, either in raising living standards or in ultimately benefiting the countries which have indulged in it.

Marx predicted that the growing gap between the wealth of the possessing classes and the workers it employs would ultimately produce a conflict fatal to capitalism in each individual capitalist State.

This conflict between the rich and the poor has now been transferred on to the international scene, but for proof of what is acknowledged to be happening it is no longer necessary to consult the classical Marxist writers. The situation is set out with the utmost clarity in the leading organs of capitalist opinion. Take for example the following extracts from *The Wall Street Journal*, the newspaper which perhaps best reflects United States capitalist thinking.

In its issue of 12 May 1965, under the headline of 'Poor Nations' Plight', the paper first analyses 'which countries are considered industrial and which backward'. There is, it explains, 'no rigid method of classification'. Nevertheless, it points out:

> 'A generally used breakdown, however, has recently been maintained by the International Monetary Fund because, in the words of an IMF official, "the economic demarcation in the world is getting increasingly apparent." The breakdown, the official says, "is based on simple common sense."
>
> In the IMF's view, the industrial countries are the United States, the United Kingdom, most West European nations, Canada and Japan. A special category called "other developed areas" includes such other European lands as Finland, Greece and Ireland, plus Australia, New Zealand and South Africa. The IMF's "less developed" category

embraces all of Latin America and nearly all of the Middle East, non-Communist Asia and Africa.'

In other words the 'backward' countries are those situated in the neo-colonial areas.

After quoting figures to support its argument, *The Wall Street Journal* comments on this situation:

'The industrial nations have added nearly $2 billion to their reserves, which now approximate $52 billion. At the same time, the reserves of the less-developed group not only have stopped rising, but have declined some $200 million. To analysts such as Britain's Miss Ward, the significance of such statistics is clear: the economic gap is rapidly widening "between a white, complacent, highly bourgeois, very wealthy, very small North Atlantic élite and everybody else, and this is not a very comfortable heritage to leave to one's children."

"Everybody else" includes approximately two-thirds of the population of the earth, spread through about 100 nations.'

This is no new problem. In the opening paragraph of his book, *The War on World Poverty*, written in 1953, the present British Labour leader, Mr Harold Wilson, summarised the major problem of the world as he then saw it:

'For the vast majority of mankind the most urgent problem is not war, or Communism, or the cost of living, or taxation. It is hunger. Over 1,500,000,000 people, something like two-thirds of the world's population, are living in conditions of acute hunger, defined in terms of identifiable nutritional disease. This hunger is at the same time the effect and the cause of the poverty, squalor and misery in which they live.'

Its consequences are likewise understood. The correspondent of *The Wall Street Journal*, previously quoted, underlines them:

'. . . many diplomats and economists view the implications as overwhelmingly—and dangerously—political. Unless the present decline can be reversed, these analysts fear, the United States and other wealthy industrial powers of the West face the distinct possibility, in the words of British economist Barbara Ward, "of a sort of international class war".'

What is lacking are any positive proposals for dealing with the situation. All that *The Wall Street Journal's* correspondent can do is to point out that the traditional methods recommended for curing the evils are only likely to make the situation worse.

It has been argued that the developed nations should effectively assist the poorer parts of the world, and that the whole world should be turned into a Welfare State. However, there seems little prospect that anything of this sort could be achieved. The so-called 'aid' programmes to help backward economies represent, according to a rough U.N. estimate, only one half of one per cent of the total income of industrial countries. But when it comes to the prospect of increasing such aid the mood is one of pessimism:

'A large school of thought holds that expanded share-the-wealth schemes are idealistic and impractical. This school contends climate, undeveloped human skills, lack of natural resources and other factors—not just lack of money—retard economic progress in many of these lands, and that the countries lack personnel with the training or will to use vastly expanded aid effectively. Share-the-wealth schemes, according to this view, would be like pouring money down a bottomless well, weakening the donor nations without effectively curing the ills of the recipients.'

The absurdity of this argument is demonstrated by the fact that every one of the reasons quoted to prove why the less developed parts of the world cannot be developed applied equally strongly to the present developed countries in the period prior to their development. The argument is only true in this sense. The less developed world will not become developed through the goodwill or generosity of the developed powers. It can only become developed through a struggle against the external forces which have a vested interest in keeping it undeveloped.

Of these forces, neo-colonialism is, at this stage of history, the principal.

I propose to analyse neo-colonialism, first, by examining the state of the African continent and showing how neo-colonialism at the moment keeps it artificially poor. Next, I propose to show how in practice African Unity, which in itself can only be established by the defeat of neo-colonialism, could immensely raise African living standards. From this beginning, I propose to examine neo-colonialism generally, first historically and then by a consideration of the great international monopolies whose continued stranglehold on the neo-colonial sectors of the world ensures the continuation of the system.

1. Africa's resources

AFRICA is a paradox which illustrates and highlights neo-colonialism. Her earth is rich, yet the products that come from above and below her soil continue to enrich, not Africans predominantly, but groups and individuals who operate to Africa's impoverishment. With a roughly estimated population of 280 million, about eight per cent of the world's population, Africa accounts for only two per cent of the world's total production. Yet even the present very inadequate surveys of Africa's natural resources show the continent to have immense, untapped wealth. We know that iron reserves are put at twice the size of America's, and two-thirds those of the Soviet Union's, on the basis of an estimated two billion metric tons. Africa's calculated coal reserves are considered to be enough to last for three hundred years. New petroleum fields are being discovered and brought into production all over the continent. Yet production of primary ores and minerals, considerable as it appears, has touched only the fringes.

Africa has more than 40 per cent of the world's potential water power, a greater share than any other continent. Yet less than five per cent of this volume has been utilised. Even taking into account the vast desert stretches of the Sahara, there is still in Africa more arable and pasture land than exists in either the United States of America or the Soviet Union. There is even more than in Asia. Our forest areas are twice as great as those of the United States.

1

If Africa's multiple resources were used in her own development, they could place her among the modernised continents of the world. But her resources have been, and still are being used for the greater development of overseas interests. Africa provided to Britain in 1957 the following proportions of basic materials used in her industries:

tin ore and concentrates	19%
iron ore	29%
manganese	80%
copper	46%
bauxite	47%
chrome ore	50%
asbestos	66%
cobalt	82%
antimony	91%

French imports from Africa include:

cotton	32%
iron ore	36%
zinc ore	51%
lead	85%
phosphates	100%

To Germany, Africa provided:

copper imports	8%
iron ore	10%
lead ore	12%
manganese ore	20%
chrome ore	22%
phosphorites	71%

Yet in none of the new African countries is there a single integrated industry based upon any one of these resources.

Although possessing fifty-three of the world's most important basic industrial minerals and metals, the African continent tails far behind all others in industrial development. Gauged

2

on the production of primary products output in the total economic activity, by comparison with the country of most advanced production, the United States of America, the facts can be seen at a glance.

Country	Year	Agriculture Forestry Fishing	Mining	Industry and Manufacture	Construction	Transport and Communications	Commerce	Public Administration and Defence	Others
Algeria	1958	21	3	11	6	6	19	22	12
Congo (L.)	1958	26	16	12	6	9	7	14	16
Kenya	1958	42	1	10	4	9	13	10	11
Morocco	1958	34	6	18	4	*	15	10	13
Nigeria	1956	63	1	2	11	1	4	6	3
Rhodesia and Nyasaland	1958	20	14	11	8	9	10	4	24
Tanganyika	1958	59	4	7	6	7	5	7	5
Republic of S. Africa	1958	12	13	2	5	8	12	10	20
U.S.A.	1959	4	1	30	5	8	17	13	22

From the *United Nations Statistical Year Book*, 1960 (figures are percentages).

It will be noted that in America agriculture, forestry and fishing provide a mere four per cent of the total national activity, and mining a trifling one per cent. On the other hand, industry, manufacture and commerce provide 47 per cent. In the African countries included in the table, which are, with the

* Included under 'Others'.

3

exception of Nigeria, those with the highest settler communities and therefore the most exploited, agriculture is predominant. Industry, manufacture and commerce lag far behind. Even in the case of South Africa, the most highly industrialised sector of the African continent, the contribution of agriculture (12 per cent) and mining (13 per cent) are equal to those of industry, manufacture and construction put together.

However, on the whole, mining has proved a most profitable venture for foreign capital investment in Africa. Its benefits for Africans have by no means been on an equal scale. Mining production in a number of African countries has a value of less than $2 per head of population. As *Europe (France) Outremer* puts it, 'It is quite certain that a mining production of $1 or $2 per inhabitant cannot appreciably affect a country's standard of living.' Affirming correctly that 'in the zones of exploitation, the mining industry introduces a higher standard of living', the journal is forced to the conclusion that mining exploitations are, however, relatively privileged isolated islands in a very poor total economy.

The reason for this is seen in the absence of industry and manufacture, owing to the fact that mining production is destined principally for exportation, mainly in primary form. It goes to feed the industries and factories of Europe and America, to the impoverishment of the countries of origin.

It is also remarked by *Europe (France) Outremer* that about 50 per cent of Africa's mining production remains in the country of origin as wages. Even the most cursory glance at the annual accounts of the mining companies refutes this claim. The excess of revenue over expenditure in many cases proves conclusively by its size that wages received by manual labour form by no means such an exaggerated proportion of value produced as 50 per cent. The considerable sums which go in highly paid salaries to European staffs in the skilled and administrative categories, part of which is returned to their own countries, must in many instances amount to the total received by African labour, to say nothing of the large amounts which swell the yearly incomes of wealthy directors who reside in the metropolitan cities of the west.

4

The assumption also ignores another important fact, namely that wages of manual workers, low as they are, are partly spent on goods manufactured abroad and imported, taking out of the primary producing countries a good part of the workers' wages. In many cases, the imported goods are the products of the companies associated with the mining groups. Frequently, they are sold in the companies' own stores on the mining compounds or by their appointed agents, the workers having to pay prices fixed by the companies.

The poverty of the people of Africa is demonstrated by the simple fact that their income *per capita* is among the lowest in the world.

Income per capita *U.S.* $, 1960–63

Under $80	$81–125	$126–200	$200–250	Over $400
Basutoland	Angola	Liberia	Algeria	South
Bechuanaland	Cameroun	Libya	Cote	Africa
Burundi	Republic	Morocco	d'Ivoire	
Chad	Congo (L.)	Swaziland	Gabon	
Congo (B.)	Gambia	Tunisia	Ghana	
Dahomey	Guinea		Mauritius	
Ethiopia	Kenya		Senegal	
Guinea de Sao	Malagasy		South-west	
Malawi	Republic		Africa	
Mali	Mauritania		Zambia	
Mozambique	Sierra Leone		Rhodesia	
Niger	Sudan		(Zimbabwe)	
Nigeria	Togo			
Rwanda	United Arab			
Somalia	Republic			
Tanganyika-				
Zanzibar				
Uganda				
Voltaic				
Republic				

In some countries, for example Gabon and Zambia, up to half the domestic product is paid to resident expatriates and to overseas firms who own the plantations and mines. In Guinea de Sao, Angola, Libya, Swaziland, South-West Africa and Zimbabwe (Rhodesia), foreign firm profits and settler or expatriate incomes exceed one-third of the domestic product. Algeria, Congo and Kenya were in this group before independence.

On achieving independence, almost every new state of Africa has developed plans for industrialisation and rounded economic growth in order to improve productive capacity and thereby raise the standard of living of its people. But while Africa remains divided progress is bound to be painfully slow. Economic development is dependent not only on the availability of natural resources and the size and population of a country, but on economic size, which takes into account both population and income *per capita*. In many African States the population and *per capita* products are extremely small, giving an economic unit no larger than a medium-sized firm in a western capitalist country, or a single State enterprise in a European socialist economy.

Africa is having to pay a huge price once more for the historical accident that this vast and compact continent brought fabulous profits to western capitalism, first out of the trade in its people and then out of imperialist exploitation. This enrichment of one side of the world out of the exploitation of the other has left the African economy without the means to industrialise. At the time when Europe passed into its industrial revolution, there was a considerably narrower gap in development between the continents. But with every step in the evolution of productive methods and the increased profits drawn from the more and more shrewd investment in manufacturing equipment and base metal production, the gap widened by leaps and bounds.

The Report of the U.N. Economic Commission for Africa published in December 1962 under the title of *Industrial Growth in Africa* states that the gap between 'the continents separated by the Mediterranean' has widened faster during the twentieth century than ever before. True, *per capita* output has increased in Africa, particularly in the last two decades, which have seen an increase of some 10 to 20 per cent. Already far ahead, the industrial countries have marked a *per capita* advance in the same period of 60 per cent, and their *per capita* industrial production may be estimated as high as twenty-five times that in Africa as a whole. The difference for the greater part of Africa, however, is even more marked, since industry on this continent tends to be concentrated in small areas in the north and south. A real transformation of the African economy would mean not only doubling agricultural output but increasing industrial output some twenty-five times. The Report makes it plain that industry rather than agriculture is the means by which rapid improvement in Africa's living standards is possible.

There are, however, imperialist specialists and apologists who urge the less developed countries to concentrate on agriculture and leave industrialisation for some later time when their populations shall be well fed. The world's economic development, however, shows that it is only with advanced industrialisation that it has been possible to raise the nutritional level of the people by raising their levels of income. Agriculture is important for many reasons, and the governments of African states concerned with bringing higher standards to their people are devoting greater investment to agriculture. But even to make agriculture yield more the aid of industrial output is needed; and the under-developed world cannot for ever be placed at the mercy of the more industrialised. This dependence must slow the rate of increase in our agriculture and make it subservient to the demands of the industrial producers. That is why we cannot accept such sweeping assessments as that made by Professor Leopold G. Scheidl of the Vienna School of Economics at a recent meeting in London of the International Geographical Congress. Commented Professor Scheidl: 'People in developing countries seem to think that all that is necessary for them to become as wealthy as the west is to build factories. Most experts agree that it is wiser and more promising to develop agriculture into self-sufficiency and on to the level of

7

a marketing economy' (*The Times*, 24 July 1964). This train of thought links up directly with that of the chairman of Booker Brothers, Sir Jock Campbell whose combine of companies is busy monopolising sugar and by-product industries in British Guiana, shipping and trading in the Caribbean and East Africa, and is now penetrating into the west of the African continent. Sir Jock Campbell asserted at the Annual address of the Africa Bureau in London on 29 November 1962 that 'agriculture was the basis of African development and that plantations were an effective method of increasing economic potential'. He considered that 'so long as industrialised agriculture employed men free to come and go, it was preferable in terms both of efficiency and liberty to the communised collective farming whose results had fallen short of expectation both in Russia and China' (*The Times*, 30 November 1962). He does not seem to have convinced the sugar workers of British Guiana, and it is a moot point whether he has been able to impress the benefits of his 'free to come and go' plantation philosophy on the workers for his companies in Nyasaland, Rhodesia and South Africa. Even the scientific supporters of the imperialist pattern are aware of the flaws in their injunctions, but they cunningly attribute the emphasis placed by the developing states upon industrialisation to political ambitions rather than to economic and social necessity. A European representative of the University of Malaya, Mr D. W. Fryer, speaking at the meeting of the International Geographical Conference to which reference is made above, said that 'an increase in the efficiency of traditional export industries in the under-developed countries was an obvious move, but it was politically unattractive. It suggested continued acceptance of the old colonial economy. . . . Industrialism was an integral part of the nationalist movement. Its mainspring was not economic but political, and political expediency was often more important than economic efficiency in the location of new industry'.

The more efficient management of primary production and improvement on a marketing level is imperialism's gain and our loss. The point has been made quite clearly by no less a person than the chairman of Bolsa (the Bank of London and South

America), Sir George Bolton. The latter was reported in *The Financial Times* of 6 March 1964 as being confident of a rise in commodity prices, which would have considerable effect on the foreign exchanges. For whose benefit? Sir George provides the answer. 'It should help the reserve currencies, sterling and the dollar,' he said. Why? Because being tied to these currencies, 'the primary producers will be accumulating their surpluses in sterling and dollar balances'. This appears to be nothing short of a direct confession of the major interest of the banking and financial world in the exploitation of the developing countries. It is interesting, therefore, to note that Bolsa's transfer agents in London are Patino Mines & Enterprises Consolidated, the American-controlled combine operating mines in Latin America and Canada, and intimately associated with the groups engaged in exploiting Africa's natural resources.

We are certainly not against marketing and trading. On the contrary, we are for a widening of our potentialities in these spheres, and we are convinced that we shall be able to adjust the balance in our favour only by developing an agriculture attuned to our needs and supporting it with a rapidly increasing industrialisation that will break the neo-colonialist pattern which at present operates.

A continent like Africa, however much it increases its agricultural output, will not benefit unless it is sufficiently politically and economically united to force the developed world to pay it a fair price for its cash crops.

To give one illustration. Both Ghana and Nigeria have in the post-war independence period enormously developed their production of cocoa, as the table on page 10 shows.

This result has not been obtained by chance, it is the consequence of heavy internal expenditure on control of disease and pests, the subsidising of insecticides and the spraying machines provided to farmers and the importing of new varieties of cocoa seedlings which are resistant to the endemic ills which previous cocoa trees had developed. By means such as these Africa as a whole greatly increased her cocoa production, while that of Latin America remained stationary.

What advantage has Nigeria or Ghana gained through this

stupendous increase in agricultural productivity? In 1954/5 when Ghana's production was 210,000 tons, her 1954 earnings from the cocoa crop were £85½ million. This year (1964/5) with an estimated crop of 590,000 tons, the estimated external earnings will be around £77 million. Nigeria has suffered a

Cocoa Bean Production

	Long Tons		Index 1949/50=100		
	Ghana	Nigeria	Ghana	Nigeria	
1949/50	248,000	99,000	100	100	1950
1950/51	262,000	110,000	106	111	1951
1951/52	211,000	108,000	85	109	1952
1952/53	247,000	109,000	100	110	1953
1953/54	211,000	97,000	85	98	1954
1954/55	220,000	89,000	89	90	1955
1955/56	237,000	114,000	96	155	1956
1956/57	264,000	135,000	106	136	1957
1957/58	207,000	81,000	83	82	1958
1958/59	255,000	140,000	103	141	1959
1959/60	317,000	155,000	128	157	1960
1960/61	432,000	195,000	174	197	1961
1961/62	410,000	191,000	165	193	1962
1962/63	422,000	176,000	170	170	1963
1963/64	421,000	217,000	170	219	1964
1964/65 (estimate)	590,000	310,000	238	313	1965

similar experience. In 1954/5 she produced 89,000 tons of beans and received for her crop £39¼ million. In 1965 it is estimated that Nigeria will produce 310,000 tons and is likely to receive for it around £40 million. In other words, Ghana and Nigeria have trebled their production of this particular agricultural product but their gross earnings from it have fallen from £125 million to £117 million.

A detailed study of production and price shows that it is the developed consuming country which obtains the advantage of the increased production in the less developed one. So long as African agricultural producers are disunited they will be unable to control the market price of their primary products.

As experience with the Cocoa Producers Alliance has shown, any organisation which is based on a mere commercial agreement between primary producers is insufficient to secure a fair world price. This can only be obtained when the united power of the producer countries is harnessed by common political and economic policies and has behind it the united financial resources of the States concerned.

So long as Africa remains divided it will therefore be the wealthy consumer countries who will dictate the price of African cash crops. Nevertheless, even if Africa could dictate the price of its cash crops this would not by itself provide the balanced economy which is necessary for development. The answer must be industrialisation.

The African continent, however, cannot hope to industrialise effectively in the haphazard, *laisser-faire* manner of Europe. In the first place, there is the time factor. In the second, the socialised modes of production and tremendous human and capital investments involved call for cohesive and integrated planning. Africa will need to bring to its aid all its latent ingenuity and talent in order to meet the challenge that independence and the demands of its peoples for better living have raised. The challenge cannot be met on any piece-meal scale, but only by the total mobilisation of the continent's resources within the framework of comprehensive socialist planning and deployment.

We have noted that in the countries of the highest settler populations, and therefore the most exploited so far in Africa (Algeria, Congo, Kenya, Morocco, Rhodesia, Malawi, South Africa, Tanganyika), agriculture is predominant. In the case of South Africa, the most highly developed area of the African continent, the contribution of agriculture and mining is together equal to that of industry, manufacture and construction. South Africa's economy is heavily bolstered by the export of its

11

mining output. Gold contributes up to 70 per cent of the total exports, which makes the economy, for all its apparent boom, and the heavily increasing foreign investment, basically almost as insecure as that of the less developed countries of the continent. For all its pushing secondary industries, its chemicals manufacture, military production, steel processing and the rest, South Africa has so far failed to lay down the basis of solid industrialisation. G. E. Menell, chairman of Anglo-Transvaal Consolidated Investment Company, which controls gold, diamonds and uranium, made a most telling statement in his annual address on 6 December 1963 to the Johannesburg shareholders' meeting. 'The nation's economy is based, to a significant degree, on wasting assets—the gold mines of the Transvaal and Orange Free State. We have become more and more aware of this in recent years as more mines near the end of their lives without any sign of new large goldfields, in spite of the many millions being spent on exploration.'

Investment in South Africa's economy comes mainly from Western capital with which local finance, not hardy enough to stand on its own feet, is strongly bound. Quick profits are the incentive, so that while Anglo-Transvaal's chairman sees the dangers to the economy, he was nonetheless happy to be able to announce that record profits were again achieved in 1963.

The whole of the economy is geared to the interests of the foreign capital that dominates it. South Africa's banking institutions, like those of most other African States, are offshoots of the Western banking and financial houses. South Africa is dominated by western monopoly even more than by any other sector of the continent, because the investments are many times greater and the dependence upon gold and other mining as the centre of the economy gears it inextricably to that monopoly. Its vulnerability is intensified by the fact that it is a supplier of crude and semi-finished products to the factories of the west on a larger scale than the rest of Africa, and an earner of greater profits for their financial backers.

Nigeria tells in a few basic figures a tale of a different kind of economic maladjustment. In 1960 agriculture, forestry and fishing accounted for 63 per cent of the economic activity; mining one per cent. The imbalance is emphasised by the extremely low ratio of two per cent for industry and manufacture, eliminating at once any comparison with the one per cent contribution of mining and four per cent of agriculture to America's total economic product. In the case of the United States, this low proportion supports a vast superstructure of industry and manufacture. In Nigeria it connotes simply a total disregard under colonialism of Nigeria's potentialities. The reason for this lies not in the fact that Nigeria is devoid of natural industrial resources, as recent findings of oil and iron confirm. It was that Nigeria's agriculture provided greater profitability for European investment than the risks that were involved in the larger capital provisions called for by mining exploration and exploitation.

In 1962 petroleum and petroleum products contributed 9·9 per cent to Nigeria's exports, but it is Shell-BP that hopes to reap most of the benefits. The bulk of these exports was in crude oil, exceeding three million tons. The oil company is aiming at an export target of five million tons of crude oil by 1965. Processing plants are in Europe, not in Nigeria.

The oil refinery going up in Port Harcourt is owned by Shell-BP; the natural gas piping is owned by Shell-Barclays D.C. & O. The oil refinery is meant to handle only ten per cent of Nigeria's crude oil output, and its products will serve only Nigeria's domestic market. Such an arrangement makes it possible not to disturb operations outside Nigeria while making super profits on Nigerian operations.

Generally speaking, in spite of the exploration costs, which are written off for tax purposes anyway and many times covered by eventual profits, mining has proved a very profitable venture for foreign capital investment in Africa. Its benefits for the Africans on the other hand, despite all the frothy talk to the contrary, have been negligible.

This is explained by the absence of industry and manufacture based upon the use of domestic natural resources, and of the trade that is their concomitant. For mining production is destined principally for exportation in its primary form. Certain

3   13

exceptions to this generalisation are to be found in South Africa, Zambia and the Congo. Some small conversion has been taking place also in countries like Morocco, Algeria, Mozambique. South Africa's copper is exported in the form of metal and a small part of its iron is sent overseas as ingots; its gold is refined. But for these exceptions, most exported minerals are shipped from Africa in their primary state. They go to feed the industries and plants of Europe, America and Japan. The ore that is to be produced in Swaziland by the Swaziland Iron Ore Development Company (owned jointly by Anglo-American Corporation and the powerful British steel group, Guest Keen & Nettlefolds) will go at the rate of 1,200,000 tons annually for ten years from 1964 to a Japanese steel combine.

When the countries of their origin are obliged to buy back their minerals and other raw products in the form of finished goods, they do so at grossly inflated prices. A General Electric advertisement carried in the March/April 1962 issue of *Modern Government* informs us that 'from the heart of Africa to the hearths of the world's steel mills comes ore for stronger steel, better steel—steel for buildings, machinery, and more steel rails'. With this steel from Africa, General Electric supplies transportation for bringing out another valuable mineral for its own use and that of other great imperialist exploiters. In lush verbiage the same advertisement describes how 'deep in the tropical jungle of Central Africa lies one of the world's richest deposits of manganese ore'. But is it for Africa's needs? Not at all. The site, which is 'being developed by the French concern, Compagnie Minière de l'Ogooue, is located on the upper reach of the Ogooue River in the Gabon Republic. After the ore is mined it will first be carried 50 miles by cableway. Then it will be transferred to ore cars and hauled 300 miles by diesel-electric locomotives to the port of Point Noire for shipment to the world's steel mills'. For 'the world' read the United States first and France second.

That exploitation of this nature can take place is due to the balkanisation of the African continent. Balkanisation is the major instrument of neo-colonialism and will be found wherever neo-colonialism is practised.

14

2. Obstacles to economic progress

SPEAKING of West Africa in 1962, the United Nations Economic Commission for Africa pointed out:

> 'Few other regions of the world show such a multitude of fairly small States both as far as production and population go. The only similar region of some importance is Central America.'

West Africa is in fact divided into nineteen separate independent States and includes two colonial enclaves possessed by Spain and Portugal. The population of the area is about a third of the total population of Africa, yet the average population of the independent countries, if Nigeria is excluded, is about 2·3 million. It is, however, illusory to regard even Nigeria as an exception to the balkanisation policy practised by the departing colonial rulers. The constitution imposed on Nigeria at independence divided the country into three regions (which have since grown to four) loosely joined on a Federal basis but with sufficient powers left to the regions to cripple overall economic planning. If the other States of West Africa are examples of political balkanisation, Nigeria is an example of economic balkanisation. Ghana, with a population of over seven million, only escaped a similar fate by the resistance put up by the Convention People's Party government to a British plan which would have created no less than five regions, some with a population of less than one million, yet each possessing sufficient powers to defeat central planning.

Kenya, which was also forced to accept at independence a similar type of constitution, has only recently been able to establish a unified regime.

When France was faced with the possibility of being forced to accept some form of independence, or at least self-government, for the territories of the old colonial federations of French West and Equatorial Africa, a series of balkanisation measures were adopted by the French Government. The *Loi-Cadre* of 1956 established the frontiers of the present French-speaking States. The dismantling process begun by the *Loi-Cadre* was completed by the referendum of 1958 on the Constitution of the French Fifth Republic. Each of the territories established by the *Loi-Cadre* was called upon to decide separately whether it wished to remain an overseas territory of France, an automonous Republic within the French Community or to be independent.

Teresa Hayter, a research assistant of the British Overseas Development Institute, in the April 1965 issue of the journal of the British Royal Institute of International Affairs has described the process:

'The territories were to make separate decisions; it was therefore they and not the Federations of West and Equatorial Africa which were legally to inherit France's powers; no provision was made for strengthening the Federal institutions and in fact they were dismantled after the referendum and came formally to an end in April 1959. The original purpose of the Federations had been to enable the colonies to pay for themselves, through a reallocation of their revenues; . . . Senghor in particular has bitterly accused France of "balkanising" Africa in the *Loi-Cadre*. . . . With the choice so loaded, only Guinea voted against the Constitution; all the others became autonomous republics, members of the Franco-African Community.'

Fearing that the example of Guinea might be followed by other states which had decided to join the Community, the

French Government removed everything of value from the territory. Administrators and teachers were withdrawn. Documents and even electric light bulbs were removed from government buildings. Financial assistance, trade support and the payment of pensions to Guinean war veterans were discontinued.

Despite the pressure placed on Guinea in this way, the remaining French States were forced by internal pressure to seek political independence. This destroyed the conception usually associated with General de Gaulle, the originator of the French Community, of a non-sovereign group of African States each separately linked to France. One after another the 'autonomous Republics' obtained international sovereignty but under such adverse conditions that they had in fact to maintain all the military, financial, commercial and economic links of the previous colonial period. In order to exist at all as independent States, these former French territories were forced to accept French 'aid' even to meet their recurrent expenses.

French 'aid' to developing countries is, in proportion to the French national income, the highest in the world and is, in absolute terms, the second highest. Nearly all of this 'aid' is absorbed by commitments in Africa, and nearly half of it goes to the fourteen States which were previously autonomous republics and whose combined population is only slightly larger than that of Nigeria. Aid of this type can dictate African relations with the developed world and, as experience has shown, can be extremely dangerous to the recipients.

French African aid originally arose from the advantage which French firms and individuals derived from the African franc zone and this has determined the framework in which the aid is still provided. So long as the relationship which the aid provided was profitable to France it naturally continued. It was in effect a levy on French taxpayers for the benefit of French individuals and firms.

The overall value of the policy to France was that in return for guaranteed markets and prices for colonial primary products, such as coffee, cocoa, groundnuts, bananas and cotton, the

17

African States had to import from France fixed quantities of certain goods, such as machinery, textiles, sugar and flour, which were then uncompetitive in price or surplus in Europe, and in addition the States were forced to limit their imports from countries outside the franc zone. While this scheme made nonsense of any plan for inter-African trade it was for a period highly profitable to France. With the fall in the world price of primary commodities these profits began to diminish, as did enthusiasm for 'aid' in France. At the present moment the most which can be said in favour of French aid is that it does not now, as it did in the past, make an actual profit for France from the less developed States of its former African empire. Teresa Hayter sums it up:

'France does not gain in its transactions with the States nor does it lose: aid, private investment, French Government expenditures and imports from them are balanced by exports to them, repatriation of capital and remittances of profits and salaries.'

This state of affairs is considered to be no longer of value to France. The Jeanneney Report published in 1964 and expressing the official French view, pointed out that the protective system of the French zone was no longer in the interests of France and the Report therefore advocated the re-deployment of French aid. In any event, France had to comply with her obligations to the European Common Market. Under the new Convention of Association which came into force in the summer of 1964, the six members of the European Common Market are to achieve in stages a free trade area and this will no longer make it possible for France to discriminate in favour of the African States nor for these States to discriminate against France's Common Market partners. Exports from these States will by the end of a five-year period have to be aligned to world prices. In consequence the primary production which they have built up on the strength of the promise of guaranteed markets and prices is likely to fail to be competitive in world conditions. It is difficult to see how Senegal in particular can manage without a French subsidy for her groundnuts, and

President Senghor has already called attention to the serious economic position into which this puts his country.

In fact, the limited neo-colonialism of the French period is now being merged in the collective neo-colonialism of the European Common Market which enables other States, hitherto outside the French preserve, to profit by the system. It also rationalises the division of Africa into economic zones based upon Europe, by drawing in four other States. The Congo (Leopoldville), Burundi and Rwanda are, as previous Belgian colonies, tied to the Belgian economic system and Somalia through its previous association with Italy is also brought in as an associated State of the Common Market.

A grouping such as this raises the wider problems of African neo-colonialism and emphasises its irresponsible nature. Of the States carved out of the former French colonies one, Guinea, has been able, with great suffering and losses it is true, to cut free from the type of neo-colonialist control imposed on the others. Mali has been forced to accept some of the rules and regulations which govern the relations of the former French colonies to France, but at least she has set up her own currency, limits transfers of money abroad and receives from France only a partial guarantee of the parity of her currency with the French franc. In the case of all the other States their currencies have been stabilised on a fixed parity with the French franc and have a total guarantee from the French Treasury. These States pay their receipts of French francs into operation accounts in the French Treasury. These accounts can be overdrawn and the States can draw on them against their own currencies to an unlimited extent. Obviously, however, whatever the theoretical position, the international financial position of these countries is subject to control in that at any time their operation accounts in the French Treasury could be blocked, as was done in the case of Guinea. Most, at any rate, of the States concerned lack the strength to stand up against such pressure as did Guinea.

Why then, it may be asked, are these powers not sufficient to enable France to persuade these States to follow present French foreign policy which is based upon a 'third force' concept? France did not support the United States and Belgium in their

19

'humanitarian' intervention at Stanleyville in the Congo. Unlike Britain and the other Common Market countries, France has openly opposed the United States policy in Santo Domingo, has recognised the Peoples' Republic of China and has recommended the neutralisation of Vietnam. Yet only a minority of the African States which would appear to be under French neo-colonial control have followed the French line. The majority of them refuse to recognise China or in any way criticise United States policy. Indeed they behave in a fashion suggestive of being under United States rather than French influence. The answer to this apparent paradox will, I believe, be found in the following chapters of this book in which I attempt to explain the power and ramifications of international financial control. Here one has a super State which can at times even override the policy wishes of the nominal neo-colonial master.

The control of the funds of the French neo-colonial African States is exercised by the administrative council of their central banks, which are composed partly of Frenchmen without whose agreement no decision in monetary policy can be taken. This French banking complex, with its absolute control of the currencies and external payments of the French neo-colonial States, could, in theory, dictate that these States follow a French policy. However, the complex is itself subject, in the manner later described, to external pressures which support United States rather than French policies where a difference of opinion arises.

Part of the value of commencing a study of neo-colonialism in its African context is that it provides examples of every type of the system. It is impossible to define the African situation in terms of independent States, divided into the non-aligned and the neo-colonialist camp, colonies and racialist States such as South Africa. In Africa, all former colonies which have now become independent, including particularly South Africa, are subject in some degree to neo-colonialist pressures which however much they wish to resist they cannot entirely escape, struggle as they may. The difference in reality is between those States that accept neo-colonialism as a policy and those which resist it. Similarly, the colonial problem of Africa is in many ways really neo-colonial. The Portuguese African territories appear at first sight only to raise the issue of freedom from colonial rule but in fact they exist as colonies only because Portugal is itself a neo-colonial State. For the last fifty years the great powers have regarded the Portuguese colonies as counters which they can exchange between themselves in order to readjust the balance of power. In 1913 the British and Germans had initialled an agreement for their division and this was only prevented by the outbreak of the first world war. In the appeasement period prior to the second world war, when it was thought that Hitler could be bought off by an offer of colonial territory, the Portuguese colonies were again regarded as the suitable bribe.

If Portugal controls these colonies now it is only because of the military strength which she derives through her NATO alliance. Portugal is however not a member of NATO because of any military assistance which she could render the alliance but because this is a convenient way by which Portuguese territory can be made available to the forces of other members of the alliance.

At the other end of the scale is the French colony of Somalia. It continues to exist as a colony not because France would resist pressure to grant it independence but because of African disunity. It is a point of dispute between Somalia and Ethiopia. African disunity maintains this colony. If it were to go to either of its neighbours it would almost inevitably provoke a conflict between them.

Rhodesia, while theoretically a colony, is really a fossilised form of the earliest type of neo-colonialism which was practised in southern Africa until the formation of the Union of South Africa. The essence of the Rhodesia system is not to employ individuals drawn from the people of the territory itself to run the country, as in the newer type of neo-colonial State, but to utilise instead an alien minority. The majority of the European ruling class of Rhodesia only came to the Colony after the second world war, but it is they and not the African inhabitants, who outnumber them 16 to 1, that Britain regards as

21

'the Government'. This racialist State is protected from out-side pressure because under international law it is a British colony, while Britain herself excuses her failure to exercise her legal rights to prevent the oppression and exploitation of the African inhabitants (of which of course she officially disap-proves) because of a supposed British parliamentary con-vention. In other words, by maintaining Rhodesia nominally as a colony, Britain in fact gives her official protection as a second South Africa and the European racialists are left free to treat the African inhabitants as they will.

The Rhodesian system thus has all the hallmarks of the neo-colonial model. The patron power, Britain, awards to a local government over which it claims to have no control unlimited rights and exploitation within the territory. Yet Britain still retains powers to exclude other countries from intervening either to liberate its African population or to bring its economy into some other zone of influence. The manoeuvring over Rhodesia's 'independence' is an excellent example of the workings of neo-colonialism and of the practical difficulties to which the system gives rise. A European minority of less than a quarter of a million could not maintain, in the conditions of Africa today, rule over four million Africans without external support from somewhere. When the settlers talk of 'inde-pendence' they are not thinking of standing on their own feet but merely of seeking a new neo-colonialist master who would, in their view, be more reliable than Britain.

As will be seen from the chapters which follow, modern neo-colonialism is based upon the control of nominally inde-pendent States by giant financial interests. These interests often act through or on behalf of a particular capitalist State, but they are quite capable of acting on their own and forcing those imperial countries in which they have a dominant interest to follow their lead. There is, however, an older type of neo-colonialism which is based primarily on military considerations.

A world power, having decided on principles of global strategy that it is necessary to have a military base in this or that nominally independent country, must ensure that the country where the base is situated is friendly. Here is another reason for balkanisation. If the base can be situated in a country which is so constituted economically that it cannot survive without substantial 'aid' from the military power which owns the base, then, so it is argued, the security of the base can be assured. Like so many of the other assumptions on which neo-colonialism is based this one is false. The presence of foreign bases arouses popular hostility to the neo-colonial arrangements which permit them more quickly and more surely than does anything else, and throughout Africa these bases are disappearing. Libya may be quoted as an example of how this policy has failed.

Libya has had a long colonial history. From the sixteenth century onwards it was a Turkish colony, but in 1900, in the heyday of colonialism, France and Italy agreed that if Italy would not oppose France occupying Morocco, France would not oppose Italy occupying Libya. So when in 1911 and 1912 France was occupying Morocco, Italy went to war with Turkey and, defeating her, annexed Libya.

Despite promises during the second world war to the people of Libya that they would never again be subjected to Italian rule, France tried at the peace settlement to have Italy reinstalled in order to support her own position in Tunisia. This solution proving impossible, Libya became nominally independent but actually under British neo-colonial control.

According to the figures collated by the British Overseas Development Institute, during the period 1945 to 1963 Libya received no less than 17 per cent of the total bilateral aid which Britain gave to all foreign countries outside the Commonwealth in that period. The Overseas Development Institute notes that 'although these payments to Libya are counted as "aid" there is no doubt that they are in essence straightforward payments to the Libyan Government in return for the use of bases'. Nevertheless, popular pressure in Libya has now made it necessary for the Libyan Government to terminate the military agreement for British bases.

These limitations on the real independence of many countries in Africa should not be allowed to obscure the very great achievements already gained in the struggle for African independence and unity.

In 1945 Africa largely comprised the colonial territories of European powers, and the idea that the greater part of the continent would be independent within twenty years would have seemed impossible to any political observer in the immediate post-war period. Yet, not only has independence been achieved but considerable progress has been made towards the establishment of African unity. To this unity there are still powerful obstacles but they are no greater than the obstacles already overcome and, if their nature is understood, they are clearly surmountable.

Already, and this will ultimately be the decisive factor, the mass of the African people support unity in the same way as they previously supported the various local movements for political independence. Many of the political leaders of French West Africa, for example, did not at first support independence. In 1946, in the French National Assembly, of which he was then a member, M. Houphouet-Boigny, the President of the Ivory Coast, claimed 'there are no separatists on these benches . . . there is a powerful bond, capable of resisting all tests, a moral bond which unites us. It is the ideal of liberty, fraternity, equality, for whose triumph France has never hesitated to sacrifice its most noble blood'. The same policy of the maintenance of unity with France was also supported at that time by President Senghor of Senegal, who said, 'The French union must be a conjunction of civilisations, a melting-pot of culture . . . it is a marriage rather than an association.'

It was mass pressure for independence which forced these leaders to reverse their previous positions and to declare themselves in favour of national sovereignty.

In the same way as mass pressure made it impossible for an African leader to oppose independence, so today mass pressure makes it impossible for him openly to oppose African unity. Those who are against it can only show their opposition in indirect ways: by suggesting that the pace towards it is too fast; that this or that plan is impracticable or that there are procedural difficulties which prevent them assisting in formulating a practical plan for it. The case for African unity is very strong and the instinct of the mass of the people right.

24

It is only when the artificial boundaries that divide her are broken down so as to provide for viable economic units, and ultimately a single African unit, that Africa will be able to develop industrially, for her own sake, and ultimately for the sake of a healthy world economy. A common currency is needed and communications of all kinds must be developed to allow the free flow of goods and services.

The Economic Commission for Africa has repeatedly emphasised the need for economic planning on a continental scale. The inadequacy of national planning can be demonstrated by a glance at the economies of, for example, Mali, the Upper Volta, Niger and Uganda. These land-locked States, which export large quantities of food products to other African States, cannot remain indifferent to the agricultural self-sufficiency schemes adopted by their neighbours. Similarly, a national government planning the establishment of a new industry may find that a neighbouring State is developing one like it. Such duplication would probably result in wasted resources if each was depending on exporting its surplus to its neighbour.

Few would argue against the need for economic planning on a national scale. How much stronger is the argument for continental planning. The modern trend is towards larger economic and political units as interdependence of nations and peoples grows. No country can be completely self-sufficient or afford to ignore political events outside its borders. Africa is clearly fragmented into too many small, uneconomic and non-viable States, many of whom are having a very hard struggle to survive. As already noted, others have had to cling to old ties with former colonial rulers and have become easy prey to neo-colonialist forces. Some of them have found themselves, whether they liked it or not, drawn into the cold war and into the rivalries between foreign powers. The Congo is a notable example.

Naturally, each national government is concerned primarily with the welfare of its own citizens. It could only be expected to agree to a policy of unification if the immediate and long-term benefits became so apparent that it would be positively

25

damaging to its citizens *not* to co-operate. We are faced here with the problem of uneven economic growth. Some African countries are richer in natural resources than others. The less fortunate will need reassuring that their interests will not suffer at the hands of the more developed States.

Past economic union experience has not been encouraging. The linking of the Rhodesias and Nyasaland benefited chiefly Southern Rhodesia. Kenya has gained principally from the East African Common Market, Uganda and Tanganyika being at best only marginal gainers. In the former French colonial federations the benefits of economic unity tended to centre in Brazzaville, Abidjan and Dakar. These examples further strengthen the argument for continentally-planned economic growth so that all States can benefit from industrialisation and other improvements made possible by unified direction. The richer countries will be able to help the poorer. Resources can be pooled and development projects co-ordinated to raise the living standards of every African.

The time factor is important. As ECA has pointed out, *now* is the time to act, before each State gets too deeply involved in major investment and structural decisions based on narrow, national markets. With each month that passes, the foreign interests of neo-colonialism get a tighter grip on Africa's economic life.

The comparatively recent penetration of American big business into Africa points once again to the danger from neo-colonialism. So also does the combining of large firms to form powerful monopolies. How can some of our smaller States hope to bargain successfully with powerful foreign combines some of which control financial empires worth more than the State's total revenue? The smaller the State, and the more formidable the foreign interests, the less likely are the conditions for economic independence to be met. For example, Ghana, because of its economic size and alternative industries, has been in a stronger position for bargaining with the aluminium companies than much smaller, and economically more limited Togo can hope to be in dealing with French phosphate interests. The domination of Africa's economy by foreign firms must be ended if we are to achieve rounded economic growth, and this can only be done through unified action.

Something in the nature of an economic revolution is required. Our development has been held back for too long by the colonial type economy. We need to reorganise entirely so that each country can specialise in producing the goods and crops for which it is best suited.

With economic unity, those countries in Africa which are beginning to establish modern industries would benefit from wider markets. We would all be in a better bargaining position to obtain higher prices for our goods and to establish adequate taxation of foreign factor earnings. In fact, a whole new pattern of economic development would be made possible. Agriculture could be modernised more quickly with more capital at its disposal. Industries on a larger and more economic scale could be planned. These could afford to make use of new techniques involving heavy capital outlay. Smaller plants planned to meet only national needs are likely to have higher costs, and are eventually less able to reduce costs than optimum-sized units.

National planning bodies would still have a very important part to play in a unified Africa. They would, for example, supply essential information about local conditions, but their work would be made easier with the experienced advice and help of a single planning body keeping an eye on Africa's interests as a whole. The research and training in development projects already being carried out by the ECA Development Institute in Dakar would be strengthened to serve both the continental and national bodies. Expensive failures due to lack of co-ordination would be avoided. A case in point is the Inga dam project which is to provide power for a sugar refinery, a plastics and hardboard (from sugar cane waste) complex in Bangui, which in turn will ship bulk plastics to a plastic products industry in Brazzaville. Obviously there should be a planning body able to phase and harmonise construction timing for the Brazzaville and Bangui plants, the power lines from Inga to Bangui and Brazzaville, and the transportation services between Bangui and Brazzaville and the dam itself.

27

In the process of obtaining economic unity there is bound to be much hard bargaining between the various States. Integration of different aspects of economic policy will proceed at different rates, and there may be disappointing delays and compromises to be worked out. But given the will to succeed, difficulties can be resolved.

In general, the broader the front on which economic unity is launched the quicker the goals and policies of a fully developed Africa can be achieved. An all-African planning body could take immediate steps towards the development of large-scale industry and power; for the removal of barriers to inter-African trade; and for the creation of a central bank and the formation of a unified policy on all aspects of export control, tariff and quota arrangements. The ECA has carried out several surveys designed to provide information to help in the making of decisions on these points.

Among immediate needs are the manufacture in Africa of agricultural machinery of all kinds to speed up the modernisation of agriculture. We need supplies of electrical equipment for use in the growing electric power production essential for industrial growth. Mining and industrial machinery must be produced in Africa to lower the costs of developing our mineral resources. Construction machinery and supplies, chemicals, fertilisers, plastics, are all urgently required, and Africa must produce them for her own requirements.

Reports of the ECA Industrial Co-ordination Missions to different regions in Africa suggest that the production of iron and steel, non-ferrous metals, engineering supplies, chemicals and fertilisers, cement, paper and textiles should be developed on an inter-African basis since their efficiency depends on large-scale production. Other industries which can run efficiently on a smaller scale can be planned nationally.

The location of the various industries will, of course, depend on many factors such as the availability of power, mineral deposits, nearness to processing plants, markets and so on. Production of aluminium and copper, for example, will have to be developed in those countries where the essential resources, ore and cheap power, are available. The manufacturing of aluminium and copper products, however, need not take place in the countries producing the metals. Similarly, the production of cotton is limited to certain climatic regions, while cotton textile industries can be developed further afield.

Every African State has some contribution to make to the economic whole. There are, for instance, no known deposits of potash in West Africa, but requirements can be met from North Africa, Ethiopia and possibly also from the Congo (Brazzaville) and Gabon. Plans for nitrogeneous fertiliser production in Zambia have already been worked out. The plant could be supplied with coal from Rhodesia (Zimbabwe) and low-cost power from the Victoria Falls. Kenya, with its large forest reserves, could become the centre of a wood distillation complex able to supply the countries of East and Central Africa with gas, acetone, methanol and tar. There are many other examples too numerous to describe.

The urgent need to plan industrial development on a continental scale must not, however, blind us to the equally important need to do the same for agriculture, fishing and forestry. In *The Role of Industry in Development: some Fallacies*, Dudley Seers has pointed out the inter-dependence of agriculture and industry:

'Materials are needed for growing industries; more important, the swelling town labour force needs to be fed, and this implies that a rising surplus of food has to be produced in the countryside. . . . To over-emphasise industry, as some countries have found to their cost, leads paradoxically in the end to a slower rate of industrialisation.'

African States are importing larger amounts of food than ever before from abroad. This trend must be stopped by a carefully planned expansion of our own agriculture.

As an industry, there can be specialisation so that each region or State concentrates on producing the agricultural products for which it is best suited. For instance, it is wasteful for each West African State to try to be self-sufficient in rice when Senegal's Casamance district would be well able to supply the need. Equally, Mali and the Upper Volta are obvious exporters of

4

fresh, tinned and processed meat, while coastal States would supply fresh, tinned and smoked fish.

A further argument for a unified agricultural policy is implied in the need to step up efforts to combat many of the obstacles to economic growth. Locusts, the tse-tse fly and plant diseases are no respecters of political frontiers. Research into their control would benefit from a pooling of brain power and technical know-how. So also would medicine and social services. How much greater the chance of wiping out major epidemic diseases like river blindness and sleeping sickness if action against them is co-ordinated and unified.

The advantage of unified military and diplomatic policies, both for our own security and to achieve freedom for every part of Africa, are so obvious as to need no comment.

Transport and communications are also sectors where unified planning is needed. Roads, railways, waterways, air-lines must be made to serve Africa's needs, not the requirements of foreign interests. Communications between African States are quite inadequate. In many cases it is still easier to travel from an airport in Africa to Europe or America than to go from one African State to another.

Economic unity to be effective must be accompanied by political unity. The two are inseparable, each necessary for the future greatness of our continent, and the full development of our resources. There are several examples of major unions of States in the world today. In *Africa Must Unite* I described some of the more important ones, and warned against the danger of regional federations in Africa.

Africa today is the main stamping ground of the neo-colonialist forces that seek the domination of the world for the imperialism they serve. Spreading from South Africa, the Congo, the Rhodesias, Angola, Mozambique, they form a maze-like connection with the mightiest international financial monopolies in the world. These monopolies are extending their banking and industrial organisations throughout the African continent. Their spokesmen push their interests in the parliaments and governments of the world and sit on the international bodies that are supposed to exist for the promotion of world peace and the welfare of the less-developed countries. Against such a formidable phalanx of forces, how can we move? Certainly not singly, but in a combination that will give strength to our bargaining power and eliminate so many of the duplications that give greater force and greater advantage to the imperialists and their strategy of neo-colonialism.

Decolonisation is a word much and unctuously used by imperialist spokesmen to describe the transfer of political control from colonialist to African sovereignty. The motive spring of colonialism, however, still controls the sovereignty. The young countries are still the providers of raw materials, the old of manufactured goods. The change in the economic relationship between the new sovereign states and the erstwhile masters is only one of form. Colonialism has achieved a new guise. It has become neo-colonialism, the last stage of imperialism; its final bid for existence, as monopoly-capitalism or imperialism is the last stage of capitalism. And neo-colonialism is fast entrenching itself within the body of Africa today through the consortia and monopoly combinations that are the carpet-baggers of the African revolt against colonialism and the urge for continental unity.

These interests are centred on the mining companies of South and Central Africa. From mining they ramify into an involved pattern of investment companies, manufacturing concerns, transport, public utility organisations, oil and chemical industries, nuclear installations and many other undertakings too numerous to mention. Their enterprises spill across the vast African continent and over the oceans into North America, Australia, New Zealand, Asia, the Caribbean, South America, the United Kingdom, Scandinavia and most of western Europe.

Connections, direct and indirect, are maintained with many of the giants of American industry and finance. They are supported by leading bankers, financiers and industrialists in the United Kingdom, France, Belgium, Germany, America and elsewhere. The rotas of their directorates are filled with names that have a familiar ring for those who have the least knowledge of international finance and industry. Names like Oppenheimer, Hambro, Drayton, Rothschild, d'Erlanger, Gillet, Lafond,

Robiliart, van der Straeten, Hochschild, Chester Beatty, Patino, Engelhard, Timmins are ubiquitous. Others, equally powerful in the interests they dominate, avoid the publicity of lengthy lists of their directorships, either by complete absence from the pages of directories anxious to advertise their glories, or by coyly hiding their eminence behind a lonely announcement with name and address.

These intricate inter-connections of the great imperialist monopolies expose the real forces that are behind world events. They indicate also the pattern which links those events to the developing countries at different points of the globe. They reveal the duality of the interests that force the developing countries to import goods and services which are the products of companies combined in the monopoly groups directly exploiting their natural resources or intimately associated with them. This is the double edge to the guillotine that cuts off Africa's wealth from Africa, to the greater enrichment of the countries which absorb her primary materials and return them to her in the form of finished products.

In their new-found independence, it is to these very same monopolistic groups that the new African States are obliged to turn to supply the requirements arising from the need to lay the foundations for their economic transformation. The policy of non-alignment, whenever it is exercised, imposes the obligation to 'shop around', but since capitalism has come to the peak of monopoly, it is impossible for any of us to avoid dealing with monopoly in some form or another. But it is in the nature of our arrangements with the monopolies that the freedom or other-wise of the African States lies. Where we establish and maintain the integrity of our financial institutions and keep our basic projects free from imperialist control, we leave ourselves room to manoeuvre away from the neo-colonialism that, unfortu-nately, has closed its grip upon countries whose independence is over-shadowed by a heavy reliance upon extra-African associations. In this atmosphere of relative freedom, the giant combines that open up industrial enterprises on our soil do so on arrangements that are well screened and are part of nationally planned advancement. The national banks are really national banks, formed and run out of the country's own resources, and our other financial and economic institutions are guarded against neo-colonialist infiltration.

Unhappily, these conditions are rare in Africa. Most of the territories pass into the state of national sovereignty in unviable circumstances that inhibit even a modicum of free movement within national limits. They could be overcome, but only within the combined strength that continental unity and a central connective socialist policy, free of attachments to other continents, could give. As things are, most of our new States, alarmed at the prospect of the harsh world of poverty, disease, ignorance and lack of financial and technical resources into which they are thrust from the womb of colonialism, are reluctant to cut the cord that holds them to the imperialist mother. Their hesitancy is fostered by the sugared water of aid, which is the stop-gap between avid hunger and the hoped-for greater nourishment that never comes. As a result, we find that imperialism, having quickly adopted its outlook to the loss of direct political control, has retained and extended its economic grip (and thereby its political compulsion) by the artfulness of neo-colonialist insinuation.

The increasing expansion of productive capacity and potential output of the advanced capitalist countries has its corollary in the necessity to export on a geometrically increasing scale the finished products of industry and the excess capital that could only further inflate competition at home, but brings rapid and high returns from the industrially-starved new nations. Hence the fevered jostling for position in these areas as well as in that of raw materials monopoly, which is using Africa as the playground, not only of the cold war (an aspect of the fight of capitalism for existence against socialism), but of the competitive struggle of international monopoly. North American imports into Africa rose from 10·3 per cent in 1959 to 13·7 per cent in 1962, while those from other western countries and Japan remained the same or declined slightly. This corresponds to the increasing American investments in the continent's extractive industries and the growth of United States participation in financial establishments on this continent. American

33

banking houses are making inroads into territories formerly catered for solely by European and British banks. The French banks still dominate in the former French countries and the Belgians in the Congo; but this is frequently a front for American participation.

European financial advisers constantly counsel the African countries on the advantages that they can receive from remaining in association with the erstwhile 'mother country', while depreciating the possibilities of inter-African association. Much subtlety is employed by Lombard, the commentator of the *Financial Times*. In an article which appeared in the issue of 6 February 1964 of this influential London newspaper, a product of an industrial holding company which also produces *The Economist*, Lombard asserted that 'there is not much that African countries can do directly to help one another financially at this stage of their economic evolution'. He is therefore 'glad to see that the independent African countries are now coming to recognise that it is very much in their own interests to preserve the monetary ties with leading European countries they inherited from their colonial days. . . . They obviously entertained strong suspicion that the enthusiasm their old mother countries were displaying for allowing them to remain within their monetary areas was motivated largely, if not wholly, by consideration of self-interest. And they are inclined to assume that this implied that their own purpose would be served best by following up political independence with its financial equivalent at the earliest possible opportunity'.

Lombard assured his readers that the Africans showed wisdom when the secretariat of E.C.A., assisting the Organisation of African Unity to implement its resolution on the possibility of establishing an African clearing house and payments union, had the good sense 'to seek the advice of the distinguished American monetary authority, Professor Triffin of Yale University'. Need we be surprised that in his report the distinguished American professor pointed out that 'it would be most unwise lightly to condemn or break up financial arrangements with major trading companies and financial centres'. This, of course, we might consider neo-colonialist penetration, but to Lombard it is only one side of the picture. For there are two worlds, and the African countries 'should now strive to get the best of both worlds, by maintaining and even further developing the relations they have with the major international monetary areas and at the same time building their own financial self-help mechanisms'. How it is possible to resolve two contradictions Lombard does not volunteer to explain, but what he does confess is that this unresolvable two-way procedure 'would meet with nothing but the fullest approval from their (African) present monetary area associates'.

This says plenty and we have no difficulty in believing what it says, for the simple fact is that those who control the major international monetary areas are placing their time bombs within the 'self-help mechanisms' of the African countries. For these mechanisms are controlled by the financial monopolists of imperialism, the bankers and financiers who have been very busy in the past few years setting up establishments throughout Africa, infiltrating into the economic heart of many countries and linking with the most important enterprises that are being established to exploit the continent's natural resources on a larger scale than ever before for their own private gain.

Though the aim of the neo-colonialists is economic domination, they do not confine their operations to the economic sphere. They use the old colonialist methods of religious, educational and cultural infiltration. For example, in the independent States, many expatriate teachers and 'cultural ambassadors' influence the minds of the young against their own country and people. They do this by undermining confidence in the national government and social system through exalting their own notions of how a State should be run, and forget that there is no monopoly of political wisdom.

But all this indirect subversion is as nothing compared with the brazen onslaught of international capitalists. Here is 'empire', the empire of finance capital, in fact if not in name, a vast sprawling network of inter-continental activity on a highly diversified scale that controls the lives of millions of people in the most widely separated parts of the world, manipulating whole industries and exploiting the labour and riches of

35

nations for the greedy satisfaction of a few. Here resides the mainspring of power, the direction of policies that stand against the advancing tide of freedom of the exploited people of Africa and the world. Here is the adamantine enemy of African independence and unity, braced in an international chain of common interest that regards the likely coming together of the new nations as a major blow at its continued domination of the resources and economies of others. Here, indeed, are the real workings of neo-colonialism. Here indeed are the economic ramifications of the monopolies and combines. Their financial and economic empires are pan-African and they can only be challenged on a pan-African basis. Only a united Africa through an All-African Union Government can defeat them.

3. Imperialist finance

THESE are the hard facts of the African situation today, a process that has continued and grown since the invasion of Africa by the European and foreign powers. It has gained tremendous momentum in recent years with the growth of the struggle between the imperialist antagonists and between capitalism and socialism.

Imperialism was analysed by Lenin as the highest stage of capitalism. His exposition was written in the middle of the first world war (1916), which was waged to determine the first major revision of imperialist supremacy. He traced the unequal development of capitalism which caused the latecomers like Germany and the United States to form into cartels and syndicates before the earlier starters, and so brought them sooner to a higher stage of monopoly from which they challenged each other and the rest of world imperialism.

Monopoly capitalism by means of mergers, amalgamations, patent agreements, selling arrangements, production quotas, price fixing, and a variety of other common contrivances, had built itself into an international confraternity. However, because of its competitive character, rooted in the principle of production for private gain and the unequal development of capitalism, the struggle of the monopolies went on within the international combinations. The conflicts between the European and American financial and industrial trusts and combines for a redivision of the world's resources of raw materials and markets for investment capital and manufactured goods, exploded into war when they became too intense to contain within the limits of diplomacy. The 1914–18 war brought a re-division of the globe's colonial sectors. At the same time it created the opportunity for a socialist break in the chain of imperialism that encircled the world.

A heavy blow was dealt to international monopoly capitalism with the triumph of the Russian October Revolution. From then on it was faced not only with the struggle for hegemony within its own ranks but, which was much worse, it was forced to engage in a defensive struggle against an opposing ideology. That ideology had achieved a signal success in withdrawing a sixth of the earth's surface from monopoly capitalism's field of operations, a fact which it has never and will never forgive, and was threatening to undermine imperialism's power at other strategic spots which had softened under the blows of war. With the failure of interventionist war to subdue the new socialist State, a *cordon sanitaire* was raised around the Soviet Union to prevent the spread of socialist contamination to other parts of Europe. Fascism was encouraged to prop capitalism at points where it had been seriously damaged and was faced with popular discontent, as in Germany and Italy, and to bolster it in those outposts which were and remain semi-colonial appendages to Western imperialism, Spain and Portugal.

These devices, however, were unable to cope with the re-current crises that were tearing at the very heart of capitalism and sharpening the bitter contentions between rival imperial-isms which erupted into a second global war in 1939. From this holocaust, socialism emerged as a much more threatening challenge to imperialism than ever before. At the same time we, the peoples of imperialism's 'far flung empires', had come to realise that we could have control over our own destiny and began to make our bid for independent nationhood. Thus imperialism came to be challenged on another front, the colonialist front, at a time when science had heightened the capabilities of the productive machinery of capitalism, thereby increasing its need for raw materials and markets for new chemically-produced primary materials, manufactured goods and overseas employment of growing capital surpluses. Challenged thus by anti-colonialism and socialism, imperialism is now engaged in a 'to-the-death' trial for survival against the forces that are antagonistic to it and that are building up across the globe even while the internecine struggle within itself is becoming more and more brutal. In this multi-sided struggle, imperialism has been forced into the use of many artifices to maintain itself in being by continuing the colonialist process without the benefit of colonial control.

The great colonial powers were able to monopolise external trade and agricultural and industrial primary materials production in their respective subject territories. The colonies of such a lesser industrialised nation as Portugal, however, which has for centuries been a pawn of Britain and became a semi-colony of British finance, were dominated by British capital, together with the international banking groups with which it is associated. Belgian financial domination of the Congo, because of the close connections of Belgian banking institutions with such international houses as Rothschild, Lazard Frères, and Schroder in their turn linked with the Morgan and Rockefeller groups, was shared with British, French and American finance.

The tribute drawn off by way of colonial and semi-colonial exploitation enabled the capitalist classes of the metropolitan countries to pass some of the crumbs to their working classes and thereby buy them off (especially the trade union and political leaders) when the class conflicts in their societies got critical. At the same time, the competition for sources of raw materials, and the export of capital and commodities intensified as productive methods improved and goods came out of the factories on a more and more massive scale.

The uneven development of capitalism brought new contenders into the field who joined in the rivalries that had grown up with the original scramble for colonies. These deepened until they erupted in the two world wars, which, notwithstanding all the pious claptrap about their being wars fought for the maintenance of democracy were, in reality, wars fought for the redivision of the world by monopoly capitalism. 'War', Clausewitz has told us, 'is the continuation of policy by other means.' What the powerful trusts were unable to achieve by 'peaceful' competition, their domination over larger and larger areas of the world, they embroiled their countries into military action to achieve for them. This not only gives them a wider sphere of exclusive operation but undermines the power of competing monopolies.

This redivision of the world is not confined to the less developed sectors but extends to highly industrialised areas. The important industrialised region of Alsace Lorraine was a coveted prize of the German invasions of France in the wars of 1871 and 1939. Hitler's campaign against Czechoslovakia was inspired by the desire to annex the highly developed manufactories of Bohemia and Moravia to the German trusts. French capitalists long looked with watering mouths at the rich coal mines and chemical and other industries of the Saar, so close to the iron ore range of Lorraine, and seized the opportunity of the 1919 peace arrangements to appropriate them to France as a reparations award. A later plebiscite won the Saar back to Germany. After the second world war, agreement between the de Wendel-Schneider-Krupp trusts achieved a customs union between the German State of the Saar and France, which actually makes the Saar a dependency of the de Wendel coal and steel empire.

World war two ended in the defeat of Hitler and a temporary rebuff to German capitalism, which had to submit to a revitalising injection of American monopoly finance. At the same time an upheaval was taking place in the colonial world such as to make Winston Churchill remark that he had not been made Prime Minister of Britain to preside over the liquidation of the British Empire. All the fair, brave words spoken about freedom that had been broadcast to the four corners of the earth took seed and grew where they had not been intended. Colonial emancipation became the dominating phenomenon of the mid-twentieth century, just as abolition of slavery was of the corresponding period of the nineteenth, with just as

40

crucial consequences in national and international politics and economics.

Post-war capitalism, which had already received one devastating blow after the first world war in the rise of the Soviet Union, took another crushing defeat in the establishment of socialist regimes in a number of countries in central and eastern Europe and in China. Large sources of raw materials and financial investment and commodity markets were withdrawn from its field of exploitation. Domestic reconstruction at first occupied the attention of the European countries. The United States, having already achieved a tremendous headstart by its late intervention into the war, its physical immunity from attack, and the enormous spurt given to its productive and inventive capacity as a main supplier of war materials and services, took over from Britain the leading role in international financial monopoly.

As a result of its primacy in the financial sphere, United States foreign policy turned in a completely opposite direction from its pre-war position of 'splendid isolation' to one of domination in world affairs. The outcropping of new States from colonial submergence raised the pivotal problem of how to retain these countries within the colonial relationship once open control was removed. Thus has opened up a new phase in imperialism, that of the adaptation of colonialism to the new condition of the elimination of political over-lordship of colonial powers, the phase in which colonialism is to be maintained by other means.

This is not to say that the old outright form of colonialism is completely scrapped. There is plenty of evidence to show how tenaciously imperial powers cling to their colonial territories. Vietnam, Korea, Suez, Algeria, are all examples of how far imperialist nations will go to hold on physically to colonies, an attitude reinforced by the interference of America as a leading protagonist in the struggle for the world monopolist control of finance capital. This struggle has been given an ideological content by invoking anti-communism as the mainspring of the battle to bring the socialist sector of the globe back into the exploitive control of Western financial monopoly.

Cuba is the outstanding example of the extremist lengths to which these power groups will go in the effort to reimpose their grip where they have been ejected and to maintain what they consider a strategic bastion in the struggle for the renewal of dominion over the socialist anti-imperialist world.

Control of fuel resources is a prime motivator in the frantic competition between monopolies. The Saar was bandied between France and Germany because of its important coal resources. Similarly, the battle for oil has gone on since before the first world war. Middle Eastern oil, in fact, became an important objective of that war, and the struggle continued after the war by diplomatic and economic means inside the national boundaries and on the international plane. Rockefeller supremacy in oil has been stoutly contested by the Morgan groups, which have extended their influence by breaking into the Anglo-Dutch holdings, a one-time preserve of the Rothschilds, Lazard Frères, the Deutsche Bank, and their associates.

The frenzied battle for oil monopoly has been a cardinal factor in the suppression of popular movements in colonial and semi-colonial areas of the Near, Middle and Far East, in Latin America and North Africa. The series of events in Iran, Iraq, Kuwait, Aden, Saudi Arabia, Cuba, Venezuela, Brazil, Brunei, and Algeria, that have erupted in violence, revolution and war have been largely stimulated by the struggle for control of oil. Oil finds in European centres, such as Groningen in Holland, have drawn the competition into well industrialised centres, just as the competition for coal and iron did.

Competition between the oil combines is not confined to production, but extends into the distribution of petroleum products and the new by-product industry of petro-chemicals. A fierce struggle is going on all over the world as a result of the sharp increase in the quantity of oil consumed and the territorial expansion of consumption. The oil industry has from its outset been dominated by the most powerful banking interests, the Rockefellers, Morgans, Rothschilds, because of the spiralling profits it provides. Today, even with the larger royalties the oil combines have been obliged to pay to the oil-producing countries, their profits are still mounting prodigiously.

Oil trust reserves run into billions. Much has been used in investments abroad, America far and away exceeding all others. To financial reserves from oil must be added those amassed from metal and other raw materials' monopolies; from monopoly of food supplies and vast industrial and agricultural empires; from the monopoly network of distribution and distributive agencies; from military preparations and the several wars that have been fought with colonial peoples since the end of the second world war; from the development of nuclear instruments of destruction and the frenzied race for leadership in the realm of space research.

Capitalism contains many paradoxes, all of them based in the concept of commodity production: the few rich and the many poor; poverty and hunger amid superabundance; 'freedom from hunger' campaigns and subsidies for restriction of crop output. But perhaps the most ludicrous is the constant traffic in the same kinds of goods, products and commodities between countries. Everyone is busy, as it were, taking in the other's washing. This is not done out of need, but out of the compulsion of profit-making and monopoly extension. The European Common Market has become the apotheosis of this process, as well as the dumping ground of international investment, dominated by the giant American banking concerns and their British satellites.

The European Community, of which the European Common Market is only one aspect, is by no means a new concept. It was foreshadowed by Hobson in his critique of imperialism as 'a European federation of great powers which, so far from forwarding the cause of world civilisation, might introduce the gigantic peril of western parasites, a group of advanced industrial nations, whose upper classes drew vast tribute from Asia and Africa, with which they supported great masses of retainers, no longer engaged in the staple industries of agriculture and manufacture, but kept in the performance of personal or minor industrial services under the control of a new financial aristocracy.' It is collective imperialism.

This is precisely what has happened. Competition between the monopolies has produced the phenomenon of vast advertising and public relations organisations which busy themselves selling not only goods and services but personalities as well. These organisations and the media through which they operate —the press, radio, cinema, television—and the businesses dealing with the packaging of goods, employ huge armies of people in what are nothing more than parasitic jobs which would have no place in a sane society producing for consumption instead of profit. As things are, enormous sums are invested and earned by the financial interests that participate in the promotion of these enterprises.

But this is only a tiny facet of the fevered financial activity which is going on today in the capitalist world. Every week, every day, with almost monotonous regularity, we see the same names repeating themselves as bidders for large companies; as underwriters and issuers of new shares or holders of debentures; as combiners in new financial institutions for more universal methods of investment; as participants in new factories and ventures that will extend monopoly in fresh directions and more territories.

They are especially industrious in the countries of the 'Six' and others which still hope to push into the Common Market as direct or associate members. The lowering of trade barriers was the signal for their entry. For practical purposes, some of the key European countries are financial servants of the dominant banking monopolist groups, the Morgans and the Rockefellers. Despite all the power pertaining to such important banks as the Société Générale de Belgique, Banque de Bruxelles, Kredietbank, Banque Lambert, to such important industrial-finance groups as Solvay, Boel, Brufina-Cofinindus, Petrofina—Belgium, with its appendage Luxemburg, is in reality a financial colony of American investment capital. Thirty-nine new companies were established in Belgium in 1959 by foreigners. In the year 1961 the number of new 'foreign' companies set up had grown to 237. Sums invested from abroad had swollen from 2,457 million Belgian francs in 1959 to 6,664 million Belgian francs in 1961. Of this last figure, almost 60 per cent, that is 3,979 million Belgian francs, was furnished from American sources. Henry Coston, in his revealing book on the ramifications of banking finance, *L'Europe des Banquiers* (p. 174), declares that this enterprise is not limited to the territory of the kingdom, and that the Belgian ex-colonies have not been ignored. 'One might even ask if the sanguinary events in the Congo were not caused by the merciless struggle going on between rival financial groups', he concludes.

American finance capital, of course, had a field day in Germany during the post-war occupation. German industry and finance, already linked to American industry and finance by cartel and trust arrangements, became even more heavily penetrated by the powerful United States monopoly groups. The giant German banks, Deutsche Bank, Dresdner Bank, Diskonto Gesellschaft, Commerzbank; the mighty German trusts, Krupp, Bayer, Badische Anilin & Soda Fabrik, Hoechst, and Siemens are all strung to American capital and in many ways subordinate to it. Italian banks and industry are in much the same position. The Banco Commerciale Italiano, Banco di Roma, Mediobanca, Credito Italiano, all are in several ways tied up with American finance capital either directly or indirectly. Examples can be stretched across the world, to Japan, Canada, Australia, and New Zealand. This financial dependence upon America has been put by Lord Bearsted, chairman of M. Samuel & Co. at the 1963 annual meeting, when he reported the 16⅔ per cent acquisition of the company's shares by the Morgan group. 'We will not be the first merchant bank to have part of its capital owned by American interests'.

This piteous statement is a public confession of Europe's subservience to American financial monopoly, a monopoly expressed in the strategic and political alliances that bind European capitalism to American capitalism. European statesmen are deeply conscious of their inferior standing but, in the main, feel there is little they can do to adjust the position. Resentment, however, there is, and in France it has expressed itself in General de Gaulle's stand on an individual French nuclear striking force; in his overtures to Adenauer, former

German Chancellor; in his attempts to exclude Great Britain from the Common Market as the long arm of the United States; and more recently in the overtures to China and his tour in Latin America. All these are efforts to arrest America's dominance of Europe and to exert French independent action on the international front. Such attempts, however, have little chance of success, nor can they make but a passing impression upon the world scene. They are in reality expressions of the deep competitive conflicts within capitalist-imperialism, which exist below the surface federations and alliances, conflicts rooted in the unequal development of the contestants, in the unequal development of capitalism.

Britain, as the forerunner of the industrial revolution, became the workshop of the world, the carrier of the world's goods, the foremost thruster for imperialist control from the City of London. Her decline set in with the upsurge of the younger, more vigorous capitalist States of Germany and America. The two world wars were a test of their strength against the older established capitalist countries and against each other. The United States came out triumphant both times. Still, the City of London is only slowly giving way to Wall Street as the symbol of world money power. It hopes to resuscitate itself by spreading into the European Common Market, even though it must do so in alliance with, and subordination to, American financial monopoly. Surplus capital in France was more heavily invested in the less advanced countries of Europe—Russia, Poland, Hungary, Rumania— than that of either Britain or Germany, although they, too, had large investments in the same European heavy industries, armaments, mines and oil fields. Everybody, however, turned to the primary producing countries of the world, alienating some as outright colonies under political rule, subserving and exploiting others as spheres of investment on a semi-colonial pattern.

Because of their late start, German and American capitalism pressed forward with the amalgamation of industrial combines and the monopoly of finance capital more hurriedly than did either Britain and France, whose supremacy on the colonial plane assured their hegemony, inter-related at several points even while competitive, on the international financial level. German financial monopoly took a beating in the defeat of 1918, when the colonial world was re-divided, and again in 1945. American capitalism on the other hand, owing to geographical and territorial advantages (the last inherent in its political union), continued to make rapid strides and was the real victor of both world wars. Expansion of American financial and industrial monopoly, however, was not confined to Europe. The balance of western financial power began to tilt towards Asia and Africa, a process that has been speeded up since the end of the second world war, with the breakdown of colonial rule.

The many consortia which are being established in the majority of the new States revolve largely about the same financial and industrial groups that have rooted themselves firmly since the inception of colonial rule. Such changes as there are correspond with the changes of influence that have occurred within the groups themselves. The dominating influence is held by the ubiquitous American formations of Morgan and Rockefeller, with their British and European associates following behind. Dying colonialism is reviving in the international coalitions of neo-colonialism. These coalitions of competing organisms reflect the global character that financial monopoly has attained under the dominance of the most powerful imperialism, that of America. They are also a sign of the struggle for survival of the older imperialisms against the fierce questing of the more powerful aggressiveness of American imperialism, whose vaster productive force is driving it outwards more and more.

Attempts are made to sweeten the well-known aims of rapidly disintegrating political colonialism: the maintenance of less developed areas of the world as the providers of cheap raw materials, spheres of investment, and markets for expensive finished goods and services. The finished goods and services, now that the populations of the new nations are asserting demands for a rising standard of life, are taking on a different character and over-spilling into categories formerly neglected. Land-clearing equipment, hydro-electrical projects, road reconstruction, housing, schools, hospitals, harbours, airports, and all the ancillary and supplementary services they call for, are providing new fields of capital investment and profit for financial monopoly, both at home and abroad. They are also keeping in handsomely paid employment a large army of so-called experts, technical and professional people, not always of the highest calibre.

New sources of extractive and agricultural commodities are also attracting large capital investment sums. Former dependence upon domestic sources of many minerals in the metropolitan countries is giving place to their importation from abroad. Miners in the copper and iron ore producing regions of the United States, for example, are being thrown out of work not only because of automation, but also because bigger profits are being obtained from the greatly stepped-up mining of base materials in Africa and Asia. In some places, their semi-processing also offers greater margins than can be got in the areas of more expensive labour. Puerto Rico and other Latin American countries that offer cheap labour are fast becoming centres of manufactured consumer goods, frequently processed from imported raw materials and sent to the United States to compete with American-produced commodities at only slightly reduced, or the same, prices. This gives greater profits still to finance capital.

The intricate process of balancing returns from domestic investment against the outflow of capital into more profitable foreign investment is creating serious rifts in the internal economic position of every Western capitalist country. This is felt particularly in the balance of payments position. Even the United States, whose reserves of gold and foreign exchange were so vast that they have carried her through a growing outward current over a long period, has now reached the stage when, like her less fortunate European counterparts, she is herself entering upon an adverse balance of payments crisis.

Despite the rise in national production and increased productivity, the problems of agriculture even in such rapidly rising economies as Western Germany, Italy and France bedevil the economic situation. In America, the farming small-holder still lives close to and even below the poverty line, while the extensive mechanised farms of banker-financed companies are spoon-fed by a bankers' Government. Guaranteed prices for produce that goes into government-paid and government-built storages make large-scale farming in the United States highly profitable to finance capital, which passes on to the government the burdensome problem of what to do with unsold surpluses resulting from high prices.

The need of further outlets for the products of agriculture as well as of the industrial and commercial complexes that are coming under increasing electronic control, and hence acquiring a greatly increased potential, is forcing Western capitalism, particularly American capitalism, into greater and more intensive involvement in highly industrialised foreign countries. The recent 'chicken' farce played out against the background of de Gaulle's anti-American policy which led Franco-German opposition to a continuation of cheaper American poultry importation into Europe, is just one of the lighter examples of the fierce competition going on to unload the output of bank-financed vigorously mechanised mass production. It highlighted for a moment the intrinsically paradoxical nature of the European Market as a monopolistic organism putting up a strong resistance to a dominant competitive monopoly. The competitive tug-of-war is exemplified in the retaliative higher tariffs that have now been put upon French and German small cars imported into the United States, which have lost their main advantage over the home produced article in the consequent higher price.

Facts and figures prove that trade and investment between the highly industrialised countries are outpacing those with the less developed regions. They effectively support the case that imperialism is not confined to the primary producing sectors of the world. However, the salient fact is that the profit rate from the exploitation of the less developed areas is greater than that received from the more industrialised countries. In the latter, the competition between the monopolies is fiercest and domestic interests, even those which are linked with international finance monopoly, all the time offer the stoutest resistance to the invading ones. Yet, and this is precisely due to their imperialist character, the dominating world financial groups are able to make their constant incursions into the national monopolies, and so deepen their hegemony over larger and larger parts of the globe.

How much easier then it is for imperialist finance to edge its way more and more into the developing countries where colonial rule has broken, or is breaking, down. Under the necessity of seeking greater and greater capital sums for geological explorations and the opening up of new fields of extractive materials, international finance was called to the aid of the national finance of the respective imperialist countries. This process was stimulated by the fact that the national financial monopolies had already proceeded to the stage of international alliance with the onset of imperialism, a process that has manifoldly quickened in the present epoch of rising nationalism and socialism. Thus, at this present time, all the instruments and mechanics of international imperialism, expressed in monopoly coalitions, are brought to bear in a general descent upon the new, needy countries.

This new wave of predatory invasion of former colonies operates behind the international character of the agencies employed: financial and industrial consortia, assistance organisations, financial aid bodies, and the like. Friendly co-operation is offered in the educational, cultural and social domains, aimed at subverting the desirable patterns of indigenous progress to the imperialist objectives of the financial monopolists. These are the latest methods of holding back the real development of the new countries. These are the paraphernalia of neo-colonialism, superficially proffering aid and guidance; subterraneously benefiting the interested donors and their countries in old and new ways.

There are several definitions of 'aid', as B. Chango Machyo in his *Aid and Neo-Colonialism* has pointed out.

'The definition varies with different blocs. Thus the U.N. has its own definition, the imperialist camp has its own, so has the socialist camp, and probably the non-aligned camp might also have one. But, generally speaking, there are two main definitions: one by the U.N. and another as understood by the so-called donor countries. According to the U.N., "economic aid consists only of outright grants and long-term lending, for non-military purposes, by Government and international organisations". But the so-called aid-giving countries include in the term "aid", private capital investment and export credits, even for relatively short periods, as well as loans for military purposes.'

As Professor Benham in *Economic Aid to Underdeveloped Countries* remarks: 'It is pleasant to feel that you are helping your neighbours, and at the same time increasing your own profits.' Before the decline of colonialism what today is known as aid was simply foreign investment.

4. Monopoly capitalism and the American dollar

THE 'end of empire' has been accompanied by a flourishing of other means of subjugation. The British Empire has become the Commonwealth, but the proceeds from the exploitation of British imperialism are increasing. Profits of British tin companies have ranged as high as 400 per cent. The latest dividends to British diamond shareholders are close to 350 per cent. On one occasion Mr Nehru declared that British profits from independent India had more than doubled and British capital investment in his country rose from Rs. 2,065 m. in 1948 to Rs. 4,460 m. in 1960. Total British investments in Africa have soared to $6,500 m., the French to about $7,000 m. and American to $1,100 m. A recent survey made plain the plunder of British monopolies. It listed 9 out of 20 of Britain's biggest monopolies as direct colonial exploiting companies: Shell, British Petroleum, British American Tobacco, Imperial Tobacco, Burmah Oil, Nchanga Copper, Rhokana Corporation, Rhodesian Mines and British South Africa, five of which are directly engaged in chiselling away Africa's natural resources. The others are busily increasing their trading. Their total of £221 m. net profits was over half the combined net profits of the top twenty monopolies. Incredibly the list leaves out two of the world's greatest combines, those states within a state—Unilever and Imperial Chemical Industries —whose operations are based heavily in their overseas exploitations. The United Africa Company leads for Unilever in

Africa; about a third of I.C.I. and its subsidiaries operate overseas.

Sir Alec Douglas Home, former Prime Minister of Britain's Tory government, in a speech made on 20 March 1964, professed himself ignorant of the meaning of neo-colonialism. While Sir Alec was talking, Britain was engaged in what its press was busy describing as 'major crisis areas' all over the world, putting down 'troubles' inspired and perpetrated by neo-colonialism: Aden and Southern Arabia against Yemen; Borneo and Sarawak against Indonesia; Cyprus, British Guiana; 'maintaining law and order' in Kenya, Tanganyika, Uganda, for the recently independent governments. Is this the end of imperialism? Not according to *The Economist*, mouthpiece of Britain's business interests, which felt compelled to comment:

'Military bases, routes to the East, frontier skirmishing, putting down mutinies—all this has a nineteenth-century ring quite naturally disturbing to those who had hoped that the end of colonialism meant the end of military involvement east of Suez. The knobbly truth of the matter turns out to be that for the moment Britain has as many military commitments in that area as it ever had before colonies were replaced by Commonwealth.' (*Economist*, 23 May 1964.)

The intention is to hold back the progress of the developing countries. Where circumstances favour the establishment of ventures of a more than token industrial character, the aim is to see that they are made haltingly. The over-riding objective is to induce a merely fractional increase in the industrial scope of the new nations in order that they may continue to provide the sinews of imperialism's greater concentration of forces for the final tussle of strength within itself and against socialism. What is remarkable is that the major part of the less developed world, and here we must include the U.S.S.R., chose and is choosing the socialist road to national progress. There are, in addition, countries like India where the political system, though patterned on the bourgeois democracies of capitalism, nevertheless proclaims socialism as the socio-economic objective. The nations that have reached their present peaks by passing through the various stages of capitalism cling desperately to the system that has brought them to the heights of imperialism. Each, perched perilously on a narrow summit, must put up a constant battle to guard its own pinnacle.

Greater intensity is infused into the struggle by the resurgence of rivals, of whom Germany and Japan are the most virile. Both of them have benefited from strong injections of American capital, and U.S. monopolies are drawing off considerable profits from the running that is being made by these two countries in world competition, pointing the contradictions among the interests involved. Competing against American imperialism, German and Japanese monopolists are frequently in alliance with their U.S.A. opposites, who often put them forward in imperialism's general offensive against Africa, where open United States private investment might be regarded with more suspicion than others. Germany, moreover, is now second to the U.S.A. in the scale of so-called assistance to the developing countries. Since capitalism is the embodiment of the philosophy of self-interest, the ostensible allies of America's monopolists must use the position of strength into which they are being thrust to promote their own growth.

This struggle for ascendancy among the imperialisms is continuous and involves a constant search for renewal of the sinews of strength. Alongside the battle for imperialist supremacy, there wages the fight against the ideological camp of socialism, into which the warring imperialists make an all-out effort to trail the developing countries as their appendages. In this way the anti-communist campaign is used to further imperialist aims. Leaders of monopoly capitalism everywhere build up in the public mind an image of the system in socio-cultural terms by which they transform it into an idealised harmonious civilisation that must be cherished at all costs. They harp upon a way of life that may be altered only to its detriment, and stress its continuity as a major principle in the fight against communism. When Harold Macmillan as Prime Minister of Britain told the South African parliament that 'what is now on trial is much more than our military strength or our diplomatic and administrative skill—it is our way of life', he epitomised the metaphysical transmutation of economic impulses into a social philosophy. This, in spite of his reference to 'winds of change' blowing across Africa. He echoed the several statesmen of the West, any of whom could have made the statement and, indeed, have at different times and in almost identical words, 'The great issue in this second half of the twentieth century is whether the uncommitted peoples of Asia and Africa will swing to the East or to the West.' All the powerful imperialist nations are decided that the new States shall develop along the capitalist path, the provisioners of imperialism's vital needs, the source of its super profits. National liberation and the obvious advantages of socialist development for nations evolving out of a colonialist domination and without the capital means for making that development, are major factors determining imperialist strategy towards these nations, in both the interests of its internal struggle and in the fight against socialism.

All countries, even the most deeply involved in monopoly imperialism, have a State sector. Indeed, State involvement in private economy has become an essential part of its process. It should cause no surprise, therefore, that developing countries, particularly in view of the small accumulations of local private capital, are obliged to centralise their economies. The size of the State sector and its planned expansion, however, must depend on the economic system which is chosen, capitalist or socialist. The aim of the imperialist powers, in the application of their aid programmes, is to turn the State sector into an appendage of private capital. In view of the process that has been evolved in the imperialist countries, it would be surprising if this were not so. The declared basic policy of the Agency for International Development (formerly International Co-operation Administration) is 'to employ United States assistance to aid-receiving countries in such a way as will encourage the development of the private sectors of their economies. Thus, I.C.A. will normally not be prepared to finance publicly owned industrial and extractive enterprises, although it is realised that there may be exceptions. . . .'

Development in the new countries along non-capitalistic lines must be frustrated in the interests of Western imperialism. A series of articles which appeared in *The* (London) *Times* in April 1964 outlined the pattern and made no secret of its reasons: 'The two great objects of Britain's foreign policy must be to prevent the non-communist world from being penetrated by Communism ... and secondly, to prevent her own access to trade and investment in any part of the world from being barred or limited.' Naturally enough, as the articles conclude, 'both these objects lead straight into the "neo-colonial" issue—the struggle for influence, commercial and political, over the non-communist countries outside Europe and North America'. Thus succintly does the writer in *The Times* expose the true character of the ideological struggle between monopolies. Leading this ideological struggle, because she leads the inter-imperialist struggle, is the U.S.A. As the world's leading imperialist power, America lays successor claim to the so-called vacua which the retiring colonial powers are said to leave behind as they give way to nationalist governments. Vietnam and Congo are very obvious symbols of this policy of rabid neo-colonialism. They are also examples of bitter antagonisms between American and other imperialisms. According to *France Observateur* (issue of 4 June 1964), 'The darkest accusations are made by the U.S. against French business circles operating in S. Vietnam. ... American experts in Asian affairs assert that French planters are not content with paying their mite to the South Vietnam National Liberation Front. They will even lend assistance and hide the guerillas pursued by the Government's army.'

In spite of its policy of open aggression in many parts of the globe, the United States frequently poses as the 'anti-colonial' power in condemnation of British imperialism. 'The pose is thin, and the mask continually falls, even often over critical anti-colonialist resolutions pressed by the Afro-Asian and socialist majority in the United Nations, when the United States and Britain find themselves alone, or only with France, Portugal, South Africa and Australia voting against or abstaining.'* In the last nine years American investments on this

---

* *British Colonial Policy and Neo-Colonialist Rivalries*, R. Palme Dutt, International Affairs, Moscow, August 1964.

continent have trebled, growing at a faster rate than in any other area. In 1961 alone American monopolies profited by some £11·2 m. which they took out of Africa.

The rising tide of nationalism in the colonial territories was remarked by the shrewder operators of United States finance capital as America's opportunity to insinuate itself into what were the jealously guarded preserves of rival imperialisms. Anti-imperialist stirrings had begun to show themselves in Asia and Africa before the outbreak of the last world war. As hostilities progressed, America came out more and more openly for the ending of colonial rule. Press and other public propaganda harked back to America's own fight against colonialism. The remembrance was linked in people's minds with the budding nationalist movements that were bringing overt pressure for independence around the globe. War-torn Europe would provide part of the answer to America's need to export investment capital and goods; but territories newly released from the political power of rival imperialisms would offer practically virgin fields.

A fabulous growth in American monopoly capitalism occurred during the first forty years of the present century. United States foreign investments vied with those of Europe, overtook and surpassed them. In 1900, American private foreign investments were small by comparison with Europe's— $500 m. to Britain's $12,000 m. and France's $600 m. By 1930 the growth rate of America's foreign investments had already overleaped those of Britain, standing at $17,000 m. against the latter's $19,000, and way ahead of France's $7,000 m. America's foreign investment position was supreme by 1949— $19,000 m. against Britain's $12,000 m., the level at which it had opened the century. France's level had sunk to $2,000 m. The first world war eliminated Germany's foreign investments and reduced those of France; the second world war eliminated Germany, Italy and Japan. The American Government, moreover, had added $14,000 m. to its monopolists' $19,000 m. of private foreign investments. The Government loans 'are political loans rather than direct profit-making investments. But they enhance the position of United States finance-capital, by providing markets for surplus goods and by increasing profits of private American investors in the borrowing countries'.* The second world war gave explosive momentum to American capitalism and helped it to increase its overseas investments and exports of manufactured goods to the colonial preserves of European and Japanese imperialism. In the decade 1938–48 America's share of the imports into these territories rose from 11 per cent to 25 per cent. Her African trade in the period went from $150 m. to $1,200 m., at which figure it represented almost 15 per cent of all Africa's foreign trade.

American monopoly's appetite was whetted by the income of $18,000 m. by which it had profited from its foreign investments in the period 1920–48. The prospects in 1948 looked even richer, and proved so. Between 1950 and 1959 private American firms invested $4,500 m. in the developing countries and made three times as much. Net profits came to $8,300 m., to which can be added millions of dollars in trading profits, interest on loans, freight charges and other ancillary operations. All of this was helped along by Marshall Aid (the Economic Co-operation Administration), born out of the marriage between the American State and monopoly. The dollar was brandished as the universal cure-me-quick for Europe, bringing fat super profits to its American owners. In the confusion and devastation left by war, they were to slip unobtrusively into the cosy corners from which the European imperialists would be edged out both from Europe and its territories overseas. American financial and industrial capital used the opportunity which Europe's post-war weakness offered to draw upon its resources. It fed on war-ruined Europe, though not to the same degree as Western imperialism exploited the colonial and semi-colonial world. The powerful German metallurgical and chemical trusts, Vereinigte Stahlwerke and I. G. Farben, were broken down. The West German State established in 1949 came under a military occupation that controlled its foreign trade, its foreign policy and defence. Of the factories which had escaped wartime destruction, some were dismantled. Many of Germany's best scientists and technicians

* See *American Imperialism*, Perlo, pp. 28–29.

were lured to America and Britain. The secrets and patents of the large trusts were appropriated, the archives of the most important bank, the Deutsche Bank, turned over to the occupying forces by Dr Hermann J. Abs, Hitler's despoiler of Yugoslavia, who was saved from the death to which he was condemned first by the British and then by the American military authorities. Germany was being made safe for the democracy of its imperialist conquerors. The Marshall Plan was used to push American imperialist penetrations into the fragmented German industries and financial institutions, into which it bought heavily. Large sums were also handed out to French and Belgian mining concerns in order to tighten the links with American capitalism and support its domination.

An eye also had to be kept on the socialism that was advancing in Europe and Asia. Before the opening of the 1950s the cold war began to hot up. It was felt that the threat of heavy German competition which had inspired the limitations put upon it by the victorious imperialisms could be cushioned by drawing Germany into Western strategy and by greater participations from United States capital. Germany's position in the metallurgical and chemical fields began to change as that country was drawn into the over-all pattern of Western defence.

More energetic exploration for metal and mineral resources was undertaken in Africa and elsewhere. Africa's raw materials are an important consideration in the military build-up of the NATO countries, in which are included those of the European Common Market. Their industries, especially the strategic and nuclear factories, depend largely upon the primary materials that come from the less developed countries. Post-war Europe sustained a precarious shortage of basic supplies for its steel manufactures. Belgium needed more rich ores, Sweden more coal and coke, which America supplied in return for fine ores. Britain lacked pig iron and scrap, her coke was short and inferior. Both France and Germany had fallen behind in coke supplies. Production of Lorraine coal was declining because of lack of equipment, German coal because the Ruhr was producing less. Investment in industries 'with a high value production', that is, the mineral transformation and heavy industries, while providing the opportunity to influence the European economies and hence their policies towards United States' ideological domination, did not give the same scope for the quicker and larger profits that production of primary products in the emergent countries offered.

The Point Four Programme supported the Marshall Planners in opening up Africa to United States capital and its European associates. Before the second world war only three per cent of America's foreign investments were in Africa and less than five per cent of the continent's trade was with the United States. Firestone interests in Liberian rubber and small participations in South African and Rhodesian mines accounted for most of the $200 m. invested in Africa. As the war pushed into this continent, military bases and trade connections were established by the Americans, from which they pursued their greater penetrations after the end of the war. E.C.A. (Marshall Plan) funds financed American exploration groups, sent in the best colonial tradition to prepare the way for mining companies and military expeditions. It was announced by E.C.A. in July 1949 that 'American experts with Marshall Plan aid are probing Africa from the Atlas Mountains to the Cape of Good Hope for agricultural and mineral wealth', and later on that 'opportunities for American capital participation were disclosed in French North African lead mining, French Cameroon tin mining, French Congo lead-zinc mining. . . .' An E.C.A. loan to Mines de Zellidja, a French concern under the aegis of the Penarroya company, the fourth largest lead and zinc producer in the world, enabled Newmont Mining Corporation (an American mining and crude oil concern with 30 per cent of its interests in South Africa and Canada) to buy into the company and manage its operations.

Europe's post-war instability was turned to United States' account in the new division of Africa. In the fall of 1949, after America had forced currency devaluation upon the European countries, a committee of leading British and American bankers was formed to push U.S. investments in Africa and other parts of the still remaining British Empire. A similar committee with similar purpose was established two months later between American bankers and those of France. The hand of these establishments is seen today all over Africa in the consortia that are fast laying a grip on the continent's riches. Rockefeller, Morgan, Kuhn Loeb and Dillon Read institutions; the big British banks, Barclays, Lloyds, Westminster, Provincial, the investment houses pivoted around Hambros, Rothschild, Philip Hill; the French banks, Banque de Paris et des Pays Bas, Banque de l'Union Parisienne, Banque de l'Indochine, Union Européen Industrielle, Banque Worms, Crédit Lyonnais, Lazard Frères, etc., and the leading German and Italian banks.

These and their associates are the financial institutions that dominate the monetary and fiscal sectors of many of the newly independent States. They support the new industrial revolution of automation, electronics and nuclear and space development, in which America plays the lead and which has swept U.S. imperialism to its present ascendancy. American groups dominant in the mining and ore processing and finishing industries are involved directly or through their bankers and financing houses in ventures with leading European producers and their financial backers. The finance-capitalists who control the leading corporations in the extractive, metallurgical, chemical, nuclear and space industries of the west are to be seen stretching out across the seven seas and taking command of the sources of primary materials in Asia, Oceania, Australia, New Zealand, Central and South America, and Africa. U.S. investments in Canada in 1962 went up by nearly $700 m., mostly for developing iron ore properties. An additional $270 m. invested in other developed countries went mainly to Australia and Japan. Latin American investments of United States capital increased by $250 m. in 1962. In the previous year the increase was over $400 m. The U.S. Department of Commerce reported that private American investments and assets overseas reached $60,000 m. at the end of 1962 and advanced a further $3,000 m. in the first six months of 1963. Private investors in the United States added $4,300 m. in 1962 to their holdings of assets and investments abroad.

Direct private American investment in Africa increased

between 1945 and 1958 from $110 m. to $789 m., most of it drawn from profits. Of the increase of $679 m. actual new money invested during the period was only $149 m., United States profits from these investments, including reinvestment of surpluses, being estimated at $704 m. As a result African countries sustained losses of $555 m. If allowance is made for grants for 'non-military' purposes, estimated then by U.S. Congress at $136 m., Africa's net total losses still reached $419 m. Official American statistics put the gross profits made by U.S. monopolies in Africa between 1946–59 at $1,234 m., though other estimates place them at $1,500 m. Whichever way they are looked at, it requires no great mathematical mind to make out from these figures the almost hundred per cent profitability on investment in Africa.

The avid explorations that have gone on apace in the last two or three decades for additional reserves of all the metals and minerals that are important for modern industrial supremacy have been instigated by the drive for monopoly, upon which supremacy and its super-profits rest. A recent example makes the principle clear. Alcan Industries, a British associate of Alcoa (Aluminium Company of America) through Alcan (Aluminium Ltd. of Canada), according to a *Sunday Times* headline (issue of 18 October 1964), wrapped up 'the last of the foil'. That is, Alcan Industries paid £5½ m. to take over the last independent firm (Fisher's Foils) in British aluminium foil making, having already swallowed most of the rest. This was done, it is said, to bring about 'rationalisation'. But in boardroom talk it has another meaning, 'sewing up the industry'.

Part of the objective of gaining control of industries and new-found raw materials' sources is to deprive rivals of their use. The manipulation of artificial scarcity is another of monopoly's tactics for maintaining profits. For three years until mid-1964 the big copper companies were running production at between 80 and 85 per cent of capacity to keep up prices. Steel production, too, was held back to something like 80 per cent of capacity. Exploitation under imperialism does not, nor will, always follow upon the finding of new sources of raw materials. Whoever monopolises the major sources of supply controls output by having the decisive voice in what deposits shall or shall not be worked, and to what degree.

Monopoly allows the monopolists to manipulate the economies of other countries in their interests. In the case of bauxite, for instance, Mellon-dominated Alcoa is sovereign and has drawn into its orbit the other major producers, Kaiser and Reynolds. Because of the tremendous cost of building power plants, upon which the conversion of bauxite into alumina depends, the exploitation of all known reserves of this ore by private capital would defeat the prime incentive of monopoly—profit—for the super-abundant production that would result would depress prices. West Africa is exceptionally rich in bauxite, but the individual countries are not equally favoured with the power to develop resources. Ghana is providing hydro-electric power which could be used to convert alumina in both Ghana and Guinea. This would be a welcome co-operative effort within the framework of a united continental economy.

Another weapon that is held over the heads of the primary producing countries is the threat of using synthetic alternatives, and the replacement of traditional metals by others. Synthetic diamond plants have been established by De Beers, the world's monopolist in natural diamonds, by the Belgian company, MIBA, which controls Congo's natural diamonds, the largest supplier in Africa, by the General Electric Corporation in the U.S. and by Japan. The price of copper was held down by the main producers on the London metal market at a period of recession in its marketing because of the likely use of aluminium in its place for certain purposes, while plastics, on the other hand, are frequently proposed as an alternative to aluminium. Vast sums are expended in research for new materials and in scientific invention of labour-saving machinery and equipment. Thus metals that are being threatened with substitution are at the same time being developed for a wider variety of finished goods. Such research projects and the resultant re-equipment of factories and industries which must be done if the original investment is to be justified, calls for tremendous capital sums which frequently can only be met from the assets of financial and insurance establishments. Consequently, banks and insurance companies dominate industrial finance and exercise a leading role in the push for monopolist ascendancy. The banks and insurance companies have been foremost in the process that has brought monopoly to its present peak, and it is their financial power that supports the increasing movement towards greater and greater concentration of monopoly.

Today, competition in the thrust to secure and hold monopoly over whole industries and sources of raw materials has intensified to the point where mergers are taking place at a dizzy rate. The struggle is grimly tense and in the ding-dong battle for domination a truce is arranged at critical points, by which influence is divided with mutual consent. Harmony, however, is more apparent than real. The struggle for re-division is proceeding all the time, and the changes that take place within the combining organisations are observed to be more and more frequent.

Present-day monopoly is highly variegated and spread out. While it draws its strength from its monopolistic position, it is on the other hand seriously exposed to the dangers that face a multiple organism that stretches its limbs to extremity in different directions. A fracture at any one point can lead to a disjunction which may unbalance the structure. And the monopoly's rivals are always on the alert to spot its most exposed parts in order to deliver a blow that will enable the most relentless competitor to insinuate into the broken organ. Hence monopoly, having passed through the stages of cartelisation, combine, trust and syndicate, is today more and more making use of a further protective safeguard. That is the consortium, through which it aims at immobilising the rivals and disarming the associates who are permitted to join this most ravishing of imperialist contrivances. Usually in a consortium there is a dominant party, either directly or through (and with) affiliates and associates, which enables it to exert the largest influence upon the affairs of the consortium. Furthermore, each of the parties to the consortium will have its own string of appendages or even a principal standing outside the consortium. All continue the fight outside, while those within exercise their efforts to enlarge the importance of their share of the group activities. For example, as a monopoly it will be in control of a complex of companies connected at many levels with the production of primary materials, their processing from the original state right through all the stages of transformation into a variety of semi-finished and finished goods from the most ordinary article to the most complicated and delicate equipment and heavy plant and machinery. The monopoly does not restrict itself to a single raw material, though it will be pre-eminent in one or two. Nor does it restrict itself to any particular department of manufacture or enterprise that may be ancillary to its basic activities, though here again it may specialise in certain lines. Many monopolies branch into real estate and land development projects, as construction and contracting work bring quick and high returns and high rents. This form of capital investment is growing rapidly in the present era of enlarging industrialisation and the growth of new towns, and extends to large-scale agriculture.

In Africa the consortium is making the most sinister penetrations. It extends from the monopolistic amalgamations of American and European finance-capital, particularly those combined within the European Common Market, where financial consortia have been set up as the most effective means of profiting from the competitive struggle that is spiralling within this so-called unifying organisation. The prime objective is to monopolise Africa's sources of raw materials, not, as it is claimed, to assist the African countries to develop their economies. For the materials are carried off largely in their raw state or as concentrates to enhance the productive output of the imperialist countries and to be returned to them in the form of heavy equipment for extractive industry and the infrastructure for carrying the resources away.

It is out of the revenue from the trade in these materials that the African countries look to amass part of the capital that will make it possible for them to utilise these same commodities in the service of their own development. Paradoxically, however, these precious counters in Africa's future are meantime being used to widen the economic gap between her and the highly industrialised countries, which are hurriedly exploiting the opportunity to make good deficiencies in their economies. Since those who are carrying on the exploitation are also the monopolists who manipulate the markets for primary products at the one end and the price for the final products at the other, the countries of origin must be pinned down to a long wait before they can tackle on a major scale the capital problem facing all the developing countries of seriously raising the standard of life of their people, if they make no effort to gird their resources in a more practical and self-supporting manner. This is the answer to those pious economists who assure us that what matters is not what is taken out of our lands but what is left behind.

The reply has been given by the Commission for Aid to Development of O.E.C.D. in its estimate that if the industrial countries continue to increase their gross national product by three per cent per annum, it will take the less developed countries two hundred years at least to catch up with their standard of living, assuming that the unindustrialised nations reach an annual increase of five per cent. Yet how problematical the achievement of this five per cent remains in the light of the drain on resources from the less developed countries to the highly developed ones. In most African countries the rate of rise in the domestic product has barely kept pace with the rate of population growth of two and a half to three per cent. It is the less developed countries that continue to carry the burden of the increasing development of the highly developed. Firestone, for example, has taken $160 m. worth of rubber out of Liberia in the past quarter century. In return the Liberian Government has received a paltry $8 m. The average net profit made by this American company is three times the entire Liberian revenue.

From south to north, financial and industrial consortia have spread across Africa, busily staking out claims to mineral, metal and fuel resources, to forest and land produce, and erecting extractive and primary conversion industries in which they are entrenched as stanchions. In Algeria, for example, the really big investment stampede coincided with the war of national liberation. Between 1951 and 1955 there was an inrush of French and French-American investment greater than ever before. Win or lose, the financial and industrial interests were entrenching themselves within the Algerian economy. Throughout Africa the industrial giants are supported by financial institutions which dominate the monetary and fiscal sectors of so many of the independent States. Most heavily engaged are the mammoth banking and insurance institutions and the multi-millionaire companies they control, bolstered by the international institutions like the World Bank and its affiliates. These formidable alliances radiate from the United States, Britain, Germany, France, Holland, Italy, Sweden. They move around the metallurgical and chemical combines with the E.C.S.C. (European Coal and Steel Community), such as Sollac, G.I.S. (Groupement de l'Industrie Sidérurgique), Sidelor (Union Sidérurgique Lorraine), Usinor (Union Sidérurgique du Nord de la France), Krupp, Thyssen, Kuhlmann, Pierrelatte, Farbwerke Hoechst, Bayer, BASF (Badische Anilin & Soda Fabrik), I.C.I. They are in the assemblages of bankers such as Consafrique (Consortium Européen pour le Développement des Ressources Naturelles de l'Afrique), situated at the same address as the International Bank in Luxembourg; Eurofin, Compagnie Bancaire, Finsider, Cofimer, Union Européenne Industrielle et Financière, and others.

Powerful American corporations like Bethlehem Steel, United States Steel, Republic Steel, Armco Steel, Newmont Mining, Johns Manville, Union Carbide, Olin Mathieson, Alcoa, Kaiser, crop up among all the post-war primary materials producing projects on this continent. Their alliances are spread among the leading metallurgical and financial companies of Europe in combinations that mask the underlying competition. This competitiveness erupts to the surface when circumstances cause a breakdown in the facade of peaceful co-existence between rival imperialists operating in the sovereign States of others, to which they make assumptions of power and use as pawns in the struggle for monopolistic supremacy. Gabon is vocal testimony to these assertions. Mass discontent with the existing regime which led to the disorders of February 1964 was the occasion utilised by France to warn the United States that she would brook no encroachment on the claims she lays to the manganese, uranium and oil riches of this, her former colony. Neglected under the colonial regime, these resources have assumed inestimable value to France in the struggle against the advance of American imperialism in Europe in the new epoch of atomic rivalry. France sent in paratroopers to force the issue of whose pawn Gabon would remain. United States Steel may have the dominant participation in Comilog (Cie de l'Ogooue), which is working on the bed of the vastly rich Franceville manganese deposits, but France, through the Cie des Mines d'Uranium de Franceville, controls the uranium field at Mounana, and is urgently occupied in the attempt to foil the aspirations of the American oil barons to undisputed access to Gabon's offshore petroleum reaches.

5. The truth behind the headlines

REALLY to understand what goes on in the world today, it is necessary to understand the economic influences and pressures that stand behind the political events. The financial columns of the world's press give, in fact, 'the news behind the news'. Every few days we come upon such newspaper announcements as: 'Morgan Grenfell participates in new French bank'; or 'African Banking Group'; or 'Consortium gains voting power in Hulett' (South African sugar monopoly); or 'New factoring company set up in Germany'.

These are newspaper headlines actually taken at random. However, when examined even briefly, the facts reveal an attenuated line of connection between powerful financial groups that exert the most decisive pressure upon the happenings of our time. The facts relate to the men and interests directly involved or indirectly connected with the rearrangements the articles cover. Not that the full facts are ever revealed. On the contrary, they are more often concealed, and it takes knowledge of the careers of the personalities and groups which the articles link to see behind them the inevitable direction of the reported arrangements and their intrinsic meaning in terms of economic and political power.

Let us take the item of the Morgan Grenfell participation in the new French bank (*Financial Times*, London, 18 December 1962). Morgan Grenfell & Co. acts effectively as the London end of the important American banking house of

J. P. Morgan & Co. which, in 1956, already owned one-third of the British company. It should not, therefore, surprise us to learn that the new 'continental' bank in which Morgan Grenfell is participating is called Morgan et Cie; more especially, since 70 per cent of the capital of 10 million new francs is held by the Morgan Guaranty International Finance Corporation, and 15 per cent by Morgan Grenfell. What about the remaining 15 per cent? This is divided between two Dutch banks—Hope & Co. of Amsterdam and R. Mees & Zoonen of Rotterdam—with both of which the Morgan group has had close association over many years. This association has been drawn even closer by the acquisition in March 1963 of a 14 per cent in both of them by the Morgan Guaranty International Banking Corporation, a subsidiary of Morgan Guaranty Trust.

How was this done? Through the purchase of stock in Bankier-compagnie, a company that consolidated the activities of the two Dutch banks, which, nevertheless, continue to do business under their own names. This form of one in two is the accepted formula by which the great combinations attempt to delude the world about their compact formations.

Chairman of Morgan et Cie is Mr Pierre Meynial, vice-president of Morgan Guaranty Trust in Paris, whose brother, Mr Raymond Meynial, is a director of the Banque Worms. Vice-president of Morgan et Cie is the Rt. Hon. Viscount Harcourt, K.C.M.G., O.B.E., a managing director of Morgan Grenfell and chairman of four important British insurance companies—British Commonwealth, Gresham Fire & Accident, Gresham Life Assurance, and Legal & General.

'French African banking move' captions an item of rather less than eight lines in the *Financial Times* of 26 July 1963, which informs us shortly that 'the network of the Banque Commerciale Africaine in Senegal, Ivory Coast, Cameroun and Congo Republic has been taken over by Société Générale, France's second largest bank'. It is in the single comment the newspaper allows itself that we find the grist: 'The arrangement will result in a substantial increase in the volume of deposits held by Société Générale'.

Société Générale was founded under Napoleon the Third in 1864. One of its chief participants was Adolphe Schneider, a member of the Schneider iron and steel empire, who was at the same period also one of the regents of Banque de France. Both Banque de France and Société Générale have now been nationalised. This means in effect that the French Government has a direct interest in the network of the Banque Commerciale Africaine that Société Générale has taken over.

Nationalisation does not stand in the way of the closest association with the world's most powerful private banking institutions, as the facts given under the title 'African banking group' (*West Africa*, 22 September 1963) illustrate. The title, however, is misleading. There is little that is 'African' about the group, the body mainly concerned being the Bankers International Corporation, a subsidiary of Bankers Trust Company, which shares with Morgan Guaranty Trust the commercial business of J. P. Morgan & Co. The others are Société Générale and other unnamed European financial institutions.

This combination of Western banks, topped by the long-armed Morgan interests, is to extend the formation of banks in just those territories where Société Générale has acquired the interests of Banque Commerciale Africaine, namely, Ivory Coast, Senegal, Cameroun and Congo (Brazzaville). The American Federal Reserve Board has given its approval to the Morgan extension, as have the governments of the African countries concerned. Comment is unnecessary, since we can readily accept the view of the senior vice-president and head of the international banking department of the Bankers Trust, Mr G. T. Davies, who happily announced that participation in these four nations will substantially increase the scope of Bankers Trust company's activities in Africa, a continent in which we are vitally interested. The news item concludes with the information that Bankers International Corporation has equity interests in the Liberian Trading & Development Bank (Tradevco), and in the United Bank of Africa, Nigeria.

The fact that another sugar consortium (*Financial Times*, 8 November 1962) has managed to obtain over 50 per cent of

71

the ordinary shares and thereby the majority voting power in the South African sugar monopoly of Sir J. Hulett & Sons appears, on the surface, to be entirely unrelated to the other newspaper items we have already scrutinised. But let us go on with our examination.

Behind the combination of sugar companies that has gained ascendancy in the Hulett monopoly are visible the hands of two important South African share issuing and underwriting houses, Philip Hill Higginson & Co. (Africa), and Union Acceptances Ltd.

Harold Charles Drayton is the dominating personality in the Philip Hill chain of financial and investment companies, based in London. Harry F. Oppenheimer of South Africa is chairman of Union Acceptances. Among Mr Drayton's company appointments are those of chairman of European & General Corporation, Second Consolidated Trust, and director of Midland Bank and Midland Bank Executor & Trustee Co., Eagle Star Insurance Co., Standard Bank, Consolidated Gold Fields of South Africa and Ashanti Goldfields Corporation.

Mr Oppenheimer, among his more than seventy company appointments, includes those of chairman of African Explosives & Chemical Industries, Anglo American Corporation of South Africa, De Beers Consolidated Mines, and First Union Investment Trust. He is a director of African & European Investment Co., Barclays Bank D.C.O., British South African Co. and Central Mining & Investment Corporation.

Deputy chairman of Anglo American Corporation is Sir K. Acutt, who is also a director of British South Africa Co. and Standard Bank. Co-director with the deputy chairman of Anglo American Corporation on British South Africa Co. is Mr Robert Annan, who sits beside Mr Drayton on the board of Consolidated Goldfields. Mr Annan also has the distinction of being an extraordinary director of Scottish Amicable Life Assurance Society.

A colleague of Mr Drayton's on both the Midland Bank and the bank's Executor & Trust Co. is the Rt. Hon. Lord Baillieu, K.B.E., C.M.G., who happens to be at the same time deputy chairman of the Central Mining & Investment Corporation, on which Harry F. Oppenheimer is to be found. Lord Baillieu sits also on English Scottish & Australian Bank.

Another director of Standard Bank is Mr William Antony Acton, whose close ties with the banking world are seen in his deputy chairmanship of the National Bank and directorships on the Bank of London & Montreal, Standard Bank Finance & Development Corporation, Bank of London & South America and Bank of West Africa. It is certainly not sheer coincidence that Lord Luke of Pavenham has a seat with H. C. Drayton on the board of Ashanti Goldfields and occupies a directorship on the Bank of London & South America, on which Mr Acton is seated. Nor can it be by mere chance that Mr Esmond Charles Baring, former director and London agent of Anglo American Corporation and associated with a number of other companies in the Oppenheimer group, is a member of the family that operates the merchant house of Baring Bros. and maintains the closest links with the investment world.

Other important personages who graced the board of British South Africa Co. in 1963 were the late Sir Charles J. Hambro, P. V. Emrys-Evans, and Viscount Malvern, P.C., C.H., K.C.M.H. Sir Charles Hambro was the senior director of the Bank of England. He chaired the biggest of the City of London's merchant banks, the £176 million Hambros Bank, and presided over Union Corporation, the South African mining finance group which embraces numerous of the Anglo American interests associated with the Harry F. Oppenheimer concerns.

The Standard Bank of South Africa crops up once more among the directorships of Lord Malvern, which includes Scottish Rhodesia Finance and Merchant Bank of Central Africa. The last-named bank is a creation of the Rothschild banking group, in which one finds Banque Lambert, one of the important Belgian banks, some 17·5 per cent of whose interests are concentrated in Africa, notably in the Congo. The bank also has an interest in another Rothschild creation, the Five Arrows Securities Co., an investment house operating in Canada, and under Rockefeller influence. Mr Paul V. Emrys-Evans, British South Africa Co.'s vice-president, is now president of Oppenheimer's expansive Anglo American Corporation, and also upon that of Barclays Bank D.C.O. A seat on Rio Tinto Zinc Corporation brings Mr Emrys-Evans into the company of Lord Baillieu, its deputy chairman, and his associations with H. C. Drayton.

Several of the leading British banks and insurance companies and some of their European associates participate in the Standard Bank. Its chairman, Sir Frank Cyril Hawker, used to represent the Bank of England, and its vice-chairman, Sir F. W. Leith-Ross, represents the National Provincial Bank. W. A. Acton's banking associations have already been outlined above. H. C. Drayton brings in the interests of his own financial groups, as well as those of the Midland Bank and Eagle Star Insurance. Sir E. L. Hall Patch, a director of the Standard Bank of South Africa who resigned at the July 1963 annual general meeting, is a director of Commercial Union Assurance Co. Sir G. S. Harvie-Watt is an associate of H. C. Drayton on Eagle Star Insurance and the Midland Bank. He is chairman of Consolidated Gold Fields and a director of American Zinc Lead & Smelting Co. of the U.S.A.

John Francis Prideaux brings the interests of the Commonwealth Development Corporation into the bank, as well as those of Westminster Bank, the Bank of New South Wales and sundry other financial and investment concerns. William Michael Robson as vice-chairman of the Joint East & Central African Board of the Standard Bank, brings to bear all those vested interests joined in the Board, while he represents separately the investments of the finance holding, merchant, shipping and plantation companies of the Booker Bros. McConnell group, which has a monopoly grip upon the economy of British Guiana. Charles Hyde Villiers holds a brief for Banque Belge Ltd. and Sun Life Assurance Society. Banque Belge Ltd. is the London outlet of Banque de la Société Générale de Belgique and controls in its turn, among others, Banque du Congo Belge, Belgian-American Banking Corporation, Belgian-American Bank & Trust Co., Continental American Fund (Ameri-fund) of Baltimore, U.S.A., and Canadafund Co., Montreal, Canada.

The headline, 'New factoring company set up in Germany' (*Financial Times*, 4 October 1963), has a superficially innocuous look. However, the briefest glance at the text takes us at once right into the world of international banking. For we meet extensions of British and American capital that have stimulated and supported an international factoring venture which has expanded in a very short time across four continents. The focal point is a Swiss holding company, International Factors AG. of Chur. Its nominal capital is Sw. Frs. 6,000,000 (about £490,000). It has now established activity in Germany, where a company, International Factors Deutschland, has been set up in conjunction with three German banks, the Chur company retaining 50 per cent of the capital. Of the rest, 20 per cent is held by the Frankfurter Bank, 25 per cent by Mittel-rheinische Kreditbank Dr Horback & Co., and five per cent by a private bank in Frankfurt, George Hauck. Frankfurter Bank's portion, however, will be enlarged by the fact that it has acquired a 51 per cent stake in Horback & Co., by way of a share exchange.

The heavy banking interests behind the international factoring venture, which has affiliates in Switzerland, Australia, South Africa, Israel, and now Germany, are the First National Bank of Boston, and M. Samuel & Co. of London. A holding company under Samuel influence, Tozer Kemsley & Milbourn (Holdings), is a third. The First National Bank of Boston, once firmly inside the great Morgan financial empire, has, since 1955, come increasingly under Rockefeller influence, though it still has significant ties with Morgan. It is joined with Chase National Bank (Rockefeller) in the American Overseas Finance Corporation.

Chairman of M. Samuel & Co. is Viscount Bearsted, a director of the Rothschild creation, Alliance Assurance Co. and its affiliate, Sun Alliance Insurance. Chairman of both these insurance companies is Mr T. D. Barclay, a director of Barclays Bank, Barclays Bank (France) and British Linen Bank, a Barclays Bank affiliate.

At the beginning of February 1963, the First National City Bank of New York, through International Banking Corporation, institutions controlled by the Rockefeller interests, bought a 16⅔ per cent share in M. Samuel & Co., represented by 600,000 ordinary shares, at a cost of £1,900,000. First National City placed the chairman of its executive committee, R. S. Perkins, upon the Samuel board. The shot in the arm injected by the Rockefeller capital has enabled the Samuel banking firm to spread itself into the European Market, where it has joined the European bankers association brought together by the important French bank, Banque de Paris et des Pays-Bas. This is Groupement d'Etudes pour l'Analyse des Valeurs Européennes, whose purpose is to canalise what is called 'institutional investment'.

The house of M. Samuel has also been placed in charge of managing another Common Market organisation, domiciled in London, New European & General Investment Trust, in which it is associated with Banque Lambert, Banque de Paris et des Pays-Bas, the prominent German banking house of Sal Oppenheim & Cie., the Dutch bankers, Lippmann, Rosenthal & Co., the Credito Italiano of Italy, Banco Urquijo of Spain and Union de Banques Suisses of Switzerland.

We may appear to have gone at some length into the intricacies of the financial and economic interests behind some innocent-looking headlines. Yet these are in fact the merest directional indications of today's trend of ever-tightening links between a short list of incredibly powerful groups that dominate our lives on a global scale. The task of taking their detailed significance farther is the main purpose of this book.

Nevertheless, even this brief breakdown provides illuminating evidence of the serpentine interlocking of financial monopoly today. What we observe, above all, is the constant penetration of a few banking and financial institutions into large industrial and commercial undertakings, creating a chain of links that bring them into a connective relationship making for domination in both national and international economy. The influence exercised by this domination is carried into politics and international affairs, so that the interests of the overriding monopoly groups govern national policies. Their representatives are placed in key positions in government, army, navy and air force, in the diplomatic service, in policy-making bodies and in international organisations and institutions through which the chosen policies are filtered on to the world scene.

This process had already reached a high enough pitch before the outbreak of the first world war to call forth a number of important studies of its growth and potentialities. Two of these studies, *Imperialism*, by the English Liberal, J. A. Hobson, published in 1902, and *Finance Capital*, by the Austrian Marxist, Rudolf Hilferding, published in 1910, were used by Lenin as the main basis of his study of *Imperialism*, which he described as 'the highest stage of capitalism'.

It came at the stage at which competition transformed into monopoly, the so-called *combination* of production, that is to say, the grouping in a single enterprise of different branches of industry, and monopoly itself became dominated by banking and finance capital. Lenin's study was written in 1916. Since then the domination of financial monopoly has speeded up tremendously.

How is it possible that capitalism, rooted in free enterprise and competition, has arrived at a stage where competition is being eroded to the point where pyramidal monopolies exercise dictatorial rights? The possibility lay in the very fact of free enterprise itself. The spur of competition led to invention on several planes. New machinery was devised to increase output and profit, factories grew larger. Small units became unprofitable and were either driven out or swallowed up by bigger ones. Rail communication improved distribution and better ocean transport stimulated overseas trade and the bringing in of foreign raw materials.

The joint stock company that encouraged the growth of rail and ocean transport served as a forcing instrument for banking and insurance growth. New company laws assisted its extension to industrial and commercial enterprises in which the individual investor's risk was lessened by the limitation upon his liability.

Competition moved on to another level. Companies that possessed large capital or were able to call upon it on their own security were able to wield an unequal influence against weaker ones. Profits became hinged to the elimination of competition. The enormous expansion of industry at the end of last century and the beginning of the present, was accompanied by a rapid concentration into ever larger enterprises.

Combination of production was established as a cardinal feature of capitalism. Firms that had begun by concentrating upon one function of an industry spread into a group enterprise that represented the consecutive stages of raw materials processing, or were ancillary to one another. Trading houses extended their activities into distribution and then into actual production of finished goods from primary materials produced from plantations and mines they acquired in overseas territories.

Hilferding, in his classic work on the subject, *Finance Capital*, explains the reasons behind this process:

'Combination levels out the fluctuations of trade and therefore assures to the combined enterprises a more stable rate of profit. Secondly, combination has the effect of eliminating trade. Thirdly, it has the effect of rendering possible technical improvements, and consequently, the acquisition of super-profits over and above those obtained by the "pure" (i.e. non-combined) enterprises. Fourthly, it strengthens the position of the combined enterprises compared with that of the "pure" enterprises, strengthens them in the competitive struggle in periods of serious depression, when the fall in prices of raw materials does not keep pace with the fall in prices of manufactured goods.'

As monopoly of industry and commerce extended, the reliance upon banking capital also increased. New methods of production, the division of factories and businesses into departments, research into the possibilities of new materials and fresh ways of employing both old and new ones—all these, while they eventually reinforced monopoly and enlarged profits, called for capital sums that only the banks and their associates in the insurance world were able to provide. Thus side by side with the process of amalgamation of industrial enterprises went the concentration of banks and their penetration into the large industrial and commercial enterprises to whose capital they heavily contributed.

From middlemen, originally performing the role of simple moneylenders, the banks grew into powerful monopolies, having at their command almost the whole means of production and of the sources of raw materials of the given country and in a number of countries. This transformation of numerous humble middlemen into a handful of monopolists represents one of the fundamental processes in the growth of capitalism into capitalist imperialism.*

Union was established between the industrialist and the banker, in which the latter dominated. In the U.S.A., for instance, the United States Steel Corporation, which was an amalgamation of several giant steel firms controlling half the steel production of the country, was controlled by J. P. Morgan's banking interests because of the large investments they had in the industry. Before the end of the first decade of the present century, the inter-volutions of industry and banking had already taken place to a high degree. In Germany, for instance, six of the biggest banks were represented by their directors in a total of some 750 companies engaged in the most diverse branches of industry: insurance, transport, heavy industry, shipping, restaurants, theatres, art, publishing, etc. Conversely, there sat on the boards of these six banks in 1910, fifty-one of the biggest industrialists, including Krupp, iron and steel magnate, armaments manufacturer and director of the powerful Hamburg-American shipping line.

Today this process has gone very much deeper, and is spreading its roots more embracingly every day. The six German banks included the four giants, the Deutsche Bank, Dresdner Bank, Disconto Gesellschaft, Commerzbank, all of which have grown even more powerful. Allied with them today, as in 1910, are the big German industrial trusts and cartels. Krupp, A. E. G. Bayer, Badische Anilin & Soda Fabrik, Farbwerke Hoechst (the last three the components into which the great I. G. Farben was broken by the allies at the end of the second world war), the explosives and armaments manu-

* *Imperialism*, Lenin, p. 45.

facturers connected with the massive I.C.I. and its continental affiliate, Solvay. For example, the Deutsche Bank is now Germany's leading bank and is placed as eleventh among the foremost in the world. In 1870 the Deutsche Bank had a capital of 15 million marks which it had been able to increase to 200 million by 1908. In 1962 it disposed of funds amounting to 1,100 billions of old French francs.

The rule of the financial oligarchy is maintained through the principal device of the 'holding company', often established with a purely nominal capital but controlling direct and indirect subsidiaries and affiliates utilising vastly superior finances. Assuming that a 50 per cent holding of the capital is sufficient to control a company (sometimes it can be and is considerably less), it is possible with an investment of, say, £100,000 to control tens of millions in subsidiary and interlocked enterprises.

Concentrated in the hands of a few, finance capital exercises a virtual monopoly, by reason of which it exacts enormous and ever-increasing profits from company flotations, share underwritings, debenture holdings, state loans, and bond issues. The Deutsche Bank, for instance, adopts a specific procedure for gaining control of enterprises and drawing in fresh profits. When participating in the launching of new ventures or extensions of already existing ones, it finds the whole of the required capital from its own and associated resources. When the formation is complete, the shares are unloaded at a premium, the bank holding just sufficient to give it a commanding voice in the direction of affairs. At the same time, it takes a profit on the original capital.

Flotation of foreign loans provides one of the highest yielding fields of monopolist profits. Usually a borrowing country is lucky if it gets more than nine-tenths of the loan sum. Frequently it is less, particularly if it is a developing country. Liberia's loans are a revealing and classic example of how monopoly finance operates in conjunction with governments to increase its profits.

In Liberia, in 1904, President Arthur Barclay reported that the English seven per cent loan of 1871, originally £100,000, of which only £27,000 actually reached the Liberian Treasury because of certain official defalcations, was the largest item of the country's indebtedness and would require three years' revenue to cover it. A desperate Liberian Government succeeded in arranging an international loan of $1,700,000. This was subscribed by British, French, Dutch and German banking houses associated with the United States financial institutions of J. P. Morgan, the National City Bank, First National Bank of New York and Kuhn Loeb & Co.

In this instance, the most arbitrary means were used in applying and securing repayment of the loan. An American Receiver General was appointed by the United States and sub-receivers by Britain, France and Germany, an arrangement which continued until America took over full control of Liberia's finances during the first world war. Little actual cash went to the Liberian Government, but fancy profits went to the banks and loan issue houses. Bonds to the value of $715,000 were delivered in London, $225,000 in Germany, $460,000 in Amsterdam and $158,000 in New York to creditors of Liberia in payment of their outstanding claims. It required reparations money from the sale of German properties in Liberia to liquidate subsequent debts incurred with the then British Bank of West Africa to try and meet the claims on this loan.

It was only after a new loan was negotiated with the Firestone Corporation of America in 1926 that the Liberian Government was able to use $1,180,669 to pay off the principal and accumulated interest on the 1912 loan. The loan offered by Firestone was in the region of $5 million, at an interest rate of seven per cent, but by 1945 still only half of this amount had been subscribed. Firestone stipulations included the abolition of the office of Receiver of Customs and its replacement by a Financial Adviser. It was under pressure of these debts that Liberia was obliged to cede large concessions for rubber planting to Firestone, and later to the Goodrich Rubber Company.

One of the principal functions of finance capital is the issue of securities on which the discount rates are ridiculously high.

81

It is also an important method of consolidating financial oligarchy. In boom periods the profits are immense. During periods of depression, the banks acquire holdings by buying up small or failing businesses, or engage in their reorganisation at a profit. Money is made by the banks and the sphere of control is extended. Financial assistance to land speculators is extended. Financial assistance to land speculators is also a means of entrenching control and inflating profits in times of industrial expansion. Ground rent monopoly merges with communications monopoly, since an important factor governing rise in land prices is good means of communication with town centres.

In his book *Monopoly: A Study of British Monopoly Capitalism* published in 1955 by Lawrence and Wishart, Sam Aaronovitch has shown how the financial resources of Britain have become concentrated in the hands of a small number of big banks and financial institutions. Between them, the 'Big Five' banks exercise immense power. In 1951 their 147 directors held 1,008 directorships of which 299, just under a third, were in other financial institutions. Of these 299, 85 were in other banks and discount companies; 117 were in insurance companies and 97 in investment trusts and finance companies.' (p. 49.)

'Talk about centralisation!' wrote Karl Marx in *Capital* (Vol. 3, Ch. 33):

> 'The credit system, which has its centre in the so-called national banks and the great moneylenders and usurers about them is an enormous centralisation, and gives to this class of parasites a fabulous power . . . to interfere with actual production in a most dangerous manner—and this gang knows nothing about production and has nothing to do with it.'

Hegemony of the money institutions over industry is assured by the vast reserves built up out of the various ways by which capital is advanced to industry at high profit and drawn from it through holding companies and interlocking directorates. This process emphasises the separation of finance capital from industrial capital. When this separation has attained major proportions and the domination of finance capital has become supreme, the stage of imperialism has been reached. This stage can be said to have been brought to maturity at the turn of the century

From free competition, the fundamental characteristic of its early stages, capitalism at its highest stage, has polarised into monopoly, expressed in syndicates, trusts and cartels, with which the capital of a small number of banks has merged. The trusts and cartels have assumed an international character and divided up the world among themselves. Monopoly extends to the control of raw materials and markets, for the possession of which, highly developed capitalism engages in an even more intense struggle

At its imperialist stage, finance capital's primary need is to find spheres of overseas investment which will return profits at a greater rate than can be obtained at home. The export of capital, therefore, becomes the dynamo of imperialism which turns the export of commodities and leads to the capture of colonies as the means of assuring monopolist control. Upon this economic process is built the political ideology, the non-economic superstructure, that infuses the battle for colonial conquest. Hilferding expressed this ideology in a single concise sentence: 'Finance capital does not want liberty, it wants domination'. Possession of colonies gives a guarantee to the financial oligarchy of the owning country of the monopoly of actual and potential sources of raw materials and outlets for manufactured goods.

6. Primary resources and foreign interests

AMERICAN and European companies connected with the world's most powerful banking and financial institutions are, with the consent of African governments, entering upon major projects designed to exploit new sources of primary products. In some cases these are allied to long-term ventures for the establishment of certain essential industries. In the main, however, they are confining themselves to the production of materials in their basic or secondary stages, with the object of transforming them in the mills and plants owned and run by the exploiting companies in the metropolitan lands.

Africa has failed to make much headway on the road to purposeful industrial development because her natural resources have not been employed for that end but have been used for the greater development of the Western world. This has been a continuing process that has gained tremendous momentum in recent years, following the invention and introduction of new processes and techniques that have quickened the output of both the ferrous and non-ferrous metal industries of Europe and America in order to keep pace with the ever-increasing demand for finished goods. Military preparations and nuclear expansion have had a considerable impact upon this demand. World output of crude steel almost doubled itself in the decade between 1950 and 1960, from 190 million tons to 340 million tons. Even the regression of 1958 which lasted through the following years failed to halt the progress, which went on in lesser degree in both Eastern and Western countries.

The general forecast is that this tempo of production will be maintained. As it comes from Western sources, it makes little allowance for expansion of African use of primary products, and envisages a continuance of the present flow as between developing source countries and highly industrialised users. Nor does it take into account the likelihood of a repressive tendency in Western economies that can certainly affect the demand for raw materials. A publication of the United Nations Economic Commission for Europe in 1959 estimated that the world production of steel between 1972 and 1975 will be in the region of 630 million tons. Before the last war most of the Western world's iron and steel output was based upon local raw materials. The post-war years, particularly since 1956, have seen an opposite trend. Something like a quarter of the raw materials (90 million tons out of 400 million) used in the world's metallurgical industries have been imported.

The countries mainly importing these raw materials are the United States, Western Europe and Japan. The Soviet Union and the developing countries have at their disposal sufficient quantities of domestic raw materials. At the present time three large areas of primary resources are being exploited for the benefit of the great producer countries. These are Africa, Canada and South America; in particular Chile and Peru and lately Venezuela. Canada has become a province of American capital investment, which draws off high profits and exploits vast resources of raw products for conversion in American plants. South America and Africa, besides offering these advantages, provide cheap labour and local governmental assistance by way of duty exemption for imported machinery and equipment as well as tax remission.

Surveys now being carried out in Africa are discovering more and more deposits of valuable raw materials. Western investigators regard them essentially as sources of exploitation for the commerce and industry of their world, ignoring completely the development of the countries in which they lie. Robert Saunal, in an article in *Europe (France) Outremer* of November 1961 surveys the possibilities of Africa as a provider of ferrous raw materials for the industries of the great metallurgica, countries. He reminds his readers that there are sources of these primary materials in Europe, such as Sweden and Spain, and that for Japan there are the countries of Asia and Oceania.

He concludes that European participation is a favourable factor in starting off the exploitation of Africa's mineral resources, but that the new productive capacities in course of development should counsel prudence and a detailed examination of the selling possibilities. These mines are bound to start off in a situation of lively competition, which must have its effect upon price levels. They need, therefore, to be subjected to close preliminary examination before being embarked upon and must depend upon agreement between the exploiting companies and the host States which will give the former a just return and the latter a stable fiscal regime for the functioning of the 'harmonised exploitation'. In short, the governments of the new States are seen in the role of policemen for the banking and industrial consortia bent upon continuing the old imperialist pattern in Western-African relationships. The 'stable fiscal regime' they will guarantee out of such exploitation will, according to Robert Saunal, be based on conditions of depressed prices arising from acute competition.

There has been a considerable increase in the production of primary materials in Africa since 1945, under the stimulus of post-war rebuilding needs throughout the world, and the exigencies of cold-war stock-piling and armaments requirements. Another driving factor has been the revolution in productive methods and management. The surge of colonial peoples towards independence must also be acknowledged as a force contributing to the extension of raw materials production.

In some cases the production of primary materials since 1945 has multiplied several times, and in most cases has doubled. The scene in Guinea shows much change, following the discovery of deposits of iron and bauxite. Diamond mining has also made noticeable progress. The Ivory Coast in 1960 was producing diamonds at an annual level of about 200,000 carats, and operations have started in the manganese fields in the neighbourhood of Grand Lahou. Calcium phosphate is being exploited in Senegal, and aluminium and oxidised sand provide some mining activity. The mining of iron ore is under way in Mauritania, where an Anglo-French consortium is planning to produce four million tons as a first stage, to be increased later to six million tons annually. Deposits are estimated at around 115 million tons of 63 per cent iron grade. Finds of very rich phosphate deposits in Senegal have brought a French-Belgian financial and mining combination into the country to carry out their exploitation. An estimated 40 million tons of raw phosphates are expected to allow a production of 13 million tons of rich phosphates through the extraction of 600,000 tons of concentrates annually for twenty years.

Phosphates have also been found in Togo, which are to be exploited by a consortium associated with the Banque de Paris et des Pays-Bas and established mining companies having connections with the Société Générale de Belgique. Manganese, uranium, oil and iron ore finds in Gabon have brought in similar consortia for their exploitation. Cameroun produces little from mining beyond some small amounts of gold, tin and rutile. Though there has been no effective change in Madagascar's position, there have been discoveries of uranium, monozite, zircon, chromium and other minerals, whose exploitation is being investigated. Iron ore finds in Algeria are estimated at 100 million tons, and we have been hearing a good deal lately about the oil and gas resources of the Sahara desert. Algeria's fields are now producing at the rate of 450,000 barrels a day (about a third of those of Iran), and Libya has reached 150,000 barrels daily, with the anticipation of achieving 600,000 barrels a day within the next five years. In Algeria's sector of the Sahara finds of minerals at Tindouf are expected to produce 50 per cent iron.

The following figures, taken from UN Statistical Year-books, illustrate the great rise in output of minerals in Africa in the post-war period:

87

			1945	1959
Morocco	Phosphates	(tons)	1,654,000	7,164,000
	Coal	(tons)	178,000	465,000
	Zinc	(tons)	900	64,700
Congo (Leo.)	Diamonds	(carats)	5,475,000 (1947 figure)	14,854,000
	Copper	(tons)	—	280,000
	Tin	(tons)	—	9,337
N. Rhodesia	Copper	(tons)	197,000	539,900
	Zinc	(tons)	15,500	30,000
	Manganese	(tons)	500	29,500
S. Rhodesia	Coal	(tons)	1,669,000	3,758,000
	Chrome	(tons)	91,300 (1938 figure)	236,500
	Asbestos	(tons)	51,000	108,600
South Africa	Gold	(kg.)	—	624,108
	Diamonds	(carats)	—	2,838,000

The highest rate of increase is in South Africa, where a production of 624,108 kg. of gold makes the Republic the producer of half the world's supplies. An output of 2,838,000 carats of diamonds in 1959, about 40 per cent of which were gem stones, puts it third after the Congo and Ghana, whose output is almost entirely of industrial diamonds, though the value received, because of its control of the industry and the number of gem diamonds, is relatively greater than that of Ghana's. She also leads in the production of chromium ore and is second in the output of lead from S.W. Africa. Even South Africa's uranium production of 7,000 tons, obtained largely from gold and copper slimes, is way ahead of the Congo's 1,761 tons.

Mining of all kinds in South Africa has reached a stage of exploitation which can be compared with that of Canada, and which is now feverishly beginning to open up in Australia, where the same companies, in alliance with American and other associated interests, are paramount. The close relationship is borne out even in the names of mines, particularly in Canada, which frequently duplicate those also to be found in South Africa and the Rhodesias.

Africa's possession of industrial raw materials could, if used for her own development, place her among the most modernised continents of the world without recourse to outside sources. Iron ore, mostly of high quality, is to be found in gigantic quantities near to the coast where it can easily be shipped abroad. As for bauxite, Africa's estimated reserves are more than two-fifths those of the whole world. They are twice those of Australia, which are placed second. Guinea alone is estimated to contain deposits equal to those of the whole of Australia, that is, over 1,000 million tons. Ghana is said to have reserves totalling 400 million tons. Sudan, Cameroun, Congo and Malawi are other known sources of considerable deposits, and the investigation of probable reserves is proceeding in Mozambique, Sierra Leone, Portuguese Guinea and in other parts of Africa.

Among the base materials essential for the production of iron and steel, manganese has a place of high importance. Besides being used for alloying with pig iron in the manufacture of special steels, it is used in the chemical industry. For certain purposes, under present-day processes, manganese is irreplaceable. It is in constant use at the rate of 18 to 20 kg. to a ton of steel. The Soviet Union and China are practically self-sufficient in the supply of this essential basic material. The other great world steel producers, the United States, Western Europe and Japan, do not have appreciable quantities in their own territories. Their principal sources of supply are Africa, India and Brazil. Of these Africa provides the greatest quantity. Angola, Bechuanaland, Congo, Ghana, Morocco, Rhodesia, South-West Africa and Egypt have been among the producing countries for some time. Others, like the Ivory Coast and Gabon, are now being added to the list.

North Africa is the world's greatest producer of phosphates.

Morocco alone exports seven million tons out of some nine million tons coming from North Africa. The U.S.A. comes next, with an export of four million tons. New producing countries which have appeared since 1957 are China, with some 600,000 tons in 1960, and North Vietnam with 500,000 tons. Senegal is a producer of aluminium phosphate, her output being about 90,000 tons a year, and Togo is now appearing on the phosphate market.

Iron ore, like oil, has become one of the more recent mineral discoveries in Africa, North and West Africa being the main centres. Among high-grade ore producers in 1960 were Liberia (68 per cent iron content), Angola (65 per cent), South Africa (62 per cent), Sierra Leone (60 per cent), Morocco (60 per cent), and Rhodesia (55 per cent, the minimum iron content for high-grade ore). There have been discoveries of higher quantities and quality since 1960. It is considered that most countries in West Africa, from Mauritania to Congo (Brazzaville) have iron ore deposits. Enlargement of the production in Liberia, Guinea and Sierra Leone is being planned. Deposits are either being placed under production or are planned for exploitation in Nigeria, Niger, Mauritania, Ghana, Gabon, Cameroun, Senegal and Congo (Brazzaville). Ghana's reserves, estimated at about a million tons, are in the Shiene area of the Northern Region, and not easily accessible, and have an average iron content of 46 to 51 per cent. It is proposed to exploit the deposits for domestic use when the Volta lake is opened up for inland transport. The Niger Republic deposits are estimated at more than 100 million tons of 45 to 60 per cent quality. They are at Say, about thirty-five miles from Niamey, at the moment distant from roads, railways and ports. These disadvantages affect also the exploitation of the known deposits in the Kandi region of Dahomey, of 68 per cent quality.

Algeria has been an iron ore producer for some time. Exploitation was undertaken there in 1913 by a French enterprise known as La Société de l'Ouenza, operating at Djebel Ouenza in the south of Constantine, close to the Tunisian border, formerly incorporated as a department of France. The company has built its own railway lines connecting its two producing centres to Oued-Keberit, to join with the Bone-Tebessa line. Its plants enable Société de l'Ouenza to export iron principally to Great Britain, Germany, Italy, Belgium and the Low Countries, and the U.S.A. Between the outset of this exploitation and the end of 1960, a total of 46 million tons of mineral has been extracted. Ouenza's personnel then included 600 European and 1,500 Algerians.

The existence of iron ore in the Sahara was first indicated in the Gara Djebilet region, some 110 miles south-east of Tindouf, in 1952. Difficulties of situation and water supply are obstacles in the way of exploitation. Nevertheless, a committee composed of representatives of the iron and steel industries of France, Belgium, Germany, Italy, Luxembourg and the Netherlands is busily investigating the possibilities, in conjunction with the French Bureau d'Investissements en Afrique.

Liberia's iron ore resources are reputed to stand at 1,000 million tons in the Nimba range and 600 million tons in the deposits near the Sierra Leone border. The Nimba iron ore mine which has been sunk and is being mined by a consortium known as LAMCO Joint Venture Enterprise (members of the consortium being Liberian-American-Swedish Minerals Company and Bethlehem Steel Corporation) is estimated to have reserves of over 300 million tons of high-grade hematite ore with an average iron content of over 65 per cent. Long-term contracts are in hand from German, French, Italian and Belgian steelworks, while a considerable part of the output will go to the powerful United States Bethlehem Steel, which has a 25 per cent participation in the venture, the other 75 per cent being taken up by LAMCO. LAMCO is said to be a company shared between the Liberian Government and foreign enterprise on a fifty-fifty basis. The non-Government participant is Liberian Iron Ore Company, a consortium of American and Swedish financial and steel interests.

Chief of these is the Swedish mining company, Grangesberg, which besides having an important stake in the LAMCO Nimba mine acts as managing agent for this joint venture, in which American capital predominates. Grangesberg, formerly holding 12/28 of the LAMCO syndicate, according to its annual report adopted at its annual general meeting held at Stockholm, on 18 May 1962, increased its participation to 15/28, giving it a majority slice of the equity.

Grangesberg owns iron ore mines in Central Sweden, as well as power stations, forest and farm properties. It also built and controls the Frovi-Ludviks Jarnvag railway undertaking, and operates the Oxelsund Ironworks, turning out pig iron and heavy plates. In addition it possesses and runs a fleet of ships which, at the end of 1961, comprised thirty-three vessels, and had on order another four for delivery in 1962 and 1963. A subsidiary, Aktiebolaget Hematit, works mines in North Africa, and others include an arms and chemical enterprise, Aktiebolaget Express-Dynamit. The Swedish Government took over holdings which Grangesberg exercised in Luossavaara-Kürunavaara AB—LKAB, but out of the purchase price of Kr. 925 million it received, the company reinvested Kr. 100 million in LKAB.

The value given to these Government-purchased holdings was almost twice as much as Grangesberg's fully paid-up capital of Kr. 495,800,000, and even without them its assets at the end of 1961 stood at Kr. 403,719,000 in addition to shares in subsidiary and other companies totalling Kr. 154,380,000. The company's net profit for the year was Kr. 38,787,251 and dividends absorbed very nearly the same amount at Kr. 35,700,000. Its iron sales increased from 1,620,000 tons in 1959 to 2,560,000 tons in 1961.

Bethlehem Steel is a heavy investment sphere for Rockefeller's profits from Standard Oil, which has been pushing to displace British-Dutch oil interests in the Far East. John D. Rockefeller the Third has made himself a specialist on the Far East, with a preference for Japan, where he was a member of John Foster Dulles' peace treaty mission in 1951. He established the Japan Society Inc. for cultural inter-change. Persistent visits and pressure have boosted Standard Oil Company's facilities in Japan, Indonesia, New Guinea and India in oil production, refining and sales. The Rockefeller interest in Japan is reflected in the link with the Sumitomo metallurgical group, which has been cemented in the Bethlehem Copper

Corporation Ltd., a 1955 British Columbia (Canada) registration. Property claims in the Highland Valley of British Columbia hold ore reserves of 3,304,000 tons grade 1·20 per cent copper and 12,723,000 tons of 0·82 per cent grade. Additional claims are held in the provinces as well as a full subsidiary, Highland Valley Smelting and Refining Co.

Total output is to go to Sumitomo Metal Mining Co. Ltd. group, which is responsible for bringing the property into production. It has bought 400,000 shares in Bethlehem and has options on further lots in connection with loan promises of $5 million and an agreement to contribute one half of the funds required for expansion. Sumitomo provides Bethlehem's vice-president and two other directors, one of whom is from the prominent Tanaka family. The first deliveries from the Nimba mine were made during May 1963 and production of 7,500,000 tons is planned for 1965.

The Nimba iron ore streaks of Liberia stretch into Guinea where prospecting is taking place in the Nimba-Simandou region, about a thousand kilometres from Conakry, close to the Liberia-Ivory Coast borders. A West European banking group representing itself as the Consortium Européen pour le Developpement des Ressources Naturelles de l'Afrique—CONSAFRIQUE—is undertaking investigations by contract with the Guinea Government. The group comprises:

> Banque de l'Indochine, Paris.
> Deutsche Bank A.G., Frankfurt/Main.
> Hambros Bank, London.
> Nederlandsche Handel-Maatschappij N.V., Amsterdam.
> Société de Bruxelles pour la Finance et l'Industrie—
> BRUFINA—Brussels.
> S.A. Auxiliaire de Finance et de Commerce—AUXIFI—
> Brussels.
> Compagnie Franco-Americaine des Metaux et des
> Minerais—COFRAMET—Paris.

The Banque de l'Indochine is closely associated with the Banque de Paris et des Pays Bas, and has links with the Société Générale de Belgique. Its original sphere of operations has been largely closed by its exclusion from North Vietnam because of

8

the socialist regime established there, while in South Vietnam it has now become subordinate to American finance. The Banque de l'Indochine, which already had a foothold in Algeria, is turning more and more to Africa, where it is grouped in several consortia, usually round the interests connected with the Société Générale de Belgique, the Banque de Paris et des Pays Bas and the Deutsche Bank, all leagued with Morgan international interests. The Banque de l'Indochine is represented on the board of Le Nickel, which exploits a variety of minerals in Asia and Oceania and has a substantial interest in Compagnie Francaise des Minerais de l'Uranium. The late H. Robiliart was another director on Le Nickel's board, as well as J. Puerarai from Penarroya and Les Mines de Huaron, whose former president was the late H. Lafond of the Banque de Paris et des Pays Bas. These and other allied French and American interests, grouped around the Société des Minerais et Metaux, Patino and American Metal Climax form the combination known as COFRAMET, several of whom received Marshall Plan credits in the post-war years.

The Deutsche Bank, which has always concerned itself with exploitation investment in the less developed areas, also has close associations with the Banque de Paris. Even during the war the Deutsche Bank did not relinquish its role of colonialist exploiter, but followed the German army into the conquered territories of Europe. Today it is busy pushing West German interests in Africa, Panama, Chile, Pakistan, Columbia and Puerto Rico. It has floated loans for Argentina, the City of Oslo and Norway. It has a holding in the Pakistan Industrial Credit and Investment Corporation Ltd. It has acted as fiduciary house for such considerable international corporations as General Motors, Philips, Royal Dutch Petroleum and Snia Viscosa. The connection with Royal Dutch Petroleum continues Deutsche Bank's association with the pre-first world war Mosul oil concession in the part of Turkey that became Iraq, while its activities on behalf of General Motors and Philips emphasise the subservient role the Deutsche Bank plays to the Morgan interests which conduct the international expansion of these vast ramified organisations. On the board of this bank sit directors of the Mannesmann steel interests of the Ruhr, also represented on another German bank, the Dresdner, which is also engaged in a number of investment ventures in Africa.

The Mannesmann steel company, one of the most important in the German Ruhr, was established in 1885. Its chairman, Dr Wilhelm Zanger, is a director of Algoma Steel Corporation Ltd. of Canada, in which the German interests were linked for some time with the Hawker Siddeley group of Great Britain. Mannesman is associated in several projects in India and elsewhere with Krupps and its Duisberg affiliate Demag. A. G. Demag works in close collaboration with the American firm of Blaw Knox & Co. This firm which makes equipment for steel mills and for chemical, petroleum and other industries falls within the Mellon sphere of interests. Hence it has links with Bethlehem Steel, which associates with the West German Steel industry, into which the Mellon interests have increasingly pushed. Both the Deutsche Bank and Dresdner Bank, with which Mannesmann is so closely tied, in alliance with the Morgan Guaranty Trust, have considerable interests in the Oppenheimer companies of southern Africa.

Hambros Bank (the late Sir Charles Hambro was the link with the Bank of England), Cable & Wireless (Holding) and Oppenheimer holding companies have valuable interests in the diamond, gold and other mining undertakings in Central and Southern Africa. A merchant bank, Hambros has long been associated with the Scandinavian investment market, and has in the past years spread its activities in Europe in anticipation of Britain's entry into the Common Market. It added a subsidiary in Zurich in 1962, Hambros Investment Company. Like many other financial institutions it has entered a growing field for finance investment, that of leasing equipment to industry. For this purpose Hambros established Equipment Leasing Company (Elco) in 1962. It also engages directly in the business of importation and distribution of motor cars and commercial vehicles from the British Motor Corporation into the United States, through British Motor Corporation-Hambros Inc., a joint fifty-fifty venture. The British Motor Corporation covers Austin, M.G., Morris, Riley,

Wolseley motors and subsidiary companies of the Nuffield and other groups. Through its acquisition of the banking firm of Laidlaw & Co., New York, Hambros is strengthening its associations with important American banking interests. Among Hambros Bank's many other interests is its connection with the bullion firm of Mocatta & Goldsmid, which increased its holdings of bullion in 1961 from £3,750,000 to £6,500,000.

Another financial-industrial group, headed by the British company, B.I.S.C. (Ore) Ltd., and including French, German and American financial participants, is already working iron ore deposits in Guinea at Kaloum, in immediate proximity to the port of Conakry. These deposits of 50–55 per cent grade ore were discovered in 1904, when construction of the railway line from Conakry to Niger was begun. Prospecting was carried out between 1919 and 1922 by the Mining Company of French Guinea. In 1948 a new company was formed to confirm previous findings. This was the Compagnie Minière de Conakry, whose plant at Kaloum is geared to an annual production of 1,200,000 tons, which can be doubled without any appreciable modifications of the set-up. Alongside its iron production, this company is multiplying its income from the establishment of a complex of industries which includes the manufacture of explosives by the L'Union Chimique de l'Ouest Africain—UCOA. Participation in the Compagnie Minière de Conakry, which is capitalised at 1,500 million Guinea francs, is as follows:

B.I.S.C. (Ore) Ltd.	30·50%
Bureau de Recherches Geologiques et Minières	24·70%
Caisse Centrale de Co-operation Economique	8·70%
Compagnie Française des Mines de Bor	7·90%
Hoesch Werke	5·00%
Rothschild Group	9·56%
Compagnie Franco-Americaine des Metaux et des Minerais—COFRAMET	2·05%
Various	11·59%

Hoesch Werke is a leading West German iron and steel firm, associated with the larger combines like Mannesmann and Phoenix-Rheinruhr, the last of which has lately effected a fusion with the Thyssen group. Before the last war Thyssen was associated with Krupp.

The West German iron and steel industry is looking increasingly for raw materials supplies for use in German plants. In other parts of the world where less developed countries are making an attempt to industrialise, they are setting up transformation foundries and rolling mills to bring to secondary and intermediate stages ores brought in from mines to which they have been granted concessions. Thus the Mannesmann affiliate in Brazil, Companhia Siderurgica Mannesmann, is to achieve a crude steel capacity of 300,000 tons from iron ores from its mines less than five miles from a new blast furnace it is erecting at Belo Horizonte. American capital has large holdings in the German iron and steel industry, in some cases a controlling one, achieved during the post-war American occupation of Western Germany.

The Morgan banks led this incursion into the West German and other European heavy industry fields, using their European agents and associates in Great Britain, France, Germany, Italy, Belgium and Switzerland for the purpose. Among these associates is the multiple Rothschild group, already flanking the Morgans in their Southern African ventures. The British section, headed by N. M. Rothschild, has, in the words of one commentator, the Hon. Peter Montefiore Samuel, a member of the London merchant banking house of M. Samuel & Co. Ltd., 're-established their ancient connections with de Rothschild Frères', which go back to the pre-Napoleonic days. The firm of M. Samuel is itself linked with the Banque Lambert of Belgium and the Banque de Paris et des Pays Bas of France, all within the investment sphere of the Société Générale de Belgique, in an investment consortium established to exploit the European Common Market. Edmund L. de Rothschild and the Hon. P. M. Samuel sit together on the board of Anglo Israel Securities Ltd. De Rothschild, a director of two insurance companies, the Alliance and Sun Alliance created by the Rothschilds, sits also on the board of the British Newfoundland Corporation, incorporated in Canada, which secured 7,000 square miles of concessionary mineral lands and an additional like extent of oil and gas concessions from the Newfoundland Government, in 1953. The corporation also holds concessions on 35,000 square miles in Labrador. The same de Rothschild further adorns the board of Five Arrows Securities Co. Ltd., of Toronto, in which Barclays Bank and Morgan associates are interested. The Hon. P. M. Samuel is a director of the Shell Oil holding company, Shell Transport & Trading Co. Ltd., as well as of other investment companies, including several operating in Central Africa, such as Heywood Investments Central Africa (Pvt.) Ltd., on which he is joined by another member of the family, the Hon. Anthony Gerald Rothschild, who also sits on the boards of other such concerns, as well as of publishing and publicity firms.

B.I.S.C. (Ore) Ltd. is also included in a consortium, Société Anonyme des Mines de Fer de Mauritainie—MIFERMA— exploiting iron ore at Fort Gouraud, Mauritania. It is estimated that there is a minimum of 100 million tons of high-grade ore of 64–65 per cent iron contained in this property on the western edge of the Sahara Desert, and it is being prepared to produce an annual output of six million tons. The British group as well as German and Italian groups have substantial holdings, but the major interest is held by a French group headed by the Bureau Minière de France d'Outre Mer. The following are the participants in this venture:

> B.I.S.C. (Ore) Ltd.
> British Ore Investment Corporation Ltd.
> British Steel Corporation Ltd.
> Compagnie du Chemin de Fer du Nord.
> Compagnie Financière pour l'Outremer—COFIMER.
> Denain-Anzain.
> Republique Islamique de Mauritanie.
> Societa Financiaria Siderurgica—FINSIDER.
> Societa Mineraria Siderurgica—FERROMIN.
> Union Siderurgique du Nord de la France—USINOR.

The company has been capitalised at 13,300 million francs CFA, and has the following affiliates:

> Société d'Acconage et de Manutention en Mauritanie— SAMMA (capital: 100,000,000 francs CFA).

Société Anonyme d'Hebergement en Mauritanie—
HEBERMA (capital: 25,000,000 francs CFA).
Société Anonyme de Transports Mauritaniens—
SOTRAM (capital: 50,000,000 drancs CFA).

And to prove that though the names may change the components remain the same, the management of the mine will be in charge of Penarroya.

Finsider is the financing organisation related with the industrial group comprising Ferromin; and the Deutsche Bank was concerned with certain share introductions made by it during 1961–2. The Compagnie du Chemin de Fer du Nord comes within the influence of the Banque de Paris et des Pays Bas, as does Union Siderurgique du Nord de la France.

Gabon, whose timber has hitherto been its main export, has shown signs of possessing iron ore deposits since 1895. Investigations were carried out from 1938 by what was then the French Overseas Mining Bureau, transferred later to the Bureau de Recherches Geologiques et Minières, and joined by the Bethlehem Steel Company. The resultant company, Société des Mines de Fer de Mekambo, was established in 1955, with the major purpose of 'creating a great centre of production capable of satisfying, at long term, a part of the anticipated needs of Western Europe's steel industry and the future requirements of Bethlehem Steel'. Thus, in the participation, Bethlehem Steel has a 50 per cent holding. The other parties to the undertaking are:

Bureau de Recherches Geologiques et Minières	12·00%
Banque de Paris et des Pays Bas	5·00%
Compagnie Financière pour l'Outremer—COFIMER	3·00%
Compagnie Financière de Suez	5·00%
Fiat Company, Italy	3·50%
German Consortium of Mekambo (German steel industry)	10·00%
French steel industry	9·00%
Belgian steel industry	2·00%
Dutch steel industry	0·50%

The undertaking is capitalised at 200 million francs CFA, and on its behalf further investigations have been undertaken by the syndicate grouped round the Bureau de Recherches and the European Coal and Steel Community, underlining the interest that the European Community and its Common Market has in Africa's primary resources. What makes Gabon's iron ore deposits so interesting is their proximity to important electrical power resources, capable of affording abundant electricity at an estimated rate of one franc CFA per kilowatt.

Fiat's inclusion in this consortium is an illustration of the inevitability of monopoly's extension into capital investment in less developed countries. Fiat is not simply an automobile producing company, but a vast industrial organisation which has penetrated deeply into financial investment in Europe and beyond. Founded in Turin in 1899, Fiat had grown in sixty-three years into the second-largest motor manufacturer in Europe and the fourth largest in the world after General Motors, Ford and Volkswagen. If Simca, which is linked with Fiat, is added to Fiat's production, it is larger than that of Volkswagen. But Fiat's growth came, not through automobile manufacturing, but through industrial production connected with armaments during the first world war, its expansion continuing in the second world war. It made profit out of the devastation that came to Italy and continued to build itself up in the post-war period under its founder, an ex-cavalry officer of a well-to-do Turin family, Giovanni Agnelli, in whom 'business genius was combined with the ruthlessness of an American railroad or oil tycoon of the old days'.

In its working year of 1960 the Fiat company had investments in other companies valued at some £26,700,000, a valuation decided by the company, since under Italian company law this is left entirely to 'the discretion of the company's accountants, and figures listed in Italian balance sheets under this heading usually bear no relation whatsoever to the market value or even to the face value of the equities and bonds held'. Cement, camera and film manufacture are among the company's ventures. A subsidiary, Unione Cementi Marchino, produces 16 million tons of cement yearly. The Cinzano vermouth which is so widely enjoyed throughout the world is among Fiat's undertakings. Its subsidiary, Impresit, is busy wherever hydro-electrical dams are being constructed. It built the Kariba dam in Rhodesia and is working on Ghana's Volta dam. Fiat owns property all over the world. Practically the whole of the Rue Blanche in Paris's notorious night-life world is owned by Fiat, as well as land, hotels and pleasure facilities in Sestriere, a leading Italian winter sports resort.

Like so many of the monopoly organisations that spread their interests over the globe and into manifold undertakings, Fiat has branched into oil, having a 22 per cent holding in Aquila, the Italian subsidiary of the Compagnie Française des Petroles. Aquila is now operating in Austria as well as Italy. Shipping also comes within Fiat's operational sweep through ownership of a couple of shipping companies. All of these ramifications, which cover more than a hundred companies inside and outside Italy, are almost all vested in the holding company, Instituto Financiario Industriale, founded in 1927, and known briefly as J.F.I. In the latter part of 1962 Fiat joined the international group comprising S.A.B.C.A.—Avions Fairey (Belgium), Breguet (France), Focke-Wulf (Germany), Fokker (Holland), Hawker Siddeley Aviation (U.K.) and Republic Aviation (U.S.A.), which submitted designs to NATO for a vertical take-off strike aircraft. Fiat had already maintained co-operation with Bristol Siddeley in the manufacture of Bristol Siddeley Orpheus turbo-jet engines for the G.91, then the standard NATO strike aircraft. And to help mould public opinion in the right direction, Fiat publishes Italy's second largest daily paper, *La Stampa*.

Compagnie Financière de Suez was in considerable difficulty after the affairs of the Suez Canal were taken over by the Egyptian Government, following the unsuccessful attempt by Anglo-French imperialism to dominate Egypt once more, and has been under pressure from its shareholders. However, the board held off the shareholders and righted its position by looking for investments which will give quick high returns. It has made certain equity purchases in Australia, but is really seeking quick profitability in Saharan oil and African primary materials. Its investment in Coparex is expected to give early good results, since this company

101

had in 1961 large reserves of oil from which it was deriving a substantial income.

Bauxite in Western and Equatorial Africa is even more plentiful than iron ore, but its exploitation is waiting upon the availability of electrical power. We have already referred to FRIA, the enterprise that has been set up in the Republic of Guinea by the consortium with the Rockefeller firm of Olin Mathieson at its head. The second largest holding in this group is held by Pechiney-Ugine. These same groups, together with Reynolds, Kaiser and Mellon's Alcan, formed another enterprise, Les Bauxites du Midi, which originally exploited other deposits at Kassa and Boke. Notice, however, was given to the company by the Guinea Government that if, within three months from 24 November 1961 Bauxites du Midi had not made arrangements to set up an aluminium factory at Boke by July 1964, as originally agreed, its installations, works and machinery would be expropriated, as well as its assets, for which reparation would be made. The Guinea Government declared that it waited for the company to renounce 'its colonial methods based on the simple extraction of minerals whose transformation would be subsequently effected outside the country of production'.

Pechiney-Ugine is also concerned with the Compagnie Camerounaise d'Aluminium Pechiney-Ugine—ALUCAM—in which a 10 per cent participation is held by Cobeal, a Société Générale de Belgique affiliate. Pechiney-Ugine's share of Alucam's total production in 1962 of 52,246 tons was 46,443 tons, obviously the most important.

Gabon's natural resources are proving immensely rich. Atomic energy commissions are busy prospecting and investigating uranium sources at Mounana in the Haut-Ogooue region, one of the most isolated in the country. The only means of access is the river Ogooue, cut by rapids over more than 600 km. of its length. At the beginning of 1959, however, a 100-km. road, constructed by the Compagnie Minière de l'Ogooue—COMILOG—put the terminus of the railway which opened in 1962 about 120 km. from Mounana, thus making it more accessible. The ore is to be mined and uranated by the

Compagnie des Mines d'Uranium de Franceville, capitalised at 1,000 million francs CFA. A participant in Comilog, the Compagnie de Mokta, is responsible for the management of the mine. Comilog is exploiting Gabon's manganese deposits at Franceville, which were first investigated by the French Overseas Mining Bureau in collaboration with U.S. Steel, the mammoth American steel firm, controlled by Morgan interests. Together with its affiliates, U.S. Steel has 49 per cent control of Comilog, to which the other parties are the frequently-present Bureau de Recherches Geologiques et Minières (22 per cent), the Compagnie de Mokta (14 per cent) and the Société Auxiliaire du Manganese de Franceville (15 per cent). The enterprise is capitalised at 2,500,000 francs CFA. United States and French monopolists are the chief parties to Comilog.

Comilog has as its principal shareholder (49 per cent) the largest steel outfit in America, and hence the world, U.S. Steel, 'a perfectly integrated iron and steel concern'. The manganese bed on which Comilog is working at Franceville in Gabon is one of the most important in the world, with estimated reserves of 200 million tons of 50 per cent ore. The French Cie de Mokta has a 19 per cent interest and, besides being concerned in operating directly the Grand Lahou manganese mine on the Ivory Coast, controls important production of iron, manganese and uranium ores through holdings in Algeria, Spain, Tunisia, Morocco and Gabon. It has, for instance, 40 per cent in the Cie des Mines d'Uranium de Franceville, which is developing the rich uranium mine at Mounana, Gabon. De Mokta is linked directly and by associates with interests radiating from Anglo-American Corporation and the great iron and steel trust of ARBED.

U.S. Steel and General Electric are world giants in their related spheres. The first, by virtue of its multiple divisions covering all aspects of the steel industry, is the sixth largest industrial company in the United States; the second is the leading producer of electrical equipment and appliances in the world, with affiliates, subsidiaries and associates all over the globe. Its plants affect many sectors of industry: radio, aviation, marine, scientific research, and turn out heavy capital goods, industrial components and materials and defence products, as

103

well as consumer goods. U.S. Steel was founded in 1901 by J. Pierpont Morgan as a holding company controlling over half the American steel industry. Since then the American steel industry has expanded by giant strides and other commanding trusts have forged ahead. But U.S. Steel leads still and today controls 30 per cent of America's steel and cement production. On the board of General Electric sits Henry S. Morgan, so that it is not difficult to find the relationship between this international monopoly and U.S. Steel in the exploitation of some of Africa's richest resources to feed the military as well as economic demands of the world's most dangerous imperialism. Operating universally, its interests are located at every crisis point of the globe.

It is said that as a result of the most complicated transaction, Tanganyika Concessions ceded to an American financial group closely associated with the leading United States banking houses 1,600,000 of its shares, as a result of which the American group probably has a majority in this British Company which owns 21 per cent of the shares of Union Minière, whose empire is the Congo.*

American interest in the Congo is motivated by very substantial investments, frequently hidden behind British, French, Belgian and West German cover, and engaging leading personalities in United States political affairs. Mr Adlai Stevenson, for instance, representing his government at U.N.O., presided over the firm of Tempelsman & Son, specialists in exploiting Congo diamonds; and Mr Arthur H. Dean, who leads America's delegations to disarmament conferences, was vice-president and still is a director of American Metal Climax, a huge consumer of uranium, since it provides 10 per cent of United States production. American Metal, according to an information blurb, forms with its subsidiaries 'a powerful international mining group, which includes, notably, Rhodesian Selection Trust Ltd.'.

The NATO powers are interested in Gabon because of her riches. At present American OFFSHORE International has been offered a drilling contract for Société de Petrol Afrique

* *France Observateur*, 9 July 1964.

Equatorial (SPAFE) with headquarters in Port Gentil. This company employs over 1,200 Africans who are all subordinate to the over 400 white people. There is no oil refinery at present in Gabon, but Gabon, Chad, Congo, Brazzaville, Central African Republic and Cameroun have agreed to establish a refinery to be financed by their respective governments and France. The first meeting of the representatives of these governments was on 22 July 1964 in Port Gentil. According to the Minister the necessary investigations are going on to start the refinery before the end of 1965. There are, I was told, many oil finds both in the territorial waters of Gabon and deep in the interior in large economic quantities to supply many parts of Africa. My information is that all the petroleum companies now distributing oil in French-speaking Africa have controlling shares in the oil production company in Gabon. Agip is not allowed to hold shares in the company. Readers will recall what caused the downfall of Mr Adoula in the Congo—oil politics. It seems to me, therefore, that two economic issues will influence the duration of French occupational forces in Gabon for many years, namely uranium and oil.

It is quite likely that Africa could provide enough phosphates not only to fertilise the abundant agricultural production that would cover its future food and industrial requirements, but to leave enough over to supply the needs of many other parts of the globe. At the moment important centres of phosphates are the Djebel-Onk deposits in Algeria, those at Taiba in Senegal, at Lac Togo in the Republic of Togo, and at Khouribga and Youssoufia in Morocco.

The Société de Djebel-Onk, with a capital of 30 million new francs, comprises the following interests:

Bureau d'Investissement en Afrique	18·00%
Caisse d'Equipement de l'Algérie	16·00%
Compagnie des Phosphates de Constantine	40·00%
Compagnie Financière pour le Developpement Economique, ca.—COFIDAL	8·50%
Sociètè Algérienne de Development et d'Expansion —SOCALDEX	8·50%

Société Algérienne de Produits Chimiques et
d'Engrais; Banque Nationale pour le Commerce
et l'Industrie Afrique; Compagnie Algérienne;
Groupe Schiaffino; Various   9·00%

The Compagnie Senegalaise des Phosphates de Taiba finds
the Government of Senegal associating with the Bureau de
Recherches Geologiques et Minières, Pechiney, Pierrefitte,
Compagnie des Phosphates de Constantine, Compagnie des
Phosphates d'Oceanie, Cofimer and the Société Auxon. The
same group, headed by the Banque de Paris et des Pays
Bas and the French interests which it represents made an
agreement in February 1963, under the signature of the
bank's director-general, J. J. Reyre, with the International
Minerals & Chemicals Corporation, by which the latter
became a partner in the consortium which is exploiting what
is said to be the world's largest high-grade phosphate mine,
near Dakar. There are several things that are noteworthy in
this arrangement.

First of all, there is something distinctly ominous in an
agreement between two foreign combinations, one of which is
a participant in a company associated with the State whose raw
materials it is exploiting. It accentuates the contemptuous
attitude towards the host country implicit in the monopoly's
purpose. International Minerals is the foremost producer of
phosphate and phosphate agricultural products in the North
American continent, with extensive phosphate mining and
chemical processing operations in Florida, U.S.A. It also owns
a potash mine at Carlsbad, New Mexico, and another
$10 million potash project in Canada. It has a market for its
products throughout the Americas and Western Europe. For
the Senegalese Government this phosphate mining project,
which is to have an output of 500,000 tons a year, has an
important place in its four-year plan. It is intended to broaden
and develop the economy. However, the purpose of the
monopolies controlling the venture is entirely otherwise. 'This
partnership bolsters our world position in regard to strategic
phosphate reserves,' Mr Reyre is reported to have said on

signing the partnership agreement with International Minerals (*West Africa*, 17 February 1962).

Phosphates deposits were uncovered in Togo about eighteen miles from the sea in 1952. Investigations had been going on since 1884 by French and British interests. It was a geological adviser of the Comptoir des Phosphates de l'Afrique du Nord who found in the Akoumape region indications of very important deposits of first quality which extend across Lake Togo. The Republic of Togo has associated itself with the Compagnie Togolaise des Mines de Benin, which is exploiting the deposits, and comprises the interests already engaged in monopolising other phosphate resources in Africa. These are the Compagnie Constantine, Penarroya, Cofimer, the Banque de Paris, Pierrefitte and the Compagnie Internationale d'Armement Maritime Industrielle et Commerciale. Capital is 1,180 million francs CFA. The first shipments were made in September 1961, when they left the new wharf of Kpeme for the United States and American-controlled plants in Japan. The plan is to produce initially 750,000 tons of concentrate yearly, a level it is intended to raise progressively to a million tons if the market possibilities are there.

There would be no lack of market possibilities if fertilisers were made available to the developing countries at prices which their purchasing power could afford. As it is, the competition in fertilisers from America and other sources is extremely keen, and the British producers, of whom Fison Ltd. and I.C.I. and Shell practically monopolise the trade in the United Kingdom, were the subject of investigation by the British Monopolies Commission in 1959. Fertilisers in the U.K. have been kept at a subsidised price level that led to serious complaints of overcharging. Fison holds 40 per cent of the U.K. market, and it has now entered into an agreement with I.C.I., whereby it will be supplied by the latter with ammonia from their new Immingham plant. This will cut costs in an effort to meet shareholders' complaints of diminishing profits.

This co-operation of the largest producers of fertilisers is going on in order to monopolise raw materials' supplies and markets, so as to sustain prices that will yield higher profits on the considerable investments involved. The chairman of I.C.I.'s Billingham Division said the company's steam naptha process has completely transformed the economics of ammonia production and has put the company in the position of being a world producer of ammonia, not just a U.K. producer.

Transportation is an important factor in the cost of fertilisers, and it is easy to appreciate that if phosphates from Africa are taken to Europe for working up and then returned in fertiliser form to Africa, packed in bags, prices cannot be economic for African agriculture. In this connection it is interesting to note that Fison have established in India, in association with the leading iron and steel firm of Tata, a fertiliser producing company, Tata-Fison Ltd., which Sir Clavering Fison, the U.K. Company's chairman, has described as now being the largest company in the industry. Fison has a partnership in Albatros Super-fosfaatbrieken N.V., of Utrecht, Holland, with which company it established fertiliser and chemical companies in South Africa. During their financial year 1961–2 the Fison-Albatros company admitted into its South African affiliate, Fisons (Pty) Ltd., a local banking undertaking, Federale Volksbeleggings Beperk, which made enough funds available to allow the South African Fison company to enter upon the exploitation of phosphate deposits at Phalaborwa in the Transvaal. Fison has other companies in South Africa concerned with agricultural chemicals and pharmaceuticals. All these companies did well during the 1961–2 year, according to Fison's chairman, who added that 'despite the difficult conditions in East Africa and the Federation of Rhodesia and Nyasaland, our companies there have maintained their position and earned satisfactory profits'. Its subsidiary in Sudan, Fisons Pest Control (Sudan) Ltd., sprayed a record cotton acreage of over one million acres and achieved profits found satisfactory by the chairman.

Canada, New Zealand, Australia, Malaya and Nigeria are all countries in which Fison have established companies for the expansion of their fertiliser and agricultural chemical markets, and they have recently begun to extend into South America and Pakistan. Plants for the manufacture of fertilisers have been erected at Zandvoorde, in Belgium, jointly with Union Chimique Belge S.A. Besides fertilisers and related chemicals manufacture, horticulture and scientific apparatus production, Fison are in the food processing and canning firm of John Brown Ltd. 'for the purpose of selling chemical know-how and plants to the U.S.S.R.'.

Oil and gas, which are becoming more and more important finds in Africa, particularly in the Sahara, are drawing the feverish competition of the predominant financial and industrial interests that are bringing monopoly into a tighter and tighter ring. Even smaller ones are pushing into this field, which, while it calls for extremely heavy initial capital for prospecting and sounding, offers the fabulous profits that have built up the fortunes of Standard Oil and Mobil-Socony for the Rocke- fellers, Gulf Oil for the Mellons, Continental Oil and Dutch- Shell for the Morgans, Texaco for the Chicago group, Hanover Bank and others. Tennessee Corporation, the Guggenheimer multiple enterprise operating nitrate and copper concessions in South America and holdings in the Congo and other parts of Africa, has extended its interests beyond uranium, fertilisers and chemicals into oil. Its Delaware subsidiary, Tennessee Overseas Co., has started upon oil exploration in Sierra Leone. C. W. Michel, Tennessee's vice-president is already connected with oil through Dome Petroleum, a subsidiary of the Americo- Canadian Dome Mines Ltd., interlocked with Tennessee by shareholding and Michel's chairmanship.

Africa is still paramountly an uncharted continent economi- cally, and the withdrawal of the colonial rulers from political control is interpreted as a signal for the descent of the inter- national monopolies upon the continent's natural resources. This is the new scramble for Africa, under the guise of aid, and with the consent and even the welcome of young, inexperienced States. It can be even more deadly for Africa than the first carve-up, as it is supported by more concentrated interests, wielding vastly greater power and influence over governments and international organisations.

7. The Oppenheimer empire

THE king of mining in South Africa, indeed in Africa, is Harry Frederick Oppenheimer. One might almost call him the king of South Africa, even the emperor, with an ever-extending empire. There is probably hardly a corner of Southern Africa's industrial and financial structure in which he has not got a very extended finger of his own or the hook of some affiliate or associate. These fingers and hooks attach the Oppenheimer empire firmly to other empires as great or greater.

Mr Harry Frederick Oppenheimer is director, chairman or president of some seventy companies. These directorships as well as those held by important colleagues and nominees, whose names recur monotonously on the boards of an ever-expanding complex of company boards, give the lie to the fiction of respectable separateness, even where there is no obvious financial connecting link. Dominating this complex of companies are the Anglo American Corporation of South Africa Ltd. and Consolidated Gold Fields of South Africa Ltd., from which radiate affiliates, subsidiaries, associates, immediately or more tenuously connected, which would provide in themselves a most interesting trade, investment and banking directory. A list of direct interests, by no means complete, would include:

> Anglo American Trust Ltd.
> African & European Investment Co. Ltd.
> Amalgamated Collieries of South Africa Ltd.

Bamangwato Concessions Ltd.
Central Mining Finance Ltd.
Consolidated Mines Selection Co. Ltd. (C.A.S.T.).
Coronation Collieries Ltd.
Consolidated Mines of South West Africa Ltd.
British South Africa Company Ltd.
Anglo Transvaal Consolidated Investment Co. Ltd.
De Beers Consolidated Mines Ltd.
Free State Development Co. Ltd.
Middle Witwatersrand (Western Areas) Ltd.
Rand Selection Corporation Ltd.
Rand Mines Ltd.
Rhodesian Anglo American Corporation Ltd.
South African Townships Mining & Finance Co. Ltd.
Vereeniging Estates Ltd.
West Rand Investment Trust Ltd.
Johannesburg Consolidated Investment Co. Ltd.
Rhodesian Broken Hill Development Co. Ltd.
Transvaal & Delagoa Bay Investment Co. Ltd.
Rhokana Corporation Ltd.
Union Corporation Ltd.
Tsumeb Corporation Ltd.
Selection Trust Co. Ltd.
Tanganyika Concessions Ltd.
Union Minière du Haut Katanga S.A.

Most of these are holding or investment outfits, established to co-ordinate a specific group of activities, but having their fingers in many other pies. It is difficult, almost impossible at times, to distinguish a delimiting line of operation. Trying to unravel the participations of the Anglo American Corporation and Consolidated Gold Fields of South Africa, for instance, leads often to the same involvements. Yet there must be a demarcation line, not only to preserve the semblance of autonomy, but to avoid a duplication of tasks and responsibilities in the interests of industrial and financial economy and profits.

As a matter of fact there is a constant rearrangement of organisational structure, either as a result of the acquisition of new interests and projects, the abandonment of exhausted

111

mines, the expansion of existing companies and alliances, but above all in order to forestall or meet competition, to stream-line the structure and to correct the tax position.

For instance, in 1961, Consolidated African Gold Fields of South Africa Corporation underwent a thorough-going re-organisation with the intention of concentrating its adminis-tration in its various spheres of operation. Reporting to the annual meeting of the corporation's activities for the year ending 30 June 1961, the chairman, Sir George Harvie-Watt, fixed the assets, at stock exchange value, at a total of approxi-mately £58 million. Sixty-six per cent of this total was represented by interests in South Africa, ten per cent in North America and six per cent in Australia. Most of the remaining 18 per cent was accounted for by interests in the United Kingdom.

To supervise these interests and the planned absorption of others, a number of changes were made in the controlling companies, so that the group structure of Consolidated Gold Fields of South Africa Ltd. now has the appearance shown in Chart 1.

Explaining the structure to the shareholders at the annual general meeting held in London on 13 December 1962, the chairman confirmed that the operational supervision of the group's interests in South Africa was the responsibility of 'our wholly owned subsidiary, Gold Fields of South Africa Ltd., which is resident in Johannesburg'. When in 1959 the group acquired both New Union Gold Fields, since renamed Gold Fields Finance (S.A.) Ltd., and the South African H.E. Proprietary Ltd., their management was also vested in Gold Fields of South Africa, although the shares of these companies were held directly by the parent company in London.

In Australia, responsibility for administration of the group's operations is exercised by Consolidated Gold Fields (Australia) Pty Ltd. Gold Fields' principal investment in Australia is represented by a majority interest in Commonwealth Mining Investments (Australia) Ltd., 'a mining finance company, which has a broadly based portfolio in Australian, North

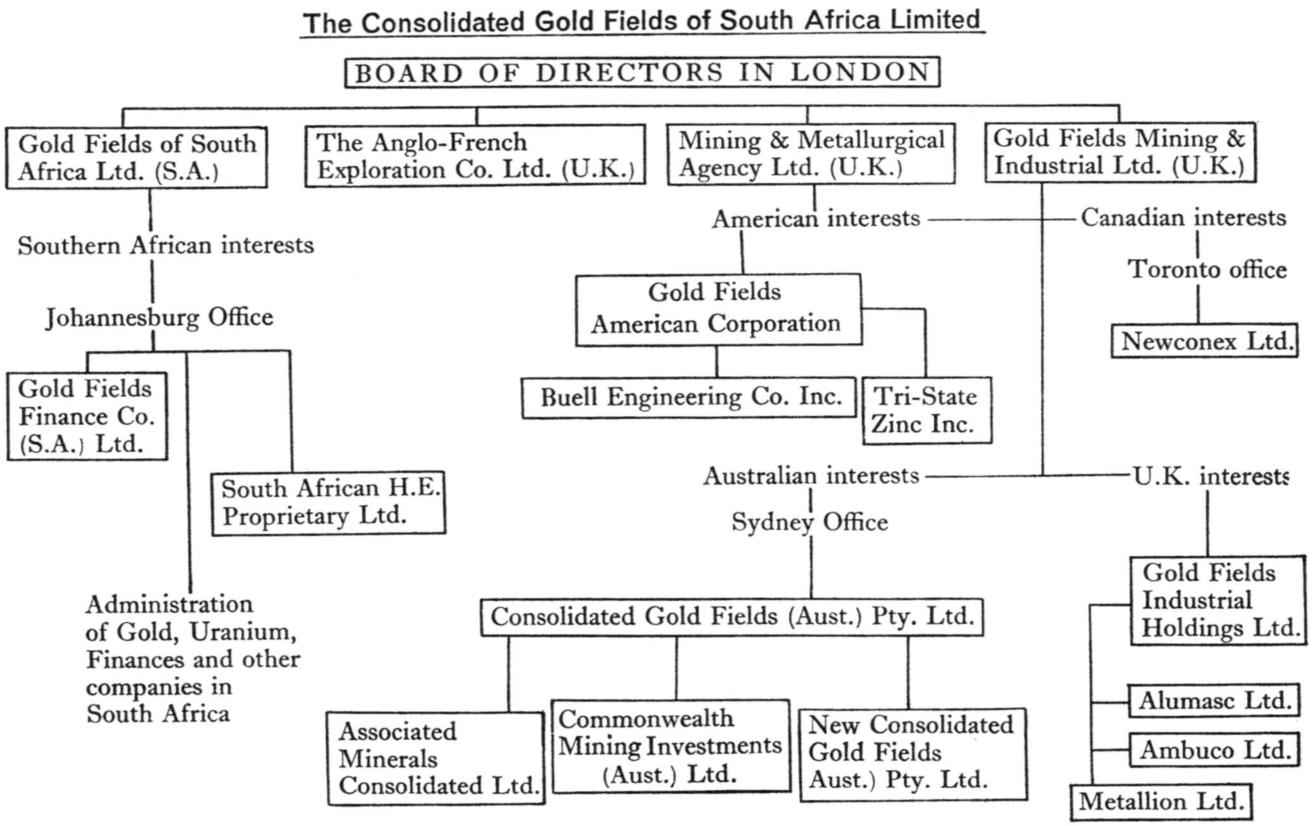

The Consolidated Gold Fields of South Africa Limited

BOARD OF DIRECTORS IN LONDON

Gold Fields of South Africa Ltd. (S.A.)

Southern African interests

Johannesburg Office

Gold Fields Finance Co. (S.A.) Ltd.

South African H.E. Proprietary Ltd.

Administration of Gold, Uranium, Finances and other companies in South Africa

The Anglo-French Exploration Co. Ltd. (U.K.)

Mining & Metallurgical Agency Ltd. (U.K.)

American interests

Gold Fields American Corporation

Buell Engineering Co. Inc.

Tri-State Zinc Inc.

Australian interests

Sydney Office

Consolidated Gold Fields (Aust.) Pty. Ltd.

Associated Minerals Consolidated Ltd.

Commonwealth Mining Investments (Aust.) Ltd.

New Consolidated Gold Fields (Aust.) Pty. Ltd.

Gold Fields Mining & Industrial Ltd. (U.K.)

Canadian interests

Toronto office

Newconex Ltd.

U.K. interests

Gold Fields Industrial Holdings Ltd.

Alumasc Ltd.

Ambuco Ltd.

Metallion Ltd.

CHART 1

113

American and other overseas investments', according to the chairman's report.

A majority interest in another Australian concern, Associated Minerals Consolidated Ltd., gives Consolidated Gold Fields a big break into the rutile and zircon industry. Associated Minerals acquired all the outstanding shares of Z.R. Holdings Ltd., a company originally formed to take possession of Zircon Rutile Pty Ltd., together with that company's share in, and advances to other companies. About the same time, Associated Minerals bought the entire share capital of Titanium Materials and the assets of Rye Park Scheelite.

Experienced enterprises like Consolidated Gold Fields do not allow others to benefit from their efforts. So 'while Associated Minerals was building up its holdings in the rutile industry', stated Consolidated's chairman, 'we felt it necessary to strengthen our position in Wyong Minerals, another rutile producer in which Commonwealth Mining already had a substantial investment. Accordingly, our wholly-owned subsidiary, Consolidated Gold Fields (Australia) Pty Ltd., made an offer in February 1962 for 50 per cent of all shareholdings in Wyong Minerals other than those held by Commonwealth Mining Investments. This offer was successful and Wyong Minerals is now a subsidiary within the group.'

Congratulations are owed to Consolidated Gold Fields on their perspicacity. Their position in the rutile field is now pre-eminent. In the words of their chairman, 'the total rutile productive capacity of our subsidiaries now represents close on one half of the total free world capacity. The expansion programme which Associated Minerals now has in hand should maintain this position.' May we be forgiven if the qualification 'free' in this context looks a trifle dulled to us?

Rutile is a much sought-after material used in the manufacture of titanium pigment. The demand had the effect of increasing its open market price by some 50 per cent in the financial year 1961/62. Zircon's price has remained stable in spite of considerably increased supplies.

A partnership with Cyprus Mines Corporation, a New York company, and the Utah Construction & Mining Co. of San

Francisco, has resulted in a joint enterprise named Mount Goldsworthy Mining Associates, to explore and work the potential of iron ore deposits of Mount Goldsworthy in north-western Australia. The construction of a 125-mile railway is involved, to end up at Depuch Island, where a major seaport is under consideration. Sir George Harvie-Watt was pleased to inform Consolidated Gold Fields' shareholders that 'negotiations are in progress with the Japanese iron and steel industry regarding the market for this ore (from Mount Goldsworthy) which is thought will be competitive in price and quality with any now available in Japan.'

In the chairman's words, the company's operations in Canada had 'taken a distinct step forward'. Their subsidiary exploration company, Newconex Canadian Exploration Ltd., was joined by a second, Newconex Holdings Ltd. A decision was made to allow the public to enjoy some of the fruits from the exploitation of their country's resources by foreign concerns. Accordingly, 36 per cent of the capital was offered to Canadians. Those who took up shares were doubtless delighted to know that the $28\frac{1}{3}$ per cent holding of Newconex Canadian Exploration Ltd. in the Mount Hundere exploration will be turned over to the holding company. A high grade deposit of lead zinc (with some silver) discovered in this south Yukon region inspired the chairman to an admission of its being 'most gratifying that so soon after its formation Newconex Holdings should be presented by Newconex Exploration with such an encouraging prospect.'

Moving southwards to the United States, a new company called Gold Fields American Corporation was formed in 1961 as a wholly-owned subsidiary of Gold Fields Mining & Industrial Ltd. Gold Fields American took over the New York organisation, set up originally in 1911, whose main function in recent years had been to provide administration for Gold Fields' Tri-State Zinc Inc. and Buell Engineering Co. Inc., as well as secretarial services for the Fresnillo Company.

Fresnillo Company was reorganised in 1961, when it transferred 51 per cent of its diverse Mexican activities to Metalurgica Mexicana Penoles S.A., under the Mexican Government's drive to have domestic control of its basic primary resources. A handsome compensation of $5,500,000 was awarded to Fresnillo, payable over a period of five years, for the cession of this holding to Compania Fresnillo S.A., in which it holds 49 per cent to Penoles' 51 per cent. Fresnillo still retains a 55 per cent interest in Somberette Mining Company, owning another gold-silver porperty in the State of Zacatecas, Mexico.

With the 'coming to the end of their profitable lives' of Tri-State Zinc's two mines in Illinois and Virginia, a replacement was sought by a new mine in the New Market area of Tennessee. This mine Tri-State are bringing into production in accordance with a joint venture agreement with American Zinc, Lead & Smelting Co. Under this agreement, Tri-State will mine and mill at least 20 million tons of zinc-bearing ores owned by American Zinc near Tri-State's New Market property. Profits from the output of a treatment plan, designed to provide a daily capacity of 3,600 tons, will be distributed on a basis varying between 50 and 60 per cent to Tri-State and 50 and 40 per cent to American Zinc, until all capital has been returned, after which profits will be distributed equally.

American Zinc's operations are closely connected with the mining and reduction of zinc and lead ores in several of the American States. It also has a 10 per cent interest in Uranium Reduction Co., and 50 per cent in American-Peru Mining Co., among several other affiliated and jointly-owned concerns. Buell Engineering Co., the other beneficiary of Gold Fields American Corporation, has been assisted to expand its fabricating facilities by taking over the entire common stock of the Union Boiler & Manufacturing Co.

Consolidated Gold Fields' interests in the United Kingdom are now grouped under Gold Fields Industrial Holdings Ltd., formerly H. E. Proprietary Ltd., as a wholly-owned subsidiary of Gold Fields Mining & Industrial Ltd. Its main operations are carried on through its own subsidiaries, Alumasc Ltd., Ambuco Ltd. and Metalion Ltd. Alumasc is a producer of die-cast aluminium casks, notably for the brewing industry. It has lately expanded into the production of aluminium high-pressure bottles for commercial uses. In 1962 Alumasc, in the words of Consolidated's chairman, 'broadened its interests geographically and industrially' by the acquisition of an Australian subsidiary, Lawrenson Alumasc Holdings Ltd., and of two United Kingdom subsidiaries, The Non-Ferrous Die Casting Co. Ltd. and Brass Pressings (London) Ltd., already well established in non-ferrous die-casting and brass pressing.

Two other U.K. organisational instruments radiate from the London directorate. These are Anglo-French Exploration Co. Ltd. and Mining & Metallurgical Agency Ltd. Anglo-French Exploration, a wholly-owned subsidiary of Consolidated Gold Fields, is an investment and financial business, holding, among others, interests in many of the principal gold-mining companies in South Africa. These interests also cover Northern Rhodesian copper mines, as well as tin-mining companies operating in the United Kingdom, South Africa and the Far East. Apex Mines Ltd. and Rooiberg Minerals Development Co. Ltd. of South Africa, and Anglo-Burma Tin Co. Ltd. are among its principals. Mining & Metallurgical Agency Ltd. was formed to look after the distribution of ores and purchase of supplies, as well as to run a shipping, insurance and general agency business. Fifty per cent of its capital is held by Consolidated Gold Fields.

Gold Fields of South Africa Ltd. is the wholly-owned subsidiary of Consolidated Gold Fields that is responsible for administering the operations of the group throughout the whole of South Africa. These are of a monumental size. For investments in the South Africa gold and platinum mines remain the major asset of the Consolidated Gold Fields group, and its principal source of income. At 30 June 1961 gold mining accounted for 71 per cent of the group's quoted investments, and the chairman assured shareholders that since the end of the second world war, Consolidated Gold Fields had invested capital sums approaching £450 million in the South African gold mines. Exploration has continued in South Africa and Rhodesia, and is in close collaboration with West Witwatersrand Areas Ltd., a company which Consolidated Gold

117

Fields floated in 1932. Since then, West Witwatersrand has itself become an important South African finance mining company with major holdings in the gold mines of the Far West Rand and Orange Free State.

West Witwatersrand produced in 1962 gold valued at over £57 million, which was twice the size of its production of ten years ago. The Harmony Gold Mining Co. Ltd., in which West Witwatersrand has a holding of 1,247,564 shares through its subsidiary Westwits Investment Ltd., also achieved a record gold output.

Apart from its interests in the Transvaal and Orange Free State gold and platinum mines, Consolidated Gold Fields has substantial holdings in South West Africa Co. Ltd., and in Rhodesia, in Bancroft Mines Ltd., Nchanga Consolidated Copper Mines Ltd., and Rhodesian Anglo American Ltd., all falling within the sphere also of Anglo American Corporation. In Ghana, Consolidated is interested in Konongo Gold Mines Ltd., which has a concession of approximately twenty square miles in the Ashanti-Akim district. On an authorised capital of £675,000, not fully paid up (7,004,175 shares of 1s. each issued out of 13,500,000), a working profit of £110,587 was achieved in 1960, increased to £130,378 in 1961, despite an advance in working costs from 86s. 6d. per ton to 88s. 2d. per ton. In 1962, Konongo Gold Mines Ltd. informed the Ghana Government that the operation of the Konongo Gold Mine would become uneconomic after April 1965. The Company were therefore contemplating ceasing operations just before that time. In view of the loss of employment that this would mean, the Government decided to purchase the mine in order to provide continued employment for the Ghanaian employees. After protracted negotiations, a purchase price of £150,000 was paid by the Ghana Government and the mine is now under the management of the State Gold Mining Corporation.

Capitalised at £15 million, Consolidated Gold Fields made consolidated profits before tax of £6,826,000 for the year to 1960/61 with dividends absorbing £1,729,299. The year 1962 proved for Consolidated Gold Fields the most profitable yet in its operations, resulting in a consolidated profit before tax of £7,030,000, while, in the chairman's own words, 'another satisfactory feature of the accounts is that dividends and interest exceeded £5 million for the first time'.

Consolidated Gold Fields' income comes largely from the specialist services which it provides to companies within its own group and those within its associated groups. Varying considerably in size, they number over one hundred, and the total market capitalisation of those quoted on the stock exchange exceeded £170 million at the end of the company's working year of 1962. It is by these means of investment and management that much larger incomes are built up than from the actual production of the mining and processing of raw materials. That is why so many of the more important mining companies, not alone in Africa but throughout the world, have coalesced into holding and investment concerns behind whom and among whom stand the most important figures in the banking and financial world.

Here we have touched only on the bare bones of the Consolidated Gold Fields skeletal structure. The flesh and brawn which clothe it are set in layers of rich fat that have created a huge corporation bulge, smugly admired by the owner, but ominous to the lean, starved African observer.

8. Foreign investment in South African mining

IT has been estimated that over 50 per cent of the foreign capital invested in Africa has been poured into South Africa. British investments probably total nearly $2,800 million, and American investments closer to $840 million. A 1957 U.S. government survey of American overseas investments shows the single most profitable area was in the mining and smelting business of South Africa, whose profits are higher than from any comparable investment in the United States. The high profits can be explained largely by the cheapness of African labour. According to the 1962 *Statistical Abstract* of the United States, U.S. miners earn an average of $2.70 an hour, which is twenty-seven times the amount earned by South African miners.

Dominant in South Africa's economy is the Anglo-American De Beers group, part of the empire of Harry Oppenheimer, which extends into South West Africa and Zambia, and is linked with mining companies in many other African states. The value of the empire has been enhanced by the discovery that uranium can be produced from the residues and slimes which surround old gold mines.

Extraction of uranium from gold ores and slimes has brought South Africa into the world's leading place as a producer of uranium. The working of slimes accumulated over the past sixty years, together with those from current gold production, is helping to prolong the life of many exhausted

120

gold mines. In 1956, 8,000,000 lb. of uranium oxide were produced in South Africa, providing exports valued at £39 million. This leaves out of account the quantities that go to the Atomic Energy Board of South Africa, with whom several of the mines have contracts. The profit made from the production of uranium oxide is running ahead of that derived from gold extraction. In fact, 'the working profits derived from uranium extraction exceeded those derived from gold extraction on the seventeen producing mines taken together, and on five of them they actually offset working losses incurred in the production of the gold'.*

Harmony Gold Mining Co. Ltd. is one of the more important gold and uranium producing companies within the Anglo American Consolidated Gold Fields' maze of interests. Its authorised capital of £5 million has been paid up to the amount of £4,500,000. Secretarial services and offices to the company are provided by Rand Mines Ltd., a company that gives executive, administrative and technical services to the South African companies of the Central Mining—Rand Mines group.

Chairman of Harmony is P.H. Anderson, a deputy chairman of Rand Mines. Other directors in common are Messrs. R. E. M. Blakeway and N. W. S. Lewin. Chairman of Rand Mines is C. W. Engelhard, who is also chairman of Rand American Investments (Pty) Ltd., and patently has a watching brief for the United States investors who more and more are infiltrating into primary materials extraction in Africa. All of Rand American's 2,371,049 issued shares of £1 each are held by De Beers Investment Trust Ltd. (now Randsel), a wholly owned subsidiary of Rand Selection Corporation since the recent re-juggling of the Rand group. Rand American owns nearly all the preference shares and a substantial interest in the issued ordinary shares of Central Mining & Investment Corporation Ltd., as well as a substantial interest in the issued ordinary capital of Rand Mines Ltd. The American link confirms the tie-up forming the Central Mining—Rand Mines group.

* *South Africa*, Monica Cole, pp. 313–15, Methuen, 1961. The quotation relates to the year 1955.

Consolidated Gold Fields and Anglo American Corporation interests converge in Harmony, in which both have appreciable holdings. By the grace of the South African Government, Harmony was able to acquire undermining and mineral rights over some 8,000 acres of land, as well as freehold ownership of farms covering approximately another 10,000 acres. These holdings being rather more than Harmony could cope with, it was found profitable to sell the right to mine precious metals on two portions of its areas on lease until 1967. This right went to another Anglo American concern, Virginia Orange Free State Gold Mining Co. Ltd. Harmony's remuneration for this friendly gesture to a sister company was a minimum £3 million payable quarterly free of interest.

Virginia Orange brings us once more into contact with the American marriage to South African mining, our first example being Mr C. W. Engelhard, an American Democrat, who, as president of Engelhard Industries, refiners of precious metals in the United States, sought after steady supplies to keep his plants working. He found them in South Africa, where he linked up with Oppenheimer, and later branched out into baser metals and other fields of profit. Mr Englehard, following Mr Oppenheimer's inspiration, has also found a niche in the Canadian, Australian and Columbian mining industries, and distributes his finished goods in Europe through companies established in Paris, Rome and London. Mr Engelhard's qualities as well as his services to the extension of American interests abroad are recognised in his membership of the U.S. Foreign Policy Association.

With Virginia Orange we are brought near to more considerable American influence than Mr Engelhard is able singly to produce, by the association of the powerful Kennecott Copper Corporation with this gold mining and uranium extracting company. Kennecott had interests in Virginia Orange which it passed over, together with those it owned in the Merriespruit (Orange Free State) Gold Mining Co. Ltd., to the reorganised concern formed in 1961 to acquire those interests. The new company bears the combination title, Virginia-Merriespruit Investments (Pty) Ltd., and the rearrangement will enable it to fulfil an outstanding uranium contract with the Atomic Energy Board of South Africa.

Mr Engelhard is a member of the Virginia-Merriespruit board by virtue of the holding directly bought into it by his Engelhard Industries of Southern Africa Ltd., and his connections with Rand Mines Ltd. and Anglo American Corporation which together with another two associates, Centramic (South Africa) Ltd. and Anglo Transvaal Consolidated Investment Co. Ltd. form the parties to the new company.

Financiers and dealers in mining and other properties in the Transvaal, Anglo Transvaal has a subsidiary, Anglovaal Rhodesian Exploration Co. (Pty) Ltd., which operates in Northern and Southern Rhodesia, its mineral prospects including coal, copper, chrome and nickel. With capital authorised at £4,337,500, not fully paid up, Anglo Transvaal is operating on an unsecured short-term loan of £1 million from the National Finance Corporation of South Africa, a private organisation with which Anglo American Corporation's friends of the international investment world are closely associated, including the house of Morgan, which has a substantial financial interest in Kennecott Copper. Among Kennecott's extensive mining engagements in Africa is a 50 per cent investment in Anglovaal Rhodesian.

Primed by Morgan friends, Kennecott knows how to take care of its manifold concerns. Hence, as consideration for cession of its interests in the Viginia and Merriespruit mines, it is to receive an amount of £3,500,000, payable in five annual instalments. This does not, however, sever Kennecott's connection with these valuable Oppenheimer-Engelhard properties. For the American copper corporation will be entitled to an interest of 20 per cent up to a maximum amount of £2,500,000 on any of Virginia-Merriespruit's net surplus that may accrue after the instalment payments on the cash consideration of £3,500,000 have been fully met. This entitlement, however, will be forfeited in the event of Kennecott taking up at a later date from the members of Virginia-Merriespruit 20 per cent of the then issued share capital.

These are the tortuous means by which financial clinches

123

are held. It is obvious that the way is being kept wide open for Kennecott's re-entry into the heart of the company. Meantime it can still feast at the table.

Kennecott is a foremost copper producer in the United States, whose shares on the 'futures' market are valued by knowing operators at around $1.48 billions, even though its present capital of 11,053,051 shares of no nominal or par value issued out of 12,000,000 authorised, have been given a stated value of only $74,806,424. The possessor of copper mines, concentrating mills, smelters, refineries, fabricating works and railways, it has smelting agreements for much of its ores with American Smelting & Refining Co., with whom it has two subsidiaries in common. American Smelting is a producer itself of copper, as well as of silver, lead, zinc and gold, in the United States, Mexico, Canada and Peru. Its interests extend to Australia and Nicaragua, and it has arrangements with Cerro Corporation, Newmont Mining Corporation and Phelps Dodge Corporation, all of whom have substantial investments in South African mining projects, including the Tsumeb Corporation of South West Africa.

The American chemical industry enters the Kennecott field of operations through a joint venture with the important Allied Chemical & Dye Corporation. The Allied-Kennecott Titanium Corporation is to produce and sell titanium metal, and has put up a pilot plant. A further break-through has been made by the acquisition of 25 per cent in Western Phosphates Inc., 7·3 per cent in the common stock of Molybdenum Corporation of America, and 50 per cent in Garfield Chemical & Manufacturing Corporation. There has been a branching out into mineral exploration in Brazil and Mexico with two subsidiaries, Kenrand Pesquisas Minerals S.A. (60 per cent Kennecott owned) and Cia. Kenmex S.A. respectively. Another subsidiary, Braden Copper Co., works a copper property in Chile.

Expansion into Canada is by way of Quebec Columbium Ltd., formed by Kennecott with Molybdenum Corporation of America to investigate a columbium property near Montreal, and Quebec Iron & Titanium Corporation, owned two-thirds by Kennecott and one-third by New Jersey Zinc Co. This latter company is linked up with the great oil organisation, Texaco Inc. in a joint enterprise, Texas-Zinc Minerals Corporation, for the construction and operation of a uranium processing mill in Utah. A uranium mine in Utah was bought in 1956 and the mill began operations in 1957, also treating ores from other mines. The uranium concentrate produced is being sold to the U.S. Atomic Energy Commission under contract. The New Jersey-Kennecott venture in Quebec Iron & Titanium is going to prove extremely valuable, as titanium is a metal that does not melt at supersonic speeds, and is accordingly in high demand for use in jet aircraft. Greece also figures in Kennecott's sphere of interests, where its 95 per cent owned Kenbastos Mining Co. Ltd. works asbestos properties. In West Africa, it has a 76 per cent holding in Tin & Associated Metals Ltd., operating a columbium and tin property in Northern Nigeria. Columbium from this mine provides most of the world's present production.

Our examination into Harmony Gold Mining Co. Ltd. has led us a long way round the world and into realms of power and prodigious wealth. This seems inevitable once we begin to trace the external interests that intertwine Africa's exploitation with that of many other parts of the world. Coming back to Harmony, it is impressive to note that this company, having a gold reduction plant capable of dealing with 200,000 tons of ore a month, also boasts a uranium extraction plant whose capacity is 120,000 tons monthly. This plant began operations in April 1955. Attached to it is a sulphuric acid plant with a daily capacity of 120 tons, which started production in January 1960.

The uranium extraction plant was erected under arrangements made with the Export-Import Bank of Washington, U.S.A., and the U.K. Ministry of Supply. A loan was obtained from the Atomic Energy Board of South Africa for the entire capital cost of the plant, exclusive of the capacity extension from 80,000 to 120,000 tons monthly. The company is under contract with the combined Development Agency, as well as with the U.K. authority alone, to supply various quantities of uranium at fixed prices, under arrangements which will allow it, without incurring extra cost, to cover by June 1965 the capital expenditure on plant.

During the year ended 30 June 1961, Harmony milled a total of 2,116,000 tons of ore, which yielded 857,794 oz. of fine gold, providing a working revenue of £10,810,496, with a working profit of £4,090,677; 2,067,100 tons of slimes treated yielded 974,349 lb. of uranium oxide, giving an estimated working profit from uranium, pyrites and acid of £2,680,233.

Accounts for the following six months to the end of 1961 showed that 2,285,000 tons of ore milled resulted in a working revenue from gold of £4,458,177. Treatment of 2,138,300 tons of slimes produced 953,100 lb. of uranium oxide, giving a working profit from uranium, pyrites and acid of £2,284,647. For the working year 1961–62 the dividend paid was 55½ per cent. Net profit for the year 1960–61 was £6,674,739, and dividends paid accounted for £2,497,500. All this can be regarded as most satisfactory for shareholders on a fully paid up capital of £4,500,000.

Messrs. Engelhard and Oppenheimer must bear a special regard for their friends in the Export-Import Bank for their ready aid in this venture, in a country that makes a mockery of human rights for its non-white inhabitants. Such ease of assistance, if extended to the less developed new nations of the continent by an international banking organisation, would help lessen the gap that the developed countries are forever deprecating but which, by these stealthy means, they serve to widen between the 'have' and 'have not' countries.

9. Anglo American Corporation Limited

BIGGEST octopus in the Oppenheimer sea of operations is probably the Anglo American Corporation Ltd. Its investments are on a threefold scale, and the list of the main ones convey but the barest idea of their very considerable range. These are more or less direct participations and do not include the more intricate holdings held through or in common with subsidiaries and others in a more far-reaching extension of interests. Principally in mining, they nevertheless branch out into processing, transport and communications, landholdings and estate, forestry and timber, industry, as well as into hydro-electrical power schemes like that of the Rhodesia Congo Border Power Corporation.

Gold, uranium, iron, asbestos and coal mines are among the corporation's most notable undertakings in South Africa, forming the solid foundation on which the Oppenheimer empire stands. Copper mining is its principal occupation in the Rhodesias, though it exploits also lead, zinc and cadmium, and has the distinction of being the only producer of coal in Rhodesia, where it controls the Wankie Colliery. Through associated companies, its interests spread out into Tanganyika, Uganda, the Congo, Angola, Mozambique, West Africa, and even into the Sahara and North Africa, as can be seen by this list of direct investments:

127

Finance and Investment Companies

African & European Investment Co. Ltd.
African Loans & Investment Ltd.
Anglo American Investment Trust Ltd.
Anglo American Rhodesian Development Corporation Ltd.
Central Reserves (Pty) Ltd.
Central Reserves Rhodesia (Pty) Ltd.
Consolidated Mines (Investment) Ltd.
Consolidated Mines Selection Co. Ltd.
Consolidated Mines Selection (Johannesburg) Ltd.
De Beers Holdings Ltd.
De Beers Investment Trust Ltd.
De Beers Rhodesia Investments Ltd.
Epoch Investments Ltd.
Jameson Mining Holdings (Pty) Ltd.
Lydenburg Estates Ltd.
Orange Free State Investment Ltd.
New Central Witwatersrand Areas Ltd.
New Era Consolidated Ltd.
Overseas & Rhodesian Investment Co. Ltd.
Rand American Investments (Pty) Ltd.
Rand Selection Corporation Ltd.
Rhodesian Acceptances Ltd.
Rhodesian Anglo American Ltd.
Rhodes Investments Ltd.
South Africa Mines Selection Ltd.
South African Townships, Mining & Finance Corporation Ltd.
Transvaal Vanadium Holdings Ltd.
Vereeniging Estates Ltd.
Western Ultra Deep Levels Ltd.
West Rand Investment Trust Ltd.
South West Africa Co. Ltd.

Diamond Mines

De Beers Consolidated Mines Ltd.
Consolidated Diamond Mines of South West Africa Ltd.
New Jagersfontein Mining & Exploration Co. Ltd.
Diamond Abrasive Products Ltd.
Diamond Development Co. of South Africa (Pty) Ltd.
Philmond (Pty) Ltd.

Premier (Transvaal) Diamond Mining Co. Ltd.
Williamson Diamonas Ltd.

Coal Mines

Amalgamated Collieries of South Africa Ltd.
Bleebok Colliery Ltd.
Coronation Collieries Ltd.
Natal Coal Exploration Ltd.
Natal Coal Exploration Co. Ltd.
New Largo Colliery Ltd.
South African Coal Estates (Witbank) Ltd.
Springbok Colliery Ltd.
New Schoongezicht Colliery.
Cornelia Colliery Ltd.
Springfield Collieries Ltd.
Transvaal Coal Corporation Ltd.
Vierfontein Coal Holdings Ltd.
Vierfontein Colliery Ltd.
Vryheid Coronation Ltd.
Wankie Colliery Co. Ltd.
Witbank Coal Holdings Ltd.

Copper Mines

Bancroft Mines Ltd.
Kansanshi Copper Mining Co. Ltd.
Nchanga Consolidated Copper Mines Ltd.
Rhodesia Copper Refineries Ltd.
Rhokana Corporation Ltd.

Gold Mines

Brakpan Mines Ltd.
Daggafontein Mines Ltd.
East Daggafontein Mines Ltd.
Free State Geduld Mines Ltd.
Jeannett Gold Mines Ltd.
President Brand Gold Mining Co. Ltd.
South African Land & Exploration Co. Ltd.
Spring Mines Ltd.
Vaal Reefs Exploration & Mining Co. Ltd.
Welkom Gold Mining Co. Ltd.

Western Deep Levels Ltd.
Western Holdings Ltd.
Western Reefs Exploration & Development Co. Ltd.
President Steyn Gold Mining Co. Ltd.
Free State Saiplaas Gold Mining Co. Ltd.

Other Mining

Highveld Development Co. Ltd.
Iron Duke Mining Co. Ltd.
King Edward (Cuperiferous) Pyrite.
Monasite & Mineral Ventures Ltd. (rare earths).
Munnik Myburgh Chrysotile Asbestos Ltd.
Rhochrome Ltd.
Rhodesia Broken Hill Development Co. Ltd.
Transvaal Manganese (Pty) Ltd.
Transvaal Vanadium Co. (Pty) Ltd.
Umgababa Minerals Ltd. (Ilmenite, rutile and zircon).
Vereenigning Brick & Tile Co. Ltd.

Prospecting

Anglo American Prospecting Co. Ltd.
Anglo American Rhodesian Mineral Exploration Ltd.
Border Exploration & Development Co. (Pty) Ltd.
De Beers Prospecting (Rhodesian Areas) Ltd.
Kaffrarian Metal Holdings (Pty) Ltd.
Kalindini Exploration Ltd.
Kasempa Minerals Ltd.
Lunga Exploration Ltd.
Prospecting & Mineral Interests Ltd.
Swaziland Rift Exploration Co. Ltd.
Western Rift Exploration Co. Ltd.

Industrial and Sundry

Anglo American (Rhodesia Services) Ltd.
Anglo Collieries Recruiting Organisation (Pty) Ltd.
Boart & Hard Metal Products (Rhodesia) Ltd.
Boart & Hard Metal Products S.A. Ltd.
Clay Products Ltd.
Easan Electrical (Pty) Ltd.

Electro Chemical Industries Ltd.
Forest Industries & Veneers Ltd.
Hansens Native Labour Organisation (Pty) Ltd.
Hard Metals Ltd.
Inter-Mine Services O.F.S. (Pty) Ltd.
Lourenço Marques Forwarding Co. Ltd.
Northern Rhodesia Aviation Services Ltd.
Peak Timbers Ltd.
Pearlman Veneers (S.A.) Ltd.
Rhoanglo Mine Services Ltd.
Rhodesia Congo Border Power Corporation Ltd.
Rhodesia Copper Products Ltd.
Rhodesian Steel Developments (Pty) Ltd.
Stone & Allied Industries (O.F.S.) Ltd.
Veneered Plywoods Ltd.
Zinc Products Ltd.

Land and Estate

Anglo American (O.F.S.) Housing Co. Ltd.
Anmercosa Land & Estates Ltd.
Cecilia Park (Pty) Ltd.
Falcon Investments Ltd.
Orange Free State Land & Estate Co. (Pty) Ltd.
Prestin (Pty) Ltd.
Welkom Township Co.

It is interesting to note among the companies two that are engaged in the enlistment of 'native labour', namely, Anglo Collieries Recruiting Organisation (Pty) Ltd. and Hansens Native Labour Organisation (Pty) Ltd. Recruiting labour for the South African mines has always been an absorbing problem in connection with which there long ago grew up an efficient organisation for importing workers not only from the reserves of South Africa itself, but also from the protectorates, the Rhodesias and Nyasaland. There are long-standing arrangements with the authorities of the Portuguese colonies, particularly Mozambique, for the recruitment of African labour for work in the mines of South Africa.

Enforcement of apartheid through the establishment of Bantustans, such as that recently gone through in the Transkei, will force the chiefs, under inducement, to supply increasing numbers of local men for the mines. There is now a plan to stop the employment of workers from Zambia, Rhodesia and Malawi, and even from the protectorates. It may well be thought that these people will be infected with the 'disease' of nationalism and hence add fuel to the fire of unrest that has been lit in South Africa itself. It is significant that Mozambique Africans are still to be allowed the privilege of enriching South Africa's mine owners by their toil, not least among them Anglo American Corporation.

This company was incorporated in 1917 to draw together a number of mining, investment and industrial companies already controlled by Mr Harry Oppenheimer, and to bring them into tighter organisation with such other interests as Mr C. W. Engelhard, chairman of Rand Mines, Kennecott Copper Corporation, and other associates. As the guardian of these interests, Anglo American acts as technical manager and secretary to an extensive number of mining and investment companies falling within its wide perimeter. In its executive, administrative and secretarial capacities, it also arranges the financial life of the many enterprises coming under its care.

The list given indicates only the barest bones of Anglo American's multifarious interests, and if we were to examine them in detail we should find ourselves reaching into a most tangled complex of arteries and sinews. Many of the undertakings are not only important in themselves but have involvements which weave together the mining, industrial and financial world of Africa with that of the rest of the world. Such organisations as the Rand Selection Corporation, Union Corporation, Rhokana Corporation Ltd., and certain others, participate in a self-perpetuating and exclusive ensemble. Inter-action and inter-penetration of interests is a predominant feature emphasising the monopolistic nature of the African mining industry, whose leaders are the powerful arbiters of the continent's industrial growth, especially south of the Sahara. It is not difficult to understand how, from this position, they and their European and American associates and financial backers

132

wield a preponderant influence upon the policies of their governments in relation to the African scene.

A look, for instance, at Rand Selection Corporation Ltd. brings us at once upon one of the principal arms of Anglo American Corporation in the working of its vast empire. Rand immediately brings to mind the vision of fevered diamond and gold rushes that followed in the wake of the young Cecil Rhodes and his brother adventurers in the late eighteen-seventies. Rhodes' quarrel with the Boers was over the fight to penetrate the interior to get at the gold of the Witwatersrand. His political leadership was assumed to make himself king of the mining wealth that had been discovered. It was, according to a committee set up in the Cape to examine Rhodes' part in the famous Jameson raid, 'in his capacity as controller of the three great joint-stock companies, the British South Africa Company, the De Beers Consolidated Mines, and the Gold Fields of South Africa, he directed and controlled the combination which rendered such a proceeding as the Jameson raid possible'.

The Jameson Raid finished Rhodes politically in South Africa. It was then he turned to what is now Rhodesia, where he made the British South Africa Company the power in the land that it has been ever since. Nor has the control of political affairs by all the great mining combines abated in any way since then. Rather has it intensified until they are the powers which control and direct affairs, not in Africa alone, but by their integration with other formidable combinations in Europe and America, they exercise great influence in these continents also and hence internationally.

De Beers and Gold Fields remain. The intervening years have, naturally, seen an extension of the opening up of mines and their exploitation, accompanied by a constant adaptation of their financial arrangements. Gold Fields heads a vast organisation of its own. De Beers has come within the periphery of Rand Selection Corporation but still controls within its own group of companies the output and distribution of most of the world's diamonds.

In its own right, Rand Selection owns around 14,890 acres

of freehold property in some of the richest mining areas of South Africa. A number of townships have been laid out by the company, in which it has leasehold rights of a high value. Certain of its rights are secured by a 92 per cent interest in South African Townships, Mining & Finance Corporation Ltd. and its wholly owned subsidiaries, African Gold & Base Metals Holdings Ltd., Cecilia Park (Pty) Ltd. and Dewhurst Farms Ltd.

Rand Selection is, however, a subsidiary of Anglo American, under whose direction its scope was enlarged at the close of 1960 to enable it to participate in any new business undertaken by Anglo American up to 1 October 1970 on an increased percentage basis. The enlargement of Rand Selection was accomplished by the contributing of shares, loans and cash to De Beers Investment Trust by Anglo American, subsidiaries of British South Africa Co., Central Mining & Investment Corporation Ltd. De Beers Consolidated Mines Ltd., and Johannesburg Consolidated Investment Co. Ltd., who have been joined by the American-controlled South African company, Engelhard Hanovia Inc., and International Nickel Co. of Canada Ltd. controlled by the American Rockefeller-Morgan groups. Rand Selection then acquired all the issued capital of De Beers Investment Trust in return for the issue of shares of its own to the Investment Trust's shareholders.

Under the arrangement, De Beers Investment has become a wholly owned subsidiary of Rand Selection. Yet at the same time by the acquisition of its holdings in Rand Selection, De Beers is now the majority holder of Rand's 33,085,365 shares issued and fully paid up of the 35 million authorised to comprise its capital of £8,270,000. It is perfectly obvious that the loans and cash advanced to De Beers by the above-listed companies were in order to enable it to facilitate its own and Rand's enlargement.

As a result of the 1962 implementation of the agreed re-arrangement, De Beers Investment is now known as Randsel Investments Ltd. Its three wholly owned subsidiaries, Rand American Investments (Pty) Ltd., Rhodes Investments Ltd. and Jameson Mining Holdings (Pty) Ltd., are now consolidated within the Rand Selection organisation. The two holding companies, Rand Selection and Randsel, shared also in 1962 in the enlargement of another Anglo American creation, Consolidated Mines Selection Co. Ltd., registered in the United Kingdom in 1897, whose interests cover the major mining activities of Southern Africa.

The assets of Consolidated Mines were jerked up to £15 million by the acquisition from companies within the Anglo American Sphere of holdings worth over £10,500,000 in the British South Africa Co., Central Mining & Investment Corporation Ltd., Johannesburg Consolidated Investment Corporation Ltd. and Selection Trust Ltd., as well as by smaller holdings in Bay Hall Trust Ltd. and Rhodesian Anglo American Ltd. In return for ceding their shares, the participating companies have acquired shares in Consolidated Mines Selection Co. Ltd.

At the same time, Rand Selection took up, in association with Anglo American, Consolidated Mines Selection and affiliated companies, an option on the purchase of 400,000 shares in Hudson Bay Mining & Smelting Co. Ltd., one of the three leading copper-gold mining companies of Canada, controlled by United States finance. Exercise of this option was made possible by loans raised in America, probably from the same interests behind Hudson Bay Mining.

Rand Selection's operations also coincide with those of Anglo American in the very important Swaziland Iron Ore Development Co. Ltd., which has concluded contracts with two major Japanese steel producers, Yawata Iron & Steel Co. Ltd. and Fuji Iron & Steel Co. Ltd., as well as with General Ore International Corporation, for the sale to them of 12 million tons of iron ore over a period of approximately ten years.

Anglo American has enabled Rand Selection to participate in the purchase from British Coated Board & Paper Mills Ltd., a United Kingdom firm, of a large holding in South African Board Mills Ltd. 'This', stated Mr H. F. Oppenheimer, in his report to the 71st annual general meeting of Rand Selection Corporation Ltd., in Johannesburg, on 26 February 1963, 'is

135

one of the leading growth companies in South Africa, and is managed by Stafford Mayer & Co., with whom the Anglo American Corporation has long been associated in the coal industry'.

Contractual arrangements with Anglo American have secured Rand Selection participation in a number of property developments in central Johannesburg. The two have also gone hand in hand in Anglo American's widespread prospecting activities and in certain development projects. Among them are explorations into the feasibility of the bushveld igneous complex of South Africa.

Here, indeed, in Anglo American, is the most ramified industrial and financial structure in Africa, powerful and commanding, the organisation that governs the fate of many millions on this continent and stretches out its influence overseas. Like all monopolies, Anglo American is never content with the existing boundaries of its empire, but is ever seeking extensions, partly because it cannot afford to be overtaken. Hence it is continually conducting a comprehensive prospecting programme in many parts of Africa and elsewhere, in order to find untapped sources of mineral wealth that can be profitably exploited.

10. The diamond groups

THE diamond industry of South Africa brought in a revenue of £93 million in 1962. Two-thirds of this was from gem diamonds, whose carat price was recently raised by the industry's controllers. Of such importance is the diamond industry to South Africa that there is no duty on the export of rough diamonds.

Diamonds are a major concern of Mr Harry Oppenheimer, and it is through De Beers and the Diamond Corporation, with their associated companies and alliances that the operations of his Anglo American Corporation stretch out from South Africa into South-West Africa, Angola, Congo, East and West Africa, to control until recently the production and sale of pretty well 85 per cent of the world's diamonds. Even the distribution of the Soviet Union's quite important production has been added, by the arrangement to dispose of 'Red' diamonds through De Beers' selling organisation.

The De Beers' group of companies, as we have seen, is controlled by Rand Selection Corporation Ltd. Tightly interwoven, it interlocks with the gem companies of Angola and Mozambique and the dominating complex that spreads across the Rhodesias and Congo. Rand Selection now dominates the administration of the group by reason of its recent acquisition of the total holdings of De Beers Investment Trust Ltd., now known as Randsel Investments Ltd.

Chief operating company is De Beers Consolidated Mines

Ltd., and still on its board is a member of the family of Solly Joel, the East End Londoner with whom Rhodes adventured into diamonds along with Alfred Beit. Consolidation of the De Beers, Kimberley and Griqualand West Mines of South-West Africa was the original purpose of the company. A considerable number of allied and even different interests have since been added. Besides the mines in South Africa, De Beers operates open-cast workings along the southern coast and in Namaqualand, South-West Africa. A 50 per cent interest is held in the Williamson Mine in Tanganyika; the other holder is the Tanganyika Government.

Among its subsidiary companies, De Beers Consolidated includes Premier (Transvaal) Diamond Mining Co. Ltd., Consolidated Mines of South-West Africa Ltd., Diamond Corporation Ltd. and De Beers Industrial Corporation Ltd. Directly and indirectly, it holds something like 40 per cent of the capital of Diamond Purchasing & Trading Co. Ltd. and Diamond Trading Co. Ltd., and 31·5 per cent of Industrial Distributors (1946) Ltd. All these purchasing and distributing companies are main avenues through which the gem and industrial diamond production of the world's principal producers are distributed. De Beers Industrial has also interests in diamond production by its control of Griqualand West Diamond Mining Co., Dutoitspan Mine Ltd., New Jagersfontein Mining & Exploration Co. Ltd. and Consolidated Co. Bultfontein Mine Ltd.

What seems at first glance to be a rather curious interest for a company engaged in the diamond industry is De Beer Consolidated's 50 per cent holding of the issued share capital of African Explosives & Chemical Industries Ltd. On closer examination it will not appear so odd. The company thought it expedient and profitable to have its own avenue for purchasing explosives used in opening up working areas on its own mines and those of associated companies. That was the original aim, but once in the explosive business it was a short road to their manufacture and expansion into serious production of chemicals, especially those allied to explosives manufacture.

138

The present-day operations of African Explosives is by no means so limited, nor is there anything innocent about them or the company's composition. Through De Beers Industrial Corporation it is jointly owned by De Beers' principal, Anglo American Corporation, and the South African branch of Imperial Chemical Industries Ltd. I.C.I.'s ramifications and its control of a number of chemicals, synthetics and manufacturing processes make it one of the most powerful monopolies in the world. It long ago reached the stage of cartelisation with other foremost chemicals and armaments organisations. Its cartel arrangements with the major chemical and plastics material company in the world, the I.E. du Pont de Nemours Corporation, link it with the modern military equipment industry that seems to issue inevitably from chemicals manufacture.

Explosives laid the foundation of the du Pont rise to power. 'Their first big order was to supply Napoleon in his vain attempt to crush Toussaint L'Ouverture and the people of Santo Domingo, and the next was for the war of the United States—against the so-called 'Barbary Pirates'.* The following quotation is from *Cartels in Action* quoted by Victor Perlo in *The Empire of High Finance*, page 195:

'This established the role of du Pont, which has continued down to the present day, when it dominates the greatest and most profitable single corporation in the world, General Motors.

Du Pont's association with I.C.I. goes back about forty years. It was in 1921 that more than half of the General Motors' shares sold by the House of Morgan were bought by Explosives Trade Ltd., a British subsidiary of the Nobel industries, with which I.C.I. was connected. Explosives were among I.C.I.'s earliest operations, and its interests in Nobel's concerns in this and other fields were subsequently absorbed into the heart of the I.C.I. empire.

Ever since that early coming together the alliance between du Pont and I.C.I. has grown more complex. Both of them

* *The Empire of High Finance*, Victor Perlo, p. 190.

had effective patent and processing rights with the great German chemical combine, I. G. Farben, and they divided the world between them. Both du Pont and I.C.I. continued to respect their arrangements with I. G. Farben during the war. Du Pont and I.C.I. have abandoned all pretence of business rivalry in numerous major foreign markets, including Canada, Argentina and Brazil. There they do business as a single, unified concern through jointly owned local companies . . . they have succeeded in cartelising these tributary chemical markets, thanks to their combined power and prestige.'

If we see I.C.I. in association with Oppenheimer companies in South Africa, this should not astonish us. Monopolies are constantly drawing together, aligned by common industrial and financial interests in a given field and at a given time. The I.C.I.-Oppenheimer combination is not restricted to African Explosives but repeats itself in association with other Oppenheimer offshoots and groups. British blessing is given to the enterprise through the secondment on contract to the company of an expert from the British nuclear arms establishment. Moreover, the military equipment produced at its factories is based on the specifications of the British army, navy and air forces.

Important though African Explosives is to the Oppenheimer combine and South Africa's military designs in Africa, it owes its existence to the diamond mining in which it was originally conceived. It is only one of the De Beers Consolidated progeny. There are several others, among them the investment company, De Beers Holding Ltd., of which it controls 84·5 per cent. On the death of J. T. Williamson, De Beers Holding contrived to secure an option on the whole of 1,200 shares constituting the capital of his mine in Tanganyika. A deal was fixed at £4,139,996, with De Beers responsible for estate duty and interest on Williamson's shares. Satisfaction of these items was made by cession of 320 shares of Williamson Diamonds Ltd. to the Tanganyika Government, which subsequently bought up a further 280. The price of £1,317,272 agreed upon for these was met, together with six per cent total interest, out of dividends received by the Government on its total holding of 600 shares.

Consolidated Diamond Mines of South-West Africa Ltd., in which De Beers Consolidated has a majority holding, has a concession covering large areas of alluvial diamond deposits in South-West Africa, valid until the close of the year 2010. This was extended by the South-West Administration from a previous expiry date of 1972. A most valuable item in the De Beers' inventory of profits is the 'De Pass' royalty owned by the South-West Financial Corporation Ltd., a full subsidiary of Consolidated Diamond Mines. This royalty gives its owner eight per cent of the gross proceeds from the sale of diamonds produced in the Pomona area of South-West Africa, in which South-West Finance possesses landed property and other mineral rights and royalties.

Participation in the diamond distributive trade comes to Consolidated Diamond Mines through the following holdings:

Diamond Corporation Ltd.—5,996,903 shares.
Diamond Trading Co. Ltd.—80,000 shares.
Diamond Purchasing & Trading Co. Ltd.—200,000 shares.
Industrial Distributors (1946) Ltd.—150,000 shares.
De Beers Holdings Ltd.—1,150,000 shares.

Its own production of diamonds has gone up from 895,744 carats in 1958 to 933,937 in 1960. Taken together with its earnings by way of royalties and investments in the diamond trade, it is small wonder that it has over the past fifteen years been able to declare the following impressive dividends:

1946–1949: 40% plus 10% bonus each year.
1950: 40% plus 20%.
1951: 125%.
1952–1958: 150% each year.
1959: 200%.
1960: 200%.

The company's fully paid-up and authorised capital stands at £5,240,000. Its net consolidated profit in 1960 was £10,734,468, after providing £4,622,731 for taxation. Dividends absorbed

£5,667,437, the major beneficiary being De Beers Consolidated. The estimated profit for 1961 was £12,848,000, after providing £5,410,000 for taxation and £168,000 for dividends on preference shares. The figure for ordinary dividend payments is not included, but it is likely to be higher than for the previous year.

Diamond Mining & Utility Co. (S.W.A.) Ltd. is associated with De Beers Consolidated by reason of a cession to the latter company of a large portion of a diamond area in South-West Africa, in exchange for a 20 per cent interest in the net profit on diamonds recovered. The company has 180,000 shares in Diamond Dredging & Mining Co. (S.W.A.) Ltd. To satisfy this purchase, Diamond Mining & Utility issued at par another 540,000 shares in July 1960, the authorised capital then being increased from £300,000 to £500,000. Its other interests are 114,400 shares in Industrial Diamonds of South Africa (1945) Ltd., which ceased operations in the spring of 1960, but retains 148,200 shares in Diamond Mining & Utility, as well as 197,900 shares in Lorelei Copper Mines Ltd., in which Diamond Mining & Utility also holds 200,000 shares. All in all, this demonstrates what might be described as a tight but cosy combination.

The most interesting hub of the whirling diamond wheel is the Diamond Corporation, whose £22 million capital is owned mainly by De Beers Consolidated Mines, Diamond Mines of South-West Africa and the ever-present Anglo American Corporation. The Diamond Corporation purchases, on periodical contract, the diamond production of the world's most important producers, usually on a specific quota basis. These diamonds are then marketed through the Central Selling Organisation, together with the output of the De Beers' group mines and those from the diggings owned and run by the South African Government, which is in the mining business on State account.

Where do the other diamond trading companies come in? Diamond Trading Company Ltd. receives and sells to the market diamonds of gem or near gem value. Industrial Distributors (Sales) Ltd. have a corner on drilling material and boart for the mines, which they sell to the market.

Close associates of De Beers also have interests in these tributary companies of the group. Société Minière du Beceka S.A., a company within the dragnet of the Société Générale de Belgique, has holdings in Industrial Distributors (1946) Ltd., Diamond Trading Co. Ltd., Diamond Purchasing & Trading Co. Ltd., Diamond Development Co. Ltd. and in another of the Société Générale's wards of the diamond world, Société Diamant Boart. Industrial Distributors, also within Société Générale's direct investment portfolio, increased its 1961 dividend by about 20 per cent over those of previous years. Beceka's association with the Congo is continued through the Société d'Elevage et de Culture au Congo (S.E.C.) and Cie Maritime Belge (C.M.B.).

Operating deposits on the Lubilash river in the Congo, which produce mainly industrial diamonds and crushing boart, Beceka has a subsidiary, Société Beceka-Manganese, working manganese deposits near a Congolese railway junction. At the beginning of 1962 Beceka-Manganese established a 500 million franc subsidiary, Société Minière de Kisenga, in which it is the chief shareholder. Kisenga has received certain concessionary and exploitation rights from Beceka-Manganese, which also participated in October 1962 in the creation of the Société Européenne des Derives du Manganese—SEDEMA. The main parties to the formation of Sedema are associates of the Société d'Entreprise et d'Ivestissements du Beceka—SIBEKA—and the Manganese Chemicals Corporation of U.S.A.

From the report of the Société Générale for 1962, a directing hand behind all this segmentation, it emerges that an extraordinary meeting of Beceka on 21 March 1962 agreed that Beceka should renounce in favour of a new company, Société Minière de Bakwanga, all its mining rights in the Congo (mainly in the Bakwanga region), and should become the Société d'Entreprise et d'Investissements du Beceka, to be known by its abbreviated form, Sibeka. The purpose of Sibeka was re-formed to cover the investigation, promoting and financing, by whatever means, in Belgium as well as in the Congo, and other foreign countries, of all kinds of enterprises, whether in mining, industry, commerce, agriculture or transport, especially those having

143

connections with mineral substances of all kinds, as well as with their derivatives and substitutes.

Within the framework of this new objective, the former participations were increased and new participations were taken up or were in course of examination, in particular certain ones having to do with the production of artificial diamonds. The principal activity of Sibeka, however, is to be its important participation in Société Minière de Bakwanga, known as Miba. Miba's production in 1961, its first year of working, was nearly 15 million carats of diamonds, which the chairman of Société Générale considered should be its normal 'rhythm', having regard to the selling market.

Sibeka has been busy in South Kasai, where other investments have been placed, including the modernisation of a 150 km. road from Bakwanga to the station at Mwene-Ditu. Société Générale's participation in Sibeka stands at 525,000 shares of no par value, and it has assisted Beceka-Manganese to place 10 million francs out of the 11 million francs it has been allotted in the 81 million franc capital of Sedema. Sibeka has taken up another 10 million francs. The object of Sedema is the manufacture of manganese composites and manganese metals for the European market.

It is not long before any endeavour to trace the companies engaged in a particular field of mining leads into associations connecting with other sectors of raw materials production. Thus our examination of the De Beers' diamond enterprises has taken us into the even vaster world of Société Générale's interests, which we shall meet again more than once in the course of our journeyings through the tangled maze of international control of Africa's basic riches. It is also significant that in almost every corner we find lurking some coupling with American major industrial concerns. In the present case, Manganese Chemicals Corporation comes immediately and directly into the picture.

Looking further into African diamond production, we find another Société Générale off-shoot operating in the Congo. Société Internationale Forestière et Minière du Congo, known briefly as Forminière, concerns itself with mining, commercial, industrial and agricultural pursuits, chiefly in Kasai. Its main preoccupation is diamond mining.

Forminière is one of King Leopold's original main concessions in the Congo. He formed the company in 1906 with the help of, among others, two American businessmen, Thomas F. Fortune and Daniel Guggenheim, the last of whom built up a fortune from mining in South America. Today Forminière is part of the vast complex dominated by Société Générale, Tanganyika Concessions and its child, Union Minière du Haut Katanga, which has the Congo's economic life in the palm of its hand, and is now greedily extended to Angola and Mozambique. Through its subsidiary, Société Internationale Commerciale et Financière de la Forminière—INTERFOR—it has sister interests with Beceka in a number of agricultural companies working plantations in the Congo on a grand scale.

Other holdings held by Forminière are in mining companies such as Société de Recherches et d'Exploitation des Bauxites du Congo—BAUXICONGO—featured also in Union Minière's lengthy list of more important interests. Oil is also included in the Société Générale's empire through Société de Recherches et d'Exploitations des Petroles—SOCOREP. This is among Forminière's investments.

The Diamond Corporation acts as the rallying centre for the merchandise offered for sale by all the large producers. In its role as the central buying organisation for the international procurers of diamonds, it is not surprising that it should have a share in some of the most important producing companies outside the South African group. Messrs H. F. Oppenheimer and H. J. Joel of its own directorate are seated on the board of the Angola Diamond Co. (Companhia de Diamantes de Angola), another two members of which, Messrs Albert E. Thiele and A. A. Ryan, adorn the Forminière board. Mr Thiele has important connections with certain powerful American groups. He began his career in 1909 with the Guggenheim brothers, one of whom was so helpful to Leopold II. Thence he graduated to the chairmanship of the Pacific Tin Consolidated Corporation and to directorates in the Kennecott Copper Corporation and its subsidiary, Braden Copper Co. Oil and nitrates are also Mr

Thiele's business. Maracaibo Oil and Barber Oil are numbered among his directorships, as are Chilean Nitrates Sales Corporation, and the chairmanship of the Feldspar Corporation. As a director of Angola Diamond and Forminière, he has most certainly not innocently strayed from his basic moorings, anchored in Guggenheim, Kennecott Copper, oil, tin and nitrates, in which the Morgans have their helping hand. The Morgan Guaranty Trust is one of the main arteries from which flows finance for the Oppenheimer combines. Morgan is also in association with the Banque Belge, the leading banking string in the Société Générale structure, and the biggest bank in Belgium. Represented on the Angola Diamond board is another Angola concern, Companhia de Pesquisas Mineiras de Angola.

Angola Diamonds has monopoly rights permitting it to work for diamonds over almost 390,000 square miles of Angola, an area almost four times the size of Ghana or Great Britain. Forty-three mines are in operation, three new ones having been opened to replace three whose reserves were running out. Prospecting is going on for further deposits, nineteen groups being at work. Direct interest in the company, registered in Portugal, is held by the Angola Government, the on-the-spot administrative arm of the Portuguese Government. It holds 200,000 shares, slightly in excess of the 198,800 held by the Société Générale. About half the African workers for the company are forced labourers rounded up by the authorities and receiving a monthly wage of around seventy escudos, equivalent to about sixteen shillings. The very handsome profits of the company are divided equally between the Province of Angola and the shareholders after six per cent has been allocated to the managing bodies.

Shareholders' profit at the end of trading, 1960, was 137,000,931 escudos, after the same amount had been reserved for the Angola Province and 15,341,649 escudos for legal reserve. Total profits, in fact, amounted to 289,343,511 escudos, of which 114,800,000 escudos had come from profits held in reserve. Interim and final dividends absorbed a sum for the year 1960 of 136,670,000 escudos.

The company pays no import duties on plant or material and

no duties on diamonds exported. It also enjoys a loan from the Angola Government of 100 million escudos, in return for the free issue of 100,000 shares of 170 escudos each to the Province of Angola in 1955. The unheard-of uneconomic rate of interest on this loan is one per cent, repayments to be completed in 1971. Angola Diamond Co. holds 16·266 per cent of the issued capital of Sociedade Portuguesa de Lapidacao de Diamantes.

Diamond Corporation has contractual arrangements for the purchase of Angola Diamond's output, which has recently been running at over a million carats and is estimated to give even higher yields, since mechanical excavators and washing plant have been installed, following the proof of extensive alluvial deposits. Gem diamonds represent 65 per cent of the output.

Diamond Corporation has broken into the Ivory Coast, with the formation of a local subsidiary to purchase diamonds on the open market of that country. How open the market will be is anybody's guess. Some of the other newly independent African countries are striving to break away from Diamond Corporation domination. Ghana has set up its own diamond market in Accra, and all sellers, including Consolidated African Selection Trust Ltd. (CAST), working a 68 square mile concession in the Akim Abuakwa district, must sell through it. Sierra Leone Selection Trust Ltd. is CAST'S subsidiary operating in Sierra Leone.

Incredible as it may sound, Sierra Leone Selection once held exclusive diamond mining rights over practically the whole of the country. In 1955, following protestations from the people, especially in the rich diamond region of Konor, the extent of its concession area was reduced to some 209 square miles, then the extent of the company's existing working. The curtailment of rights, however, was more apparent than real. The concessionary rights are for thirty years, but restricted rights were granted over a further 250 square miles, of which a hundred have since been taken up. The company is also allowed to prospect for deep deposits of diamonds anywhere in Sierra Leone, for a period of not less than ten years; and to mine them.

That the agreement was a sham is proved by the undertaking

given by the then Colonial Government not to grant before
1975 to any applicants other than Sierra Leonians, or companies
in which the beneficial interest or greater part of it is held by
Sierra Leonians, any diamond prospecting licences or leases
without first offering such licences or leases to Sierra Leone
Selection Trust. Though this virtually gives a free hand to the
company, the Government nevertheless made it a payment of
£1,500,000 to compensate for supposedly lost opportunities.
All the six million shares issued out of the 6,400,000 authorised
to make up the capital of £1,600,000 are held by CAST. What
profits the company makes are not publicly known, since
accounts are issued only to shareholders.

The chairman of both CAST and Sierra Leone Selection is
Mr A. Chester Beatty, who has as colleagues on both boards
Messrs E. C. Wharton-Tigar, T. H. Bradford and P. J. Oppenheimer. Mr P. J. Oppenheimer also sits on the board of the
Diamond Corporation, alongside Mr W. A. Chapple, who is
another colleague on the CAST board. Both these gentlemen
sit together on the London Committee of De Beers Consolidated Mines, Mr P. J. Oppenheimer also occupying a seat on
the Johannesburg Committee, on which he is associated with
Major-General I. P. de Villiers, C.B., and Mr A. Wilson, the
last-named two being also joined together on the directorate of
Consolidated Diamond Mines of South West Africa Ltd.

Mr Thomas Horat Bradford represents Selection Trust Ltd.,
of which he is managing director, on its main associated
companies in America, the Rhodesias, Canada and Venezuela.
Mr Beatty keeps company with Mr Bradford on several of these
boards. Mr Chapple's connection with the diamond world is on
a decidedly high level, if we may judge from his directorship of
the Banque Diamantaire Anversoise S.A. Antwerp, which is
still the world's major diamond-cutting centre, employing over
13,000 people in this industry. The Antwerp Diamond Bank
occupies an important strategic position. Something like 40,000
to 50,000 carats are cut in Antwerp every week, the bulk of the
rough stones coming from the Diamond Trading Company, at
the London end of the De Beers' Central Selling Organisation.
But Antwerp searches other sources for its diamond supplies

148

and in 1961 got as much as 30 per cent of its total weight in carats elsewhere.

It is only too obvious that Mr A. Chester Beatty moves among the exalted ranks of the diamond world, especially that preponderant sector of it dominated by the De Beers' group and pivoted around the Diamond Corporation and its Selling Organisation. It is therefore difficult to understand the play that Mr Beatty made in connection with the Sierra Leone Government Bill, passed towards the end of 1961, obliging all producers of diamonds in Sierra Leone to sell through the Government Diamond Office.

Mr Beatty, as chairman of Selection Trust Ltd., as well as of CAST and Sierra Leone Selection, its subsidiary, asserted that the expired contract that CAST had with the Diamond Corporation had not been renewed because of the excessive commission of 12 per cent demanded by it. CAST had offered four per cent, which had been rejected. A contract was therefore made with Harry Winston, Inc., of New York, owners and cutters of the famed Jonker diamond, who were said to be looking for a direct source of supply which would sidestep the Diamond Corporation. In view of the interconnection between Selection Trust and the De Beers' companies, including the Diamond Corporation, through interdependent shareholdings as well as directorial interweaving, it is strange to witness one of the most prominent links in the chain, Mr A. Chester Beatty, protesting his anxiety to protect Sierra Leone's interests against the Corporation, of which he is very much a part.

The protest from Mr Beatty was that if Sierra Leone Selection were obliged to submit its production to the Government's Diamond Office this would ultimately go to the Diamond Corporation, which was the Diamond Office's end purchaser, precisely what he was fighting against. Moreover, this would mean severing the contract with Winston, for which breach compensation would have to be made. Mr Beatty pointed out that his solicitude for Sierra Leone's welfare had caused him to secure a revaluation of the Diamond Corporation contract in 1957, so that an additional £2,700,000 had been received in its last three years of operation.

149

There is a curious twist here, for Mr Beatty asserts that £500,000 more in revenue would be received by the Sierra Leone Government under the Winston contract than under one concluded with Diamond Corporation. Four pertinent questions arise from this. What increased percentage of revenue was represented by the additional £2,700,000 Mr Beatty said was obtained from the Diamond Corporation on the last three years of the expired contract? How much of this came into the hands of the Sierra Leone Government, and what increased percentage of revenue did it represent for the Government? How is it that Mr Beatty could not obtain similarly advantageous terms from a new contract with Diamond Corporation? Is the eight per cent better price from Winston accurately reflected in the estimate of some £500,000 additional revenue for the Government that would accrue from a contract with Winston?

But is not all this just a facade aimed at maintaining the fiction that Selection Trust and Diamond Corporation are unrelated entities, a fiction retailed even by a press one would assume knows better? For we have the Freetown correspondent of *West Africa* declaring in that journal's issue of 27 January 1962 that 'the two European giants in the (diamond) industry— Diamond Corporation and Selection Trust—were clearly at loggerheads'. The heart of the matter really lies in Mr Beatty's complaint that the Sierra Leone Government's regulation interferes with his company's freedom, expressly laid down by the former Colonial Government in their concession agreement, to sell as they think fit. Mr Beatty, like the monopolistic interests he represents so efficiently on many boards, does not wish to recognise the winds of change that have come with African independence, giving the new nations the opportunity to order their economies in the way they consider more beneficial for their own good.

Intrusion into the diamond field has been made lately by a Texan who has more usually appeared wherever oil was bubbling. Mr Sam Collins has put his hands to gathering diamonds from the sea bed of the Chameis Reef on the South-West African coast, reported to contain a minimum reserve of 14 million carats. Mr Collins scouted round for additional capital for his Sea Diamonds Company, holding the operating company, Marine Diamonds. It was reported that Mr Oppenheimer, after watching his activities with some concern, decided to collaborate with Mr Collins. It would appear that General Mining & Finance Corporation and Anglo Transvaal Consolidated, which we have already met as part of the Anglo American complex, had engaged themselves in the venture. They were to make available additional funds up to £500,000 to equalise with a like amount to be put up by Mr Collins and the companies controlled by him. General Mining has an exchange of shares with Anglo American, and De Beers Consolidated Mines is among its portfolio of investments, as is also National Finance Corporation of South Africa, which is so helpful to a number of Oppenheimer companies in the matter of loans.

De Beers apparently had an option on 25 per cent of Sea Diamonds' equity and a first refusal on Mr Collins's holding, said to be about 80 per cent. Sea Diamonds in turn holds some 44 per cent of the share capital of Marine Diamonds, General Mining holding 25 per cent of the balance, Anglo Transvaal 16 per cent, and another Oppenheimer company, Middle Witwatersrand (Western Areas) Ltd., administered by Anglo Transvaal, seven and a half per cent. The remainder is held by the original concession holders. Middle Witwatersrand has a right of 10 per cent participation in any prospecting ventures undertaken by Anglovaal Rhodesian Exploration Ltd., of whose equity 50 per cent is held by Kennecott Copper. Everything seems to move round in circular motion within a ring that has no end. Mr Sam Collins may have acted quickly and shrewdly in staking his claim to an offshore diamond reef, and he will in all probability make a killing. But the greatest winners will certainly prove, in the long run, to be Mr Oppenheimer and his cohorts. The backstage goings-on to obtain control of what promises to be a most highly profitable venture prompted *The Economist's* Johannesburg correspondent to observe that 'the full story of the recent negotiations, if it ever emerged, might tell of a fierce struggle for control between South Africa's

151

mining magnates in the best tradition of the rough, tough early days of Kimberley and the Rand' (16 March 1963).

It is unlikely that De Beers will be able to make its way into the Japanese company now setting up plant in Japan for the manufacture of synthetic diamonds, which will initially turn out 300,000 carats a year to reach 600,000 annually. De Beers, in association with Société Minière de Beceka, have their own plant in South Africa for the manufacture of synthetic diamond grit operated by Ultra High Pressure Units. General Electric of America also has a process for turning out manufactured diamonds. The Japanese say theirs is not the same. And we have referred earlier on to Sibeka's interest in the possibility of producing artificial diamonds. There have been several attempts to create diamonds by a factory process but they have, until now, proved somewhat uneconomic. With the strong likelihood that synthetic stones which can compete in price and performance with the natural product will soon be produced, another blow may be struck at the developing producer countries of Africa.

11. Mining interests in Central Africa

IF we examine the intricacies of the Anglo-American extension through the exploitation of Africa's raw materials, we find its strong arm holding down the wealth of Rhodesia, South Africa and South-west Africa both through direct holdings as well as through those of its American Engelhard and Kennecott Copper associates and the British South Africa Company Ltd.

The British South Africa Company was a creation of Cecil Rhodes' genius in empire building. Watching the scramble for lands in South Africa in the early 1890s, he decided that unless he got in quickly, other European adventurers would take up 'large tracts of valuable country ruled by savage native chiefs in the interior of Africa'. Using his notorious agents, Rudd, Maguire, Rochford and Thompson, war was provoked between the Matabeles of what is now known as Rhodesia and their chief, Lo Benguela. Troops of the South African Company, which was granted a royal charter in 1889, went ostensibly to the support of the chief against his people. This trick of Rhodes, described by certain historians as 'adroit handling', secured the company a concession to work mineral rights in the vast expanse of land that now forms the whole of Rhodesia.

When Lo Benguela woke up to the bitter realisation of the trickery that had divested him and his people of the rights in their own land, he petitioned Queen Victoria as follows:

'Some time ago a party of men came into my country, the principal one appearing to be a man named Rudd. They asked me for a place to dig gold, and said they would give me certain things for the right to do so. I told them to bring what they would give and I would then show them what I would give.

A document was written and presented to me for signature. I asked what it contained, and was told that in it were my words and the words of these men. I put my hand to it.

About three months afterwards I heard from other sources that I had given by that document the right of all the minerals of my country. I called a meeting of my Indunas and also of the white men, and demanded a copy of the document. It was proved to me that I had signed away the mineral rights of my whole country to one Rudd and his friends. I have since had a meeting of my Indunas and they will not recognise the paper, as it contains neither my words nor the words of those who got it.

After the meeting I demanded that the original document be returned to me. It has not come yet, although it is two months since, and they promised to bring it back soon. The men of the party who were in my country at the time were told to remain until the document was brought back. One of them, Maguire, has now left without my knowledge and against my orders.

I write to you that you may know the truth about this, and may not be deceived.

With renewed and cordial greetings,

Lo Benguela.'

Who in those days gave back land filched by whatever means from 'savage native chiefs'? And who today will give them back to the people from whom they were taken unless that people insist on their return by their determined and united will expressed by a Union Government?

At the close of the nineteenth century, Rhodes, dreaming of a Cape to Cairo empire, pushed from Matabeleland into Mashonaland across the Zambesi, into the country now called

Zambia. Thus he drove a wedge between the Portuguese colonies of Mozambique and Angola. All this was done with the buccaneers of his South Africa Company, which had received three supplementary charters since the initial one was granted in 1889.

Originally the company had administrative rights over territory in Southern Africa lying to the north of Bechuanaland, to the north and west of the Transvaal and west of Portuguese East Africa. It also had rights to extend the Cape railway and telegraph systems northward and to make concessions of mining, forest or other rights, and much more besides. Its administrative and monopoly rights in Northern and Southern Rhodesia were ceded to the British Government only as late as 1923–4. Mineral rights in the Rhodesias, however, were still retained, as well as a half interest for forty years in the next proceeds of the disposal of land in North-western Rhodesia. In return, the British South Africa Company received a cash payment from the British Government of £3,750,000. The commutation of its half interest in the proceeds of land disposal was made in 1956 for an annual payment of £50,000 for the remaining eight years to run from 31 March 1957.

A cash purchase of the mineral rights was made by the Southern Rhodesia Government in 1933 for £2 million, this time from African taxpayers' money. This still left the company with its mineral rights in Northern Rhodesia which, by arrangement, it is to enjoy until 1 October 1986. However, since 1 October 1949, it was paying to the Government of Northern Rhodesia 20 per cent of the net revenue from these mineral rights, which sum was regarded as an 'expense' for the purpose of Northern Rhodesian income tax. Furthermore, 'net revenue' was defined as the profits of the company derived from its mineral rights calculated in the same manner as for the purpose of Northern Rhodesian income tax, i.e. after expenses had been charged against it. The arrangement provided for the non-imposition of mineral royalties as such in Northern Rhodesia, while Her Majesty's Government undertook to secure so far as possible that any government which became responsible during the thirty-seven-year period, that is, up to 1 October 1986, for the administration of Northern Rhodesia should be bound by these arrangements.

The British South Africa Company, in spite of recent action taken by the government of Zambia to secure mineral rights, is still extremely powerful. It owns forests, agricultural estates and real property in Zambia, Rhodesia, and in Bechuanaland. It also has mineral rights in 16,000 square miles of Malawi territory. It formed Cecil Holdings Ltd. to acquire the whole share capital of British South Africa Company's subsidiaries, with the exception of Rhodesia Railways Trust Ltd. Another formation, British South Africa Investments Ltd., acquired the greater part of the parent company's investments in 1958. Other subsidiaries include:

> British South African Company Management Services Ltd.
> British South Africa Citrus Products Ltd.
> Charter Properties (Pvt) Ltd.
> Indaba Investments (Pvt) Ltd.
> Beit Holdings (Pvt) Ltd.
> Jameson Development Holdings (Pvt) Ltd.
> British South Africa Company Holdings Ltd. (U.K.).

The British South Africa Company was divested of the greater part of its holdings in companies operating primarily in the Republic of South Africa by its participation in the 1961 exchange of shares with De Beers Investment Trust Ltd. It still retains its holding of 700,000 shares in Union Corporation Ltd.

The company's close association with Mr Harry Oppenheimer and the Anglo American Corporation in the Rhodesias is to be drawn tighter by means of a proposed share deal between them by which 1·2 million ordinary ten shilling shares of Anglo American will be exchanged for £2·5 million in £1 shares of New Rhodesia Investments Ltd., a public company registered in Rhodesia and equally owned by Mr Oppenheimer's Brenthurst Investment Trust (Pty) Ltd. and British South Africa's tributary, Cecil Holdings.

New Rhodesia Investments include: mining finance, 45·94 per cent; gold, 14·45 per cent; diamonds, 9·38 per cent; coal,

156

2·49 per cent; sundry companies, 1·9 per cent. On 31 December 1962, the market value of these holdings was put at £10,500,000 while New Rhodesia Investment's net assets stood at £12,100,000. As for Anglo American Corporation, its net assets at the end of 1961 were £114,500,000. New Rhodesia's 'important block of shares' in Consolidated Mines Selection Trust Ltd. will be increased as a result of the current financial arrangement with Anglo American, whose own share capital will be augmented from £9 million to £10 million by the creation of another two million ten shilling shares.

The complicated links between superficially separate entities are shown by their investments in concerns of common interest. New Rhodesia's major buyings into the Diamond Corporation, Johannesburg Consolidated Investment Co. Ltd. and Rhodesian Anglo American Ltd. tie up closely with Anglo American's activities in the Rhodesias and in the Congo and Portuguese territories.

Johannesburg Consolidated is concerned principally with diamonds, copper, gold and platinum. It also carries on prospecting operations, mainly in South Africa and Rhodesia. Its subsidiary companies include, among others, Barnato Brothers Ltd. and Barnato Holdings Ltd., and the important African Asbestos-Cement Corporation Ltd. An associated company, Matte Smelters (Pty) Ltd., is jointly owned by Rustenburg Platinum Mines Ltd. and Johnson Matthey & Co. Ltd. Johnson Matthey, a U.K. firm treating copper, nickel, platinum and other metals, supervised the erection of plant in the vicinity of Rustenberg to treat part of the product of Matte Smelters. Johannesburg Consolidated's last issue of shares was in 1958, when 600,000 were issued to New Rhodesia Investments.

Rhodesian Anglo American has large shareholdings in the leading copper mines of Rhodesia. These direct holdings are swollen by those of companies in which it has interest. Thus a 52·39 per cent interest in the ordinary 'A' stock of Rhokana Corporation Ltd. gives it an added interest of 17·63 per cent in Nchanga Consolidated Copper Mines Ltd., in which its direct participation is 21·429 per cent. Through its penetration of Rhokana and Nchanga, Rhodesian Anglo American has an indirect interest in Rhodesia Copper Refineries Ltd. Again, its oblique participation in Mufulira Copper Mines Ltd. via Rhokana, increases its own participation of 572,213 shares to 13·92 per cent. In Rhodesian Alloys (Pvt) Ltd. a producer of ferro-chrome, it has 263,226 shares, and in Rhodesia Broken Hill Development Co. Ltd., 1,425,905 stock units. An almost 25 per cent holding of Kansanshi Copper Mining Co. Ltd. has been secured by the acquisition of 394,209 shares. Rhodesian Anglo American's direct and indirect participation in Bancroft Mines Ltd. amounts to 24·54 per cent. Rhokana gives it an interest in Chibuluma Mines Ltd., while Rhokana in association with Nchanga leads it into Kalindini Exploration Ltd. A holding of 34,100 shares gives it a substantial purchase into Kasempa Minerals Ltd., a company carrying out prospecting operations in the western province of Zambia.

Nor are other prospecting companies ignored by Rhodesian Anglo American. Thirty-one and a half per cent of Anglo American Prospecting (Rhodesia) Ltd. has come under its control, and 333,375 shares of Chartered Exploration Ltd. Iron, steel and coal also come within its range. It owns 596,600 shares in Lubimbi Coal Areas Ltd., holding prospecting rights for coal over an area of approximately 130 square miles in the Southern Rhodesian mining district of Bulawayo. This shareholding gives Rhodesian Anglo American 65 per cent control of Lubimbi, the other 35 per cent belonging to Wankie Colliery, two million of whose shares are in Rhodesian Anglo American hands. Forty per cent gives it a major part of the Iron Duke Mining Co. Ltd., and it also has a substantial interest in the Rhodesian Iron & Steel Co. Ltd.

Sundry other interests make Rhodesian Anglo American a leading controller of Zambia's economic life. Finance and investment are included by, among others, 20 per cent of Rhodesian Acceptances Ltd., and a half share in Overseas & Rhodesian Investment Co. Ltd. Rhoanglo Mine Services Ltd., wholly owned, provides a valuable source of income for administrative and other services. Cement and clay bring it into the building and allied trades through 148,961 shares in

Premier Portland Cement Co. (Rhodesia) Ltd. and 25 per cent of Clay Products (Pvt) Ltd.

Bancroft Mines seems to provide the richest pickings for the cast-iron digestion of the Anglo American hydra. This company was formed only in 1953, to take up from 'the owners of the mineral rights, the British South Africa Co.' special grants of mining rights and prospecting rights acquired from Rhokana. Capital is authorised at £13,750,000. The British South Africa Co. took up three million shares, Rhokana 9,500,000 and Rhodesian Anglo American 74,700. There was an interchange of shares with Rhokana as well as with Rhodesian Anglo American. In 1955 an additional two million shares were subscribed for by Anglo American and British South Africa Co., who have provided loans of £2 million and £3 million respectively.

Anglo American, Rhodesian Anglo American, Nchanga and Rhokana were given an option on three million of Bancroft's ordinary shares up to 31 March 1963. In December 1961, the right was exercised on a million of the shares, of which Rhodesian Anglo American acquired 400,000.

Rhodesian Anglo American's own capital is £7 million and its consolidated net profit for the year ended 30 June 1961 was £20,590,783 after providing £11,541,475 for taxation. Dividends absorbed £5,403,535.

These tightly braided interests are of special concern to the people of Zambia and Rhodesia, whose existence and fate they dominate. Not for nothing is Mr Harry Oppenheimer enlarging his own personal stake through the proposals concerning the share exchange between Anglo American and British South Africa Co. in New Rhodesia Investments, a tributary of British South Africa's tributary, Cecil Holding. By the arrangements, British South Africa will have wider share in Anglo American's activities through the establishment of a local Rhodesian Board for the chartered company, under the chairmanship of Sir Frederick Crawford.

Sir Frederick Crawford is at present the company's resident director in Rhodesia. As a former Governor of Uganda, he brought with him his proconsular experience in the ruling of

159

'natives'. Uganda also provides as local director in Zambia, C. P. S. Allen, until recently Permanent Under-Secretary of State to its Prime Minister. Thus are imperialist agents rewarded for their services to their real masters. Opposition to the establishment of the local board was met by British South Africa Co.'s president, P. V. Emrys-Evans, with the explanation that it will provide a greater degree of autonomy for local management, and will strengthen the company's representation in Zambia. Mr Emrys-Evans is himself a director of Anglo American Corporation, as well as of Rio Tinto Zinc Corporation Ltd. Mr Emrys-Evans carries the interests of Barclays Bank D.C.O. by his directorship of the bank, and his solicitude for Rhodesia's development is implicit in his seat on the board of Rhodesia Railways Trust Ltd., a British South Africa Company subsidiary. His further connection with Oppenheimer's far-flung empire is confirmed by his membership of the London Committee of Rand Selection Corporation Ltd. The death of Lord Robins elevated him from the vice-presidency to the head of the British South Africa Co.'s board, where among his colleagues were the late Sir C. J. Hambro, Harry Oppenheimer, L. F. A. d'Erlanger and another former pro-consul, Viscount Malvern, who brings with him the blessings of the Merchant Bank of Central Africa, Scottish Rhodesian Finance Ltd., and the Standard Bank of South Africa.

A good deal of Mr Emrys-Evans' 1962 annual report to the shareholders was devoted to what is described as ill-informed criticism of the 'group's alleged policy of removing large sums of money from the country while being unwilling to invest in its development'. The attempt to rebut this criticism by the affirmation that over ten years the company had invested over £10 million in the territory, an average of over £1 million a year, would not convince Rhodesian Africans, who were well aware that the company received in gross income from its Northern Rhodesian copper royalties alone in the year 1961/2, the sum of £10,900,000. Taxation goes to the United Kingdom and South Africa, as also do dividends, which, for the year 1959–60, absorbed £4,128,863 out of a consolidated net profit of £8,148,245, arrived at after writing off almost £1 million for depreciation of investments and over £5,400,000 for taxation.

Rhodes' original links with the Rand and Kimberley mines have been knit more closely together by a thousand strands with Rhodesia and Zambia than it was possible for him to envisage at the time, though it was his overriding hope and ambition. This interwoven fabric partly provides the hangman's rope that is trying to strangle African independence and the political unification of Africa.

12. Companies and combines

To give anything like a complete account of the complicated network of foreign companies which at present governs so much of Africa's economic life, would be impossible within the space of a single book. Yet some reference to the most important of them is necessary, and in many cases their connecting interests can be shown in diagram form. Behind the facade of separateness strong connecting links bind these powerful firms together.

In East Africa, one of the most powerful concerns is Tanganyika Concessions. The name is misleading. It was actually registered in London towards the end of January 1899. Today control of the company is wielded from Salisbury, Rhodesia, whence it was removed in the latter part of 1950. Operations in Tanganyika have not yet been fully developed, though they cover two important gold mines and a mineral company, and include some prospecting. The company's writ has greater significance in Zambia, where it acquired from British South Africa Co. a concession over a large area, together with certain prospecting rights. From Zambia its activities spawn into the Congo, where it controls a mineral concession of 60,000 square miles secured from the Katanga (Belgian) Special Committee. For giving Tanganyika Concession rights over this expanse of Congolese land, the Katanga Committee enjoyed the benefit of a 60 per cent share in the royalty paid by Union Minière.

We must not for one moment, however, allow ourselves to be led into the error of thinking that Tanganyika Concessions thus permitted themselves to be 'bested' by the Special Committee. The company became a member of the Committee. In the way of financiers who, cautiously and shrewdly, do not place all their eggs in a single basket, a new organisation was created to take care of a concession covering a surface about three-fifths the size of Ghana. This is the celebrated Union Minière du Haut Katanga, whose reputation over the years has become notorious for the merciless exploitation of the Congo.

Another strategic interest of Tanganyika Concessions is the railway running from Lobito Bay in Angola up to the Angola-Congo border, operated by the Benguela Railway Company (Companhia do Cominho de Ferro de Benguela). The railway company is a creation of Tanganyika Concessions which holds £2,700,000 or 90 per cent of its £2 shares, as well as the whole of the debenture capital. The Benguela Railway, during 1961, built a branch line from the town of Robert Williams into the mining region of Guima, which was opened in August 1962. Commonwealth Timber Industries Ltd., a vast forestry and lumber concern, is also 60 per cent owned by Tanganyika Concessions.

Novobord (U.K.) Ltd., the English affiliate of Commonwealth Timber, was able, with the assistance of the African companies with which Société Générale is associated, to construct a sawmill and factory for the manufacture of fibrewood panels at Thetford in Norfolk. The factory's capacity will make possible the production of about 25 million square feet of panels yearly, the capital invested being around £2 million.

When Tanganyika Concessions was about to change its headquarters from London to Salisbury, it gave an undertaking to H.M. Treasury which no doubt had some bearing on the British government's vacillating policy in the breakdown of the Central African Federation. It must also colour its behaviour in regard to the Congo and to Portuguese rule in Africa. The undertaking provided that for a minimum period of ten years, Tanganyika Concessions would not, without consent of the British Treasury, 'dispose of or charge or pledge its interests or any part thereof in Union Minière du Haut Katanga or the Benguela Railway' except, in the case of the latter, to the Portuguese Government under the terms of the Concessions Agreement.

The limitation did not end with the expiration of the ten-year period, as a conjunctive clause provided that subsequently 'no sale or other disposal of such interests or any part thereof (except as aforesaid) shall be made without the securities proposed to be sold or otherwise disposed of first being offered to H.M. Treasury at the same price and on the same terms as have been offered to a third party'.

These provisions have given the British Government a direct concern in the operations of Tanganyika Concessions, Union Minière and the Benguela Railway which is bound to influence their behaviour in relation to the independence struggle in Southern and Central Africa. More particularly, in view of the special relations which Great Britain has had with its oldest ally, Portugal. From the point of view of the companies themselves, they must feel encouraged by this special interest of the British Government in maintaining their strategic position across the great central belt of Africa.

Tanganyika Concessions, both directly and through Tanganyika Holdings, has an important participation in Rhodesia-Katanga Co. Ltd., with which, in conjunction with Zambesia Exploring, interests were acquired in the Kakamega Goldfield, Kenya, which were transferred to Kentan Gold Areas, in which Rhodesia-Katanga has a substantial holding. Rhodesia-Katanga is indebted to the British South Africa Co. by reason of the perpetual mining rights the latter has granted it over any minerals, including coal but excluding diamonds and precious stones, which may be found in about 2,500 square miles of Zambia. Additionally, it has perpetual coal mining rights in twenty areas of 300 acres, each subject to 15 per cent interest of the British South Africa Co.

To complete Tanganyika Concessions' roster of subsidiaries, there is the wholly owned Tanganyika Properties (Rhodesia)

Tanganyika Concessions' Interests

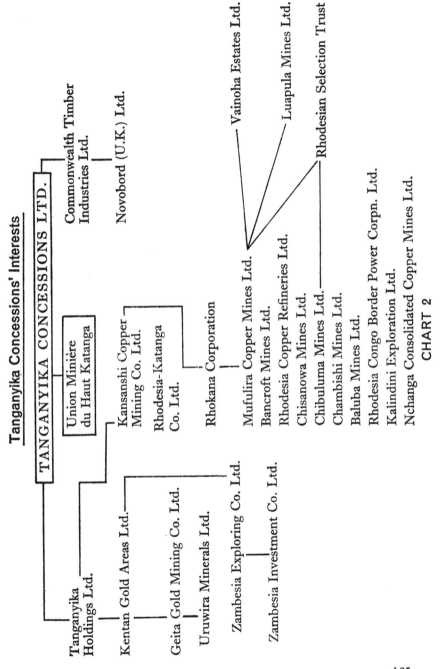

CHART 2

Ltd., registered in Salisbury, Rhodesia. It provides office and staff accommodation together with allied services, as well as holding certain investments.

Consolidated profit made by Tanganyika Concessions for the year ended 31 July 1961 was £3,296,325 out of a total revenue of £4,462,667. Its current assets are £4,380,163 in shares and debentures of Benguela Railway Co.: £5,300,318 in shares and loan to Commonwealth Timber Industries; £1,317,793 in Tanganyika Holdings; and £4,019,629 in Union Minière, whose ramifications will be examined in a later chapter.

Coming to the South-West Africa Co. Ltd. we find Anglo American Corporation and Consolidated Gold Fields merging to exploit a vast section of the wealth of southern Africa.

The South-West Africa Co. Ltd. was registered in London on 18 August 1892, and has a special grant of exclusive prospecting and mining rights over some 3,000 square miles of the Damaraland concession area of South-west Africa. This grant was made by the Administration of South-west Africa for a period of five years from 2 January 1942, and has since been renewed until 2 January 1967. The company also holds mining areas in various other districts of South-west Africa. It produces tin-wolfram and zinc-lead concentrates as well as vanadates.

Large areas of land such as those held by the South-West Africa Co. demand extremely heavy capital investment to exploit and encourage the formation of alliances between groups desirous of controlling output, distribution, and hence the prices of raw materials. Not only that, it facilitates the channelling of their processing through the allied organisations. To pursue this policy of co-ordination, the South-West Africa Co. signed an agreement with a joint Anglo American-Consolidated Gold Fields venture by which it sub-leased certain of its rights to explore and exploit its concessions. See Chart 3.

The Newmont Mining Corporation was formed in Delaware, U.S.A., on 2 May 1921. The purpose of the company is to acquire, develop, finance and operate mining properties. For this purpose a share capital of $60 million has been

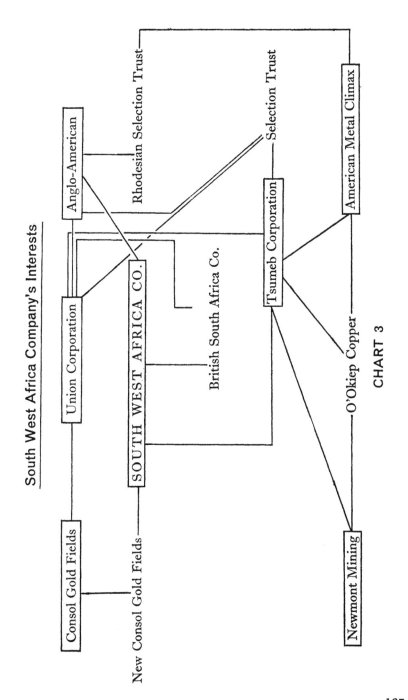

South West Africa Company's Interests

CHART 3

authorised. At 31 December 1961, 2,824,518 of the authorised six million ten-dollar shares had been issued, and paid up. Mining exploration is carried on by the company through Newmont Exploration Ltd.(Delaware), Newmont Mining Corporation of Canada Ltd. and Newmont of South Africa (Pty) Ltd. Chart 4 gives some idea of the extent of their interests.

We have already met certain of the Rio Tinto companies in Zambia and Rhodesia, and have touched upon others in connection with the Société Générale de Belgique's associations with the North American financial and industrial scene. The Rio Tinto complex is one that would be hard to miss in any attempt to examine the ramifications of the international mining world. It stretches from the United Kingdom across Spain into Africa and over the Atlantic into Canada and the U.S.A., with forays into Germany, Belgium, Austria, Australia and elsewhere. The hands of Anglo American Corporation, Consolidated Zinc Corporation and world-embracing aluminium groups are firmly clasped within it, and representatives of the Congo combination of companies adorn the directorates which bear such aristocratic names as Rothschild and Cavendish-Bentinck.

Though its original interests were mining pyrites in Spain, the Rio Tinto Co. Ltd. was registered in London in 1873. Keeping up with the times and the general trend towards combination and monopoly, the company underwent certain changes. Its directors were among the most fervent supporters of General Franco at the time of the Spanish Civil War. This devotion to the Caudillo's cause undoubtedly prospered them so that, together with their associates in the wider financial sphere, they have been able to spread their tentacles through the zinc and aluminium industry into the precious metals and general metals' fields.

In 1954 Rio Tinto transferred its Spanish assets to a company which it formed in Spain with a capital of 1,000,000,000 pesetas, under the title of Companhia Espanola de Minas de Rio Tinto S.A. For this worthy proof of its sensitiveness to Spanish patriotism, it received a compensation of 36,666,830 pesetas in settlement of profits accumulated up to 1 January

Newmont Mining's Interests

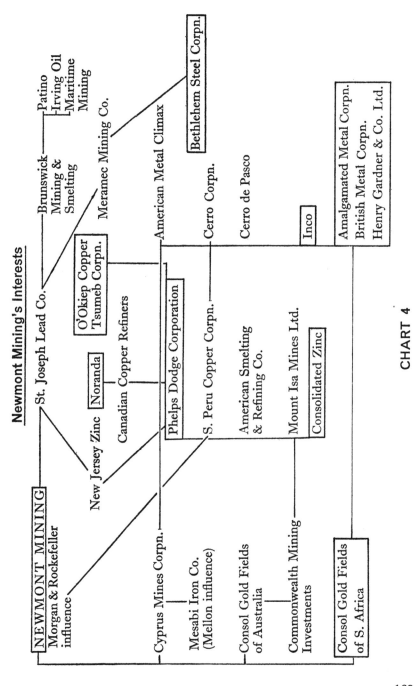

CHART 4

169

1954, and all the 333,333 'B' shares of 1,000 pesetas each in the new company. Additionally it was awarded a sterling payment of £7,666,665. Rio Tinto still draws a retainer as provider of technical and commercial services in London for the Spanish company, in which its holding of all the 'B' shares still gives it a direct interest.

Rio Tinto is now an investment holding company, whose financial operations have brought it into the forefront of industrial entrepreneurship. Africa is well up among its spheres of activity, its most important holdings on the continent being in Rhokana Corporation and Nchanga Copper Mines, where, as we have seen, it is associated with the British South Africa Co., Anglo American Corporation, Union Corporation, Tanganyika Concessions, Union Minière and Rand Selection Trust in their holdings in the important Rhodesian and South Africa mining and industrial ventures.

So tortuous and incredibly expansile are the links that tie the groups exploiting Africa's resources with those enriching themselves in other corners of the earth that we should find nothing remarkable in being led back from Rio Tinto in Africa, via some of the most powerful American and British financial forces, into Rio Tinto in Canada.

One of the most lively motivating springs of monopoly is to forestall in new or unexplored areas the entry of rival groups, and where this proves abortive or impossible, to collaborate with them. We shall see in a later chapter how Canadian Eldorado forced Union Minière to bring down the price of uranium and how their interests lock through Sogemines representation on the former's board. In the world of Western free enterprise, competition is being eroded by monopoly's role of the lone ranger after undivided profits.

Thus are African riches brought to support the manipulative ramifications of international finance-capital. Between Société Générale and Rio Tinto there is interposed a solid phalanx of interwoven power that moves out stealthily across the world.

Breaking into the aluminium world, Rio Tinto formed an alliance with Consolidated Zinc Corporation Ltd. This merger appeared superficially to bring together two powerful

RIO TINTO CO. LTD.

African Interests	U.K. Interest	Australian Interests	Canadian Interests
Rhokana Corporation	Thorium Ltd.	Rio Tinto Holdings (Australia) Pty. Ltd.	Rio Tinto Holdings Ltd.
Nchanga Copper Mines			Preston Mines Ltd.
Rio Tinto Rhodesian Holding Co. Ltd.			
Rio Tinto (Northern Rhodesia) Ltd.			
Rio Tinto (Rhodesia) Ltd.			
Rio Tinto Mining Co. of South Africa			
Palabora Mining Co. Ltd.			

controlling interest in Rio Algom

Algom Uranium
Milliken Lake
Northspan Uranium
Pronto Uranium

acquires Rio Tinto's shares in—

Anglo-Rouyn Mines Ltd.
Oceanic Iron Ore of Canada Ltd.
Rix Athabasca Uranium Mines Ltd.
Tinto Iron Mines Ltd.
Brunswick Mining and Smelting Corpn. Ltd.
Rio Tinto Dow Ltd.
Rio Tinto Canadian Exploration Ltd.
Palabora Holdings Ltd.
Rio Tinto (N. Rhodesia)—720,000
Rio Tinto (Rhodesia)—1,446,760

CHART 5

groups having no joint leading strings. This ostensible separation would mislead only the ignorant. Its subterfuge is immediately destroyed by a single glance at its combined directorate, which at once shows up the connections with South African mining and financial interests. P. V. Emrys-Evans is a prominent member, and the Rt. Hon. Lord Baillieu, K.B.E., C.M.G., deputy chairman. Lord Baillieu is also deputy chairman of the Central Mining and Investment Corporation Ltd., a leading investment and finance house within the Anglo American group of companies directed by Harry F. Oppenheimer and C. W. Engelhard. Mr Emrys-Evans is also important in his own right, being vice-president of the British South Africa Co. and a director of Anglo American.

However, the connection goes further than that. British South Africa Holdings Ltd., and some of its associates, under an agreement dated 7 December 1960, subscribed £10 million to Consolidated Zinc in the form of 5½ per cent loan stock in return for options to acquire 2,285,714 ordinary shares of £1 each in Consolidated Zinc at a price of 87s. 6d. a share. Here we enter into the intricate maze of aluminium financial policies into which Consolidated Zinc has made deep incursions by its alliance with the Kaiser Aluminium & Chemical Corporation in Commonwealth Aluminium Corporation (Pty) Ltd., commonly known as Comalco. The options acquired by British South Africa Holdings can be exercised any time between 1 June 1966 and 1 July 1968 or the date on which Commonwealth or its associated operating companies have produced a total of 200,000 long tons of aluminium ingots in the proposed new refinery to be erected by Comalco, whichever is the later.

Kaiser Aluminium's principal interest is in its wholly owned Kaiser Bauxite Co., Jamaica. In addition to its mining activities, Kaiser operates processing and chemical plants in the United States and Canada and has investments in aluminium, mining, reduction and fabricating facilities and marketing industries in the United Kingdom, South America, Africa and Asia. It operates through two fully owned subsidiaries: Kaiser Aluminium & Chemical Sales Inc. and Kaiser Aluminium

International Corporation. Like Reynolds Metals, Kaiser Aluminium only broke into the United States aluminium industry under the impetus of wartime demands for aircraft metal. Before the second world war, Aluminium Co. of America—ALCOA—was the sole domestic producer of primary aluminium.

Consolidated Zinc, with an authorised capital of £25 million, has extensive interests which make it a formidable controller of a number of important metals and allied chemical products. Formed less than fifteen years ago, in February 1949, its purposes were 'to develop, extend and carry on or finance, either itself or through any of its subsidiary or associated companies, the development, extension and carrying on of the lead and zinc mining and other or raw material producing industries and the smelting, refining and manufacturing and other industries associated therewith, throughout the world, and particularly in the Commonwealth'.

All this apparently has no connection with Africa, but we have only to look at some of the directorates to discover immediately how close the links are with the Oppenheimer network and the financial groups that associate with it.

Such are the mammoth gold-clad interests that are behind the Consolidated Zinc-Rio Tinto merger. The new holding company, Rio Tinto-Zinc Corporation Ltd., was created by a financial operation that gave shareholders of Consolidated Zinc fifty-eight ordinary shares of ten shillings each in the new company in exchange for every twenty shares of £1 in Consolidated Zinc. Rio Tinto stockholders received forty-one shares of ten shillings each in the new company for every twenty ordinary stock units of ten shillings held in Rio Tinto. Preference shares in both companies were also exchanged for preference shares in the new one.

The merger brings Rio Tinto-Zinc well into the forefront of the aluminium field, accentuating its already important position in the zinc-lead and non-ferrous metals field. It brings Consolidated Zinc more fully into the sphere of mineral exploitation in Africa by reason of Rio Tinto's holdings in some of the principal concerns operating in South Africa,

13

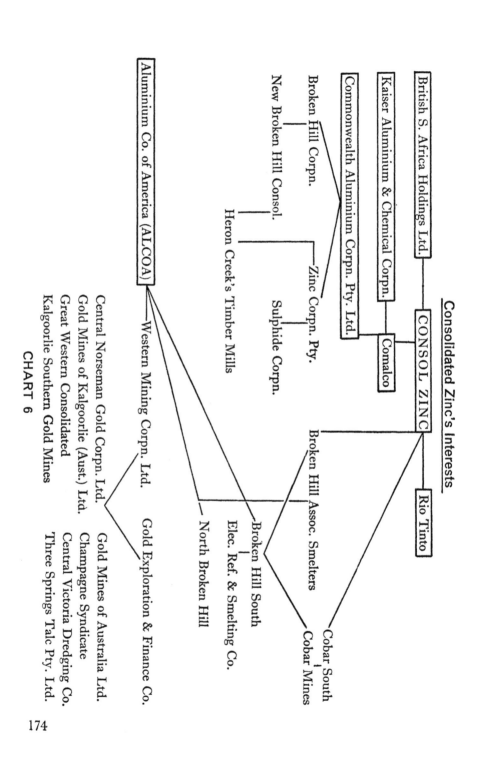

Consolidated Zinc's Interests

British S. Africa Holdings Ltd.

Kaiser Aluminium & Chemical Corpn.

Commonwealth Aluminium Corpn. Pty. Ltd.

Broken Hill Corpn.

New Broken Hill Consol.

Aluminium Co. of America (ALCOA)

Heron Creek's Timber Mills

Zinc Corpn. Pty.

Sulphide Corpn.

CONSOL ZINC

Conalco

Rio Tinto

Western Mining Corpn. Ltd.

Broken Hill Assoc. Smelters

Broken Hill South

Elec. Ref. & Smelting Co.

North Broken Hill

Cobar South

Cobar Mines

Central Norseman Gold Corpn. Ltd.
Gold Mines of Kalgoorlie (Aust.) Ltd.
Great Western Consolidated
Kalgoorlie Southern Gold Mines

Gold Exploration & Finance Co.

Gold Mines of Australia Ltd.
Champagne Syndicate
Central Victoria Dredging Co.
Three Springs Talc Pty. Ltd.

CHART 6

174

Rhodesia and elsewhere. The connections with the American, Canadian and Australian industrial and financial scenes are apparent from the foregoing very brief review. Through these interests, the Rio Tinto-Zinc combine has additional strings which lead back again to Africa.

There are some rare and localised non-metallic materials which are used in basic and secondary industries. These include asbestos, corundum, mica, vermiculite, phosphate rock, gypsum, mineral pigments, fluorspar, and silica. The most important is asbestos. It is found in three principal fibres: chrysolite, crocidolite or blue asbestos, and amosite. All three fibres have certain common characteristics. They are all non-inflammable, non-conductors of heat and electricity; they are practically insoluble in acids and are capable of being spun into textiles.

It is slight differences in these qualities that give them different uses. Chrysolite is the most resistant to fire, and its strong, fine flexible texture makes it highly suitable for asbestos textiles and for use in brake linings, clutch facings and insulation fittings. It is used also for asbestos boards and asbestos cement products. Blue asbestos has greater tensile strength and resilience, and though not so resistant to fire, withstands acids and sea-water better. It is used chiefly in the manufacture of filter cloth, boiler mattresses, insulation packings and asbestos cement products. Amosite has a fibre length of three to six inches and has greater resistance to heat than crocidolite and greater resistance to sea-water than blue asbestos. These qualities make it particularly suitable for use in spun materials and aircraft. South Africa is at present almost the only place in which both blue asbestos and amosite are found. Canada is the greatest producer of chrysolite; South Africa and Rhodesia are far behind.

The South African deposits are mainly in Swaziland and Eastern Transvaal. They are in the virtual control of a British firm, Turner & Newall Ltd., registered in 1920, which has in its hands 90 per cent of the British asbestos trade. This fact enabled it to secure an agreement in 1930 with the Soviet Union regulating deliveries to the continental market. An important producer of high grade chrysolite, the Soviet Union ceased export after the last war.

Superficially unimposing, Turner & Newall's board has as its chairman Ronald G. Scothill, who is associated with the insurance world as director of Liverpool and Globe Insurance Co. Ltd. and Royal Insurance Co. Ltd., and with finance as director of the District Bank. Its capital, however, is impressive, being authorised at £60 million with almost £50 million paid up. Originally £3 million, the increase in the size of the company's capital gives an indication of the growth of its dominance of asbestos mining and allied industries.

This capitalisation becomes more articulate when it is related to the sweep of the Turner & Newall asbestos kingdom, which is rooted in African and Canadian mines. A holding company, it has a network of subsidiaries throughout the world which manufacture and sell asbestos, magnesia and connected products. See Chart 7.

A recent survey reveals that some 60 to 70 per cent of the world's total business activity is controlled by less than two per cent of all the companies in the world. The colossal Unilever Trust is a perfect illustration of this monopolistic ratio of control.

For millions of housewives there is no such thing as a corporate entity called Unilever. There is just the daily routine of choosing between Lifebuoy and Lux, Pepsodent and Gibbs, Omo and Surf—of buying Lipton's tea, Wall's sausages and Bird's Eye frozen foods, Flytox, Stork margarine and Harriet Hubbard Ayer's cosmetics. From the viewpoint of the tax-collector also, Unilever is still not a corporate entity but two separate companies, 'Unilever Limited', the British company, and 'Unilever N.V.', the Dutch company. It has subsidiaries throughout Europe, in Belgium, Austria, Denmark, Germany, Finland, Italy, Sweden and Switzerland. In all these countries it tends to control the production of soups, frozen foods, soap, margarine, insecticides, detergents, cosmetics and edible oils. It has also powerful and century-old interests in Latin America, west, central and South Africa, India, Ceylon, Malaysia, Trinidad, Thailand and the Philippines.

Some of Turner & Newall's Interests and Connections

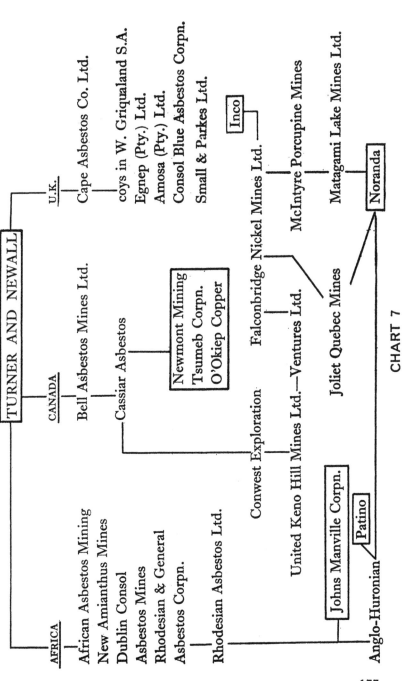

CHART 7

Unilever's most robust offshoot overseas is the United Africa Company, through which the Trust became known as the 'uncrowned King of West Africa'. The United Africa Company is the world's largest international trading company, and contrary to the belief that the liberation of colonial territories would automatically suppress monopoly capitalism, the Unilever empire continues to flourish. This is because it has known how to adapt its policy to the 'challenge of the times', as a company report puts it. And so, Unilever is applying its profit-making objectives to other more yielding sectors. It has accelerated its withdrawal from the West African merchandise and produce trade to concentrate on development in cars, engineering and the pharmaceutical sides of the business. The neo-colonialist aim is not only to export capital but also to control the overseas market. Thus attempts are subtly made to prevent developing countries from taking any decisive steps towards industrialisation, since the exploitation of the indigenous expanding market is now the prime objective. If the attempts to prevent industrialisation fail, then at all costs the Trust must secure a participation in a development it cannot prevent. And by its very nature this participation thwarts any further progress since it ensures a regular flow of payments into the coffers of monopoly capital in the form of royalties, patents, licensing agreements, technical assistance, equipment and other 'services'. It also gives priority to the assembling and packaging of foreign products often presented under the false labels of indigenous concerns. Unilever's present emphasis on the packaging industries is no coincidence.

The up-to-date Trust relies less on the amount of the dividends than on certain clauses in the Company agreements which make indigenous capital dependent on monopoly capital for the renewal of contracts and for the allocation of funds. It is significant that in a recent issue of the *New Commonwealth*, the United Africa Company has been referred to as the 'gentle giant'. Monopoly methods have become more subtle, but Lever's famous statement still seems to hold true: 'After all we are working for the permanent interests of Britain'.

13. The tin, aluminium and nickel giants

THE tin empire of Patino of Canada Ltd. and its associates spreads from South America to the United Kingdom and North America and across Africa into the Pacific and Asia. Capitalised at $10 million, Patino of Canada has issued and paid up 1,971,839 shares of $2. Of these, 47·2 per cent are held by a Panamanian financing house within the Patino group, Compania de Bonos Acciones y Negocios Industriales— COBANISA. Patino's purchase into General Tin Investments Ltd. in 1962 brought this tycoon into a large share of the United Kingdom spread in the tin-mining and dealing world. General Tin Investments is charged with acquiring and holding shares in mining, finance and industrial companies, its principal holdings being in those companies connected with the tin industry. It carries out its financing operations through a wholly-owned subsidiary, General Metal Securities (London) Ltd. A. Patino presides over both boards where he has as colleagues Count G. du Boisbouvray, J. Ortiz-Linares and E. R. E. Carter. Carter is president of Brunswick Mining & Smelting Corporation and of several other companies associated with the Patino group. Brunswick comes within the Morgan sphere of influence through the interest maintained by St Joseph Lead Co. We also know that Sogemines has concerned itself with a substantial investment with the New Brunswick Mines of Brunswick Mining. The spokes that lead out from the Société Générale de Belgique's African hub into the affairs of the most powerful financial monopolies in the world seem ever-increasing.

Patino's direct investments in Canada cover substantial holdings in Copper Rand Chibougama Mines Ltd., Advocate Mines Ltd., Nipissing Mines Co. Ltd. and Brunswick Mining. By financial jugglery consolidation of the principal Canadian companies of the group was achieved in 1960. This was done through an agreement between Copper Rand, Nipissing Mines, Chibougama Jaculet Mines Ltd., Portage Island (Chibougama) Mines Ltd., Patino of Canada and Bankmont & Co. a financial house. Copper is the chief mineral mined, but gold and silver are also produced. The Copper Rand property covers some 10,000 acres held in four concessions. Portage Island is a copper-gold property of Copper Rand, and the Jaculet mine a copper property.

Nipissing enters into the picture as a financial contributor to the development of the Portage Island property. It is the holder of a number of mining claims in Quebec and holds diverse share interests. Its operations branch into the U.S.A. though a wholly-owned subsidiary, Apalachian Sulphides Inc., with mining rights to ore deposits in the States of Vermont and North Carolina. Nipissing bought into Brunswick Mining by acquiring from a Patino subsidiary, Patino Mines & Enterprises Consolidated (Inc.), 137,143 shares and $537,429 worth of 5 per cent bonds of Brunswick, giving to Patino 1,061,145 shares of Nipissing. Patino's holdings in the Chibougama group and association with Maritimes Mining Corporation and the Irving Oil Co. Ltd. in a 40 per cent purchase of Brunswick mining shares extend the Patino empire substantially into fields other than tin.

American and Belgian mining and financial interests as powerful as Patino's have linked together with Patino of Canada in investigating and developing mineral deposits on an exclusive basis across 750 square miles of land on the north-eastern coast of Newfoundland, under rights granted to Advocate. At the end of 1960 proven ore reserves totalled 35 million tons of commercial grade. Advocate is developing asbestos under a project undertaken by Patino of Canada in conjunction with Canadian

Johns-Manville Co. Ltd., Amet Corporation Inc. and Financière Belge de l'Asbestos-Ciment S.A. The participants have agreed to place the property on an operating basis by furnishing to Advocate a total sum of $17,900,000. Canadian Johns-Manville will contribute 49·62 per cent, Patino 17·3 per cent, Amet and Financière Belge 16·54 per cent each. Advocate has been capitalised at $23 million and the parties to the agreement share in the capital ratio to the amount of their contributions, based on denominations of $100.

Canadian Johns-Manville, which is tied up with the Imperial-Commerce Bank, the largest in Canada, upon which sits a director of Johns-Manville, is a fully-owned subsidiary of the Johns-Manville Corporation of the United States. Its main interests are in asbestos, which it processes into fibre and manufactures into building and industrial materials. It is in control of Advocate's management, and has also a majority interest in and management control of Coalinga Asbestos Co. of California, U.S.A., a joint venture with Kern County Land Co. The parent Johns-Manville, of America, manufactures products from asbestos, magnesia and perlite, having manufacturing plants in America, Canada and elsewhere.

Advocate has advanced certain monies to Maritime Mining, which has close relations with Patino by reason of its associations with the purchase of the St Joseph Lead holdings in Brunswick Mining. Maritimes' share of this purchase was 46 per cent at a cost of $4,840,000. Maritime works copper on claims in New Brunswick, Canada, and properties in Newfoundland owned directly and also indirectly via a fully-owned subsidiary, Gull Lake Mines Ltd., through which it also owns all the shares of Gullbridge Mines Ltd. It has an arrangement with Falconbridge Nickel Mines giving the latter the right to a maximum one-third participation in any future financing which Maritime might undertake. Maritime and Patino of Canada share a director in W. F. James who is also on the Falconbridge board.

Quebec Metallurgical is another holding company having wide interests inside and outside Canada. These include a platinum property in South Africa's Transvaal, a small gold

181

mine in Brazil, and nickel and cobalt interests in New Cale-
donia, where, through links with Patino, it is associated with
Le Nickel.

Unfortunately for Patino, certain assets in Bolivia have had
to be relinquished under a nationalisation programme. Bolivia
was for many more years than its people cared about drained
by foreign interests of its mineral resources, in which tin predominates, but which also include silver, lead, zinc, antimony
and copper. Its oil deposits were large enough to entice
Rockefeller's Standard Oil Co., who entrenched themselves by
working a large concession, while the Guggenheim Brothers of
America, as well as British, French and others, gathered in tin
and copper over a long period, paying the Indian workers
around sixpence a day for their labour.

The properties of the Delaware incorporated Patino Mines
& Enterprises Consolidated were nationalised by the Bolivian
Government on 31 October 1952 and vested in a State-owned
property, the Corporacion Minera de Bolivia Comibol. These
Patino properties consisted of mining and placer claims, water
rights, mill sites, reduction, concentrating and hydro-electric
plants, as well as a railway connecting the mines with a point on
the main line of the Antofagasta-Bolivian Railroad Co. Ltd.
Patino Mines formed another Delaware subsidiary in 1959,
Patino Enterprises Inc.

As one of the largest entrepreneurs in the tin industry,
A. Patino has a seat on the main consolidated organisations
looking after the interests of those engaged in this field, usually
in the company of the Count of Boisbouvray and J. Ortiz-
Linares. All three of them are to be found on the board of
British Tin Investment Corporation Ltd., a United Kingdom
company formed in 1932 to take over British-American Tin
Corporation Ltd. Together with its wholly-owned subsidiaries,
Tin Industrial Finance & Underwriting Ltd. and B.T.I.C.
(Overseas) Ltd., British Tin holds large blocks of shares in the
Malayan tin-mining industry, as well as investments in com-
panies producing other metals and minerals.

General Tin Investments has a 55 per cent interest in
Eastern Smelting Co. Ltd., owning smelting works at Penang,

Malaya. A wholly-owned subsidiary of Consolidated Tin, Williams Harvey & Co. Ltd., holds 75 per cent of the issued share capital of Makeri Smelting Co. Ltd. incorporated in Nigeria in 1961. Makeri has built a tin smelter on the Jos Plateau, Northern Nigeria, which began production in December 1961. Vivian, Younger & Bond Ltd., the sole selling agents of Consolidated Tin, are well established in Nigeria.

London Tin Corporation Ltd. board does not include any of the Patino directors, but the relationship with the Patino interests are obviously established when we note on its board C. Waite, chairman and managing director of Consolidated Tin Smelters and its subsidiary Williams Harvey & Co., and a director of British Tin Investment Corporation and General Tin Investments. Mr Waite also sits on the board of Consolidated Tin subsidiaries: the Penpoll Tin Smelting Co. Ltd., Eastern Smelting Co., Wm. Symington & Sons Ltd. (rubber merchants) and that of the distributing agents, Vivian, Younger & Bond.

As director of Southern Kinta Consolidated Ltd., Southern Malayan Tin Dredging Ltd., Kamunting Tin Dredging Ltd., Malayan Tin Dredging Ltd., Mr Waite obviously represents on those boards the interests (including those of Patino) of Consolidated Tin. A director, moreover, of the Chartered Bank and a member of the London Board of British & Foreign Marine Insurance Co. Ltd., he certainly represents the financial interests supporting them. This conclusion is backed by the directorial presence of Francis G. Charlesworth on British Tin and as chairman of Malayan Tin Dredging and Southern Malayan Tin. Mr Charlesworth is also a director of certain other tin companies operating in the Malayan area, namely Kramat Pulai Ltd., Ackam Tin Ltd. and Ayer Hitam Tin Dredging Ltd. He is, moreover, a member of the board of Locana Mineral Holdings Ltd., which is honoured by including a scion of the Austro-Hungarian empire, H.I.R.H. The Archduke Robert Charles of Austria.

Locana is an investment and holding company, connected principally with the Canadian mining industry. Mr Charlesworth is a direct link with the world of tin mining and dealing

183

through his association with British Tin and its interests in Malaya. Sitting alongside Mr Charlesworth on the Locana board are Messrs N. K. Kindhead-Weekes and J. N. Kiek. Both also sit on the boards of important South African and Rhodesian companies.

Mr Kiek is chairman of Chicago-Gaika Development Co. Ltd., a company existing since 1897 and having seventeen gold claims in the Sebakwe district of Matabeleland, Rhodesia, which was at one time within the jurisdiction of the British South Africa Company. Mr Kiek's other associations are with the London and Rhodesian Mining and Land Co. Ltd., owning directly 384 gold-mining claims, base-metal claims and lands covering 757,000 acres in Rhodesia. Some of the properties are leased on a royalty basis, and ranching operations are also carried on.

Subsidiary companies of London & Rhodesian include Mazoe Consolidated Mines Ltd., Lonrho Exploration Co. Ltd. and African Investment Trust Ltd., which took over all the company's investments in 1958, except shares in subsidiaries and trade investments. Its associates include Arcturus Mines Ltd., Homestake Gold Mining Co. Ltd., Coronation Syndicate Ltd. and North Charterland Exploration Co. (1937) Ltd. Among further interests acquired by London & Rhodesian in 1961 were 90 per cent of Consolidated Holdings (Pvt) Ltd., 100 per cent of Mashaba Gold Mines (Pvt) Ltd., which operates the Empress Gold Mine at Mashaba, near Fort Victoria, Rhodesia, $36\frac{2}{3}$ per cent of Kanyemba Gold Mines and 51 per cent of Associated Overland Pipelines of Rhodesia (Pvt) Ltd., in exchange for 1,500,000 shares in London & Rhodesian and an option on another 2 million.

That London & Rhodesian Mining comes within the Oppenheimer group interests there can be no doubt, despite the separate front that is kept up. G. Abdinor, a director of Arcturus Mines, Coronation Syndicate, Homestake, Kenyemba and Mazoe, is also a member of the boards of Calcon Mines Ltd. (Northern Rhodesia), Spaarwater Gold Mining Co. Ltd. and West Spaarwater Ltd., as is also S. F. Dench, who is chairman of West Spaarwater and of Coronation Syndicate and

Kanyemba. Spaarwater Gold is among the interests of Consolidated Gold Fields, while Henderson's Transvaal Estates Ltd., of which Mr Dench is a director, comes within the Oppenheimer African Investment Trust group of holding companies, on whose board sits Mr Kiek. It is, in fact, the total owner of African Exploration Co. Ltd. which gives secretarial aid to West Spaarwater and Coronation Syndicate.

Interestingly enough, Henderson's Transvaal Estates has a fully-owned subsidiary, Henderson Consolidated Corporation Ltd., which itself has a total subsidiary, Mineral Holdings Ltd., owning freehold lands in Transvaal and Orange Free State, totalling 3,706 acres, and mineral rights over a further 689,380 acres. In addition, it has two mineral concessions in Swaziland, totalling 84,019 acres.

Another direct wholly-owned subsidiary of Henderson's Transvaal is Mineral Holdings Investments Ltd., which holds 720,000 shares in Leslie Gold Mines Ltd. and 200,000 in Bracken Mines Ltd., both of them belonging to the Union Corporation group of the Oppenheimer empire. Both mines enjoy a loan of £1 million each from the National Finance Corporation of South Africa, in which Anglo American Corporation and a number of other groups and institutions associated with it have substantial interests.

J. N. Kiek also occupied the managing director's position on Rhodesia Railways Trust Co. Ltd., and two other Oppenheimer financial concerns, Willoughby's Consolidated Co. Ltd. and Willoughby's (Investments) Ewell Ltd. Mr Kiek's associate director, N. K. Kindhead-Weekes, is a director of such important Oppenheimer enterprises as Wankie Colliery (linked with Tanganyika Concessions and Union Minière), Chibuluma Mines, Chisangwa Mines and Chambishi Mines, and also Charterland Exploration Ltd., all of them in Rhodesia. Charterland Exploration has been granted exclusive prospecting rights by British South Africa Co. over areas totalling some 118,000 square miles in Zambia.

The Patino network is shown in Chart 8. Of the organisations dominating the aluminium industry we note first the Aluminium Co. of America (ALCOA) and the aluminium

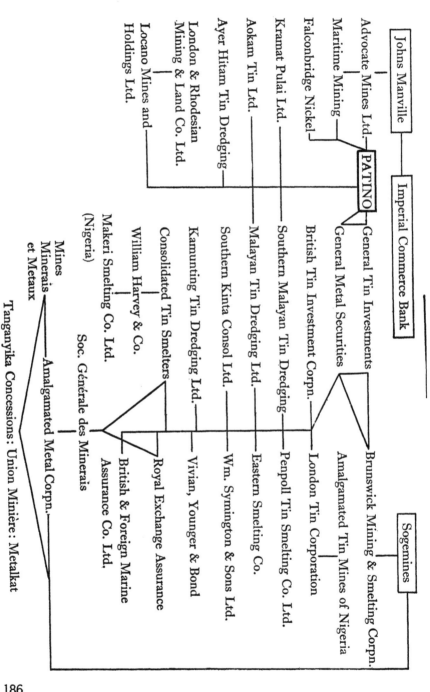

Johns Manville — Imperial Commerce Bank — Sogemines

PATINO

Advocate Mines Ltd.
Maritime Mining
Falconbridge Nickel
Kramat Pulai Ltd.
Aokam Tin Ltd.
Ayer Hitam Tin Dredging
London & Rhodesian Mining & Land Co. Ltd.
Locano Mines and Holdings Ltd.

General Tin Investments
General Metal Securities
British Tin Investment Corpn.
Southern Malayan Tin Dredging
Malayan Tin Dredging Ltd.
Southern Kinta Consol Ltd.
Kamunting Tin Dredging Ltd.
Consolidated Tin Smelters
William Harvey & Co.
Makeri Smelting Co. Ltd. (Nigeria)
Soc. Générale des Minerais
Amalgamated Metal Corpn.
Mines Minerais et Metaux

Brunswick Mining & Smelting Corpn.
Amalgamated Tin Mines of Nigeria
London Tin Corporation
Penpoll Tin Smelting Co. Ltd.
Eastern Smelting Co.
Wm. Symington & Sons Ltd.
Vivian, Younger & Bond
Royal Exchange Assurance
British & Foreign Marine Assurance Co. Ltd.

Tanganyika Concessions: Union Minière: Metalkat

CHART 8

186

empire of Mellon. This company mines bauxite in Arkansas and has subsidiaries digging and bringing out ore from far-flung places to feed the smelting and processing works in the United States. These are sited mainly in the southern States, though there are works at Massena, New York. Casting and fabricating plants are operating in twelve of the American States, while wholly-owned subsidiaries are exploring for raw materials in Europe, Central and South America, the Caribbean, Australia and Africa.

Surinam Aluminium Co. is the principal ore-producing subsidiary. It mines bauxite in the Dutch-held territory of Surinam, part of Guiana, which stretches over the north-eastern corner of the South American continent lying north of the Amazon and south of the Orinoco. Under an agreement with the Surinam Government, Surinam Aluminium has a 75-year bauxite-mining concession. It is building power facilities and will construct a 60,000-ton aluminium smelter. The eventual construction of a bauxite refinery utilising local ores is envisaged, according to the company's publicity material. Another full subsidiary is mining bauxite in the Dominican Republic and, in May 1960, mining rights were acquired over 30,000 acres of Jamaica. Chart 9 shows the extent of Alcoa's foreign interests.

Because of the anti-trust laws there is legally no direct connection between Alcoa and Aluminium Ltd., but they are both owned by the same Mellon-Davis dominated group of United States shareholders. Two brothers, Arthur V. Davis of Alcoa and Edward K. Davis of Aluminium Ltd., were for many years president of the respective companies. When the latter died in 1947 he was succeeded by his son, Nathaniel V. Davis. The size of the Davis block of shares in the Mellon aluminium companies is about a third of that of the Mellons. In 1957 *Fortune*, the American journal read by all who would be well-informed on matters of big business, listed Arthur V. Davis as one of seven persons with fortunes between $400 million and $700 million. Of the other six, four were Mellons. Aluminium Ltd's Davis is a director of the Mellon Bank.

United Kingdom provides as a subsidiary Alcan Industries

187

Alcoa's World-wide Interests

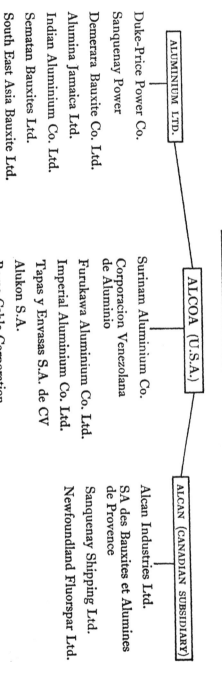

ALCOA (U.S.A.)

ALUMINIUM LTD.

Duke-Price Power Co.
Sanquenay Power
Demerara Bauxite Co. Ltd.
Alumina Jamaica Ltd.
Indian Aluminium Co. Ltd.
Sematan Bauxites Ltd.
South East Asia Bauxite Ltd.
Aluminio do Brasil S.A.
Aluminio Minas Gerais S.A.
Aluminium Co. of S. Africa

Surinam Aluminium Co.
Corporacion Venezolana
de Aluminio
Furukawa Aluminium Co. Ltd.
Imperial Aluminium Co. Ltd.
Tapas y Envasas S.A. de CV
Alukon S.A.
Rome Cable Corporation

ALCAN (CANADIAN SUBSIDIARY)

Alcan Industries Ltd.
SA des Bauxites et Alumines
de Provence
Sanquenay Shipping Ltd.
Newfoundland Fluorspar Ltd.

CHART 9

Ltd., and France contributes a further wholly-owned subsidiary in S.A. des Bauxites et Alumines de Provence, in which Aluminium Ltd. has invested some $100 million. Its mines produced 300,000 tons in 1960, from which alumina is processed. Making itself independent in the sphere of transport Alcan created Saquenay Shipping Ltd., fully financed by itself, to own and charter a fleet of ships for carrying the group's bauxite, alumina and ingot.

Though Kaiser and Reynolds set up aluminium companies as an attempt at independence from the Mellon empire, in the case of Kaiser financial alliance was formed early. Reynolds also has not found it possible to keep entirely aloof from the Mellon tentacles. Formed in mid-1928, Reynolds Metals Co. created in 1940 its subsidiary, Reynolds Mining Corporation, to work 6,100 acres of bauxite land which it had obtained in Arkansas and to mine fluorspar in Mexico, which is shipped for processing at the company's works in America.

Abroad, Reynolds owns bauxite mines and exploration tracts in north-east British Guiana, as well as in Haiti and Jamaica. The dried ores are shipped to plants in Massachusetts, Delaware, Arkansas and Texas, U.S.A., more than 3 million tons having been mined and shipped during 1961. Other subsidiaries and affiliates operate in Bermuda, Venezuela, Philippines, Mexico, Canada, Australia, Africa, Columbia and other parts of the world. Reynolds Jamaica Mines Ltd. in 1957 acquired the right from the Jamaican Government to mine bauxite for 99 years on all lands then owned or held by it under option in return for ore royalties and taxes. These lands amounted to 74,000 acres. Mining leases have been obtained on 5,822 acres.

The United Kingdom end of the Reynolds' aluminium activities is operated through British Aluminium Ltd. At one time it looked as though Mellon would take over the British company, but an alliance between Tube Investment Ltd. and Reynolds secured them 96 per cent control of British Aluminium, T.I. taking 49 per cent and Reynolds 47 per cent. The Commonwealth, Europe, Asia and Africa are embraced within the company's sphere of activities, its subsidiaries and affiliates controlling power resources, bauxite properties, processing works, even a Grand Hotel, and a pension trust, all of which are listed among Tube Investment's interests as the major parent company.

British Aluminium took over Reynolds T.I. Aluminium in mid-1961, owned at the time 51 per cent by T.I. and 49 per cent by Reynolds. Members of the Reynolds' family sit on the British Aluminium board, which accommodates W. B. C. Perrycoste, director of Ghana Bauxite Co. Ltd., a wholly-owned subsidiary of the company, registered in London in 1933. Other African interests are represented by E. F. O. Gascoigne, chairman of Tanganyika Holdings, Kentan Gold Areas, Zambesia Exploring and Zambesia Investment, all within the Tanganyika Concessions sphere. The 'objective' British press is also represented by the presence on British Aluminium's board of Sir Geoffrey Crowther, one-time editor of *The Economist* and now its deputy chairman. Commercial Union Assurance is also among Sir Geoffrey's and Lord Plowden's directorships.

FRIA Cie Internationale pour la Production de l'Alumine, Guinea, is one of British Aluminium's biggest interests in Africa, in which it holds 10 per cent of the shares. The project is to produce, initially, 480,000 tons of alumina annually, of which 10 per cent will be available to British Aluminium.

The Mellons were the original party directly interested in developing Guinea's bauxite resources but, unable to force the pressure on the newly independent African State, their people were forced to retire, having fruitlessly disbursed, according to their own estimates, some $20 million. Other partners in Fria are:

Olin Mathieson Chemical Corporation, U.S.A.	48·5%
Pechiney-Ugine, France	26·5%
Aluminium Industrie Aktiengesellschaft, Switzerland	10%
Vereinigte Aluminium-Werke A.G., Germany	5%

Olin Mathieson is within the Rockefeller sphere of influence represented on the chemical company's board by Lawrence Rockefeller, who acts for the family in its activities outside oil.

190

Control, however, is shared with the Morgans. Thus, the Mellon group gave way to an overwhelmingly more power-ful compact of interests hidden behind the Olin Mathieson facade.

The second-largest holder of Fria is a combination of the Pechiney and Ugine companies. Pechiney is an abbreviation of Compagnie des Produits Chimiques et Électrometallurgiques. Among its directors is Paul Gillet, an honorary governor of Société Générale de Belgique, chairman of Union Minière, and associate of many of the foremost concerns exploiting Africa's resources. Its chairman is Paul de Vitry, a director of the Banque de Paris et des Pays Bas. This bank, of which Henry Lafond was also a director, besides sitting with Paul de Vitry on Pechiney, operates in the Congo and South Africa. In fact it is ubiquitous in the new ventures going forward in Africa, especially those in the new States bordering the Sahara.

Pechiney, registered in Paris at the opening of the year 1896, is the continuation of a company formed over a hundred years ago in 1855 and, like the other leading mining and metallurgical companies in France, has links with the country's leading banking houses. Its proliferations are manifold, covering the production of bauxite, barytes and lignite, chemicals manu-facture, the processing of aluminium and other metals and electrometallurgical products. It manufactures almost every-thing from plastics, through iron alloys, graphite products, up to new metals and nuclear products. It holds part and total portions of affiliated companies in France and other countries in Europe, Africa and elsewhere. Its mining operations spread from north to south of France and into Africa.

Responsible today for four-fifths of France's output of alu-minium, Pechiney's trading in the metal accounts for nearly 60 per cent of its turnover. Its only sizeable French competitor is Ugine, which collaborates with Pechiney on investment policy, as we note above, and in a joint sales subsidiary, Aluminium Français. Both firms are expanding rapidly, and Pechiney has as widespread operations as the British and American aluminium companies, though the latter have greater output. It is expected that Pechiney-Ugine capacity may reach

191

300,000 tons by 1963. Pechiney uses 15 per cent of a total French power output, so that the discovery of natural gas at Lacq in south-western France made a considerable contribution to its expansion. It had pushed the aluminium sector of its exports to 37 per cent and hopes to save on its production costs by the introduction of a new process for reducing bauxite to aluminium. A pilot plant has been put into operation and its success will enable Pechiney to expand into new aluminium industries.

Through the Banque de Paris, which is said to be the biggest shareholder in the important Franco-Norwegian chemical concern, Norsk Hydro, majority-controlled by the Norwegian Government, Pechiney may become linked with the project. The Norwegians are anxious to increase their output from its present level of 200,000 tons to 600,000 tons by 1970. Already Pechiney is in consortia operating in Greece, Spain and the Argentine, and has holdings in Senegal and Madagascar projects. As a matter of fact, there is hardly a new consortium springing up in Africa today, particularly in the Mahgreb, in which Pechiney does not have an oar. It certainly has a watchful eye on the vast natural gas deposits of the Sahara, which are not uneconomically distant from the bauxite fields of Mali.

The international nickel field binds a select coterie of extractive, processing and financing concerns whose control keeps it within fairly exclusive numerical limits. Grouped around the International Nickel Co. of Canada Ltd.—INCO—Falconbridge, Sherritt Gordon Mines Ltd. of Canada and Faraday Uranium Mines Ltd. and Freeport Sulphur Co. of the United States are not geographically confined. In unravelling their engagements, we find their penetrations in Africa as well as in other parts of the world.

Inco's direct link with the Oppenheimer mining interests in Africa has already been made apparent through the interlocking directorships of Sir Ronald L. Prain and Sir Otto Niemeyer. We will see further how, through its interests in certain mines, these are connected indirectly with combinations having definite ties with the exploitation of Africa's mineral resources. It is

Reynolds Interests

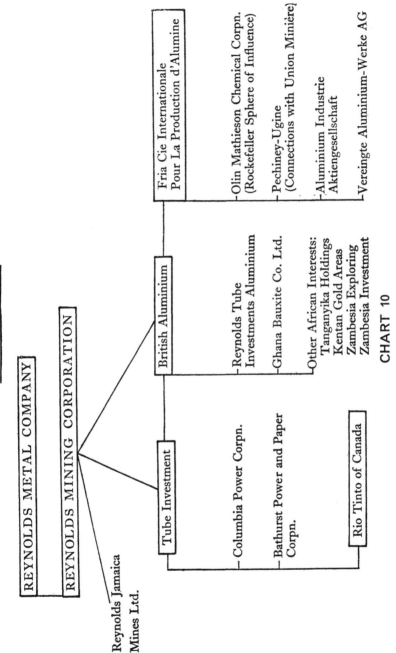

REYNOLDS METAL COMPANY

REYNOLDS MINING CORPORATION

Reynolds Jamaica
Mines Ltd.

Tube Investment

— Columbia Power Corpn.

— Bathurst Power and Paper
  Corpn.

Rio Tinto of Canada

British Aluminium

— Reynolds Tube
  Investments Aluminium

— Ghana Bauxite Co. Ltd.

— Other African Interests:
  Tanganyika Holdings
  Kentan Gold Areas
  Zambesia Exploring
  Zambesia Investment

Fria Cie Internationale
Pour La Production d'Alumine

— Olin Mathieson Chemical Corpn.
  (Rockefeller Sphere of Influence)

— Pechiney-Ugine
  (Connections with Union Minière)

— Aluminium Industrie
  Aktiengesellschaft

— Vereingte Aluminium-Werke AG

CHART 10

193

when the financial interests behind them are examined that we find the continuity of power.

The name Mond immediately brings to mind nickel, as well as explosives, chemicals and arms, and we find it linked to the most powerful international nickel organisation under the form of International Nickel Co. (Mond) Ltd. It was the founder of Brunner Mond & Co. Ltd., Ludwig Mond, who, having invented the ammonia soda process and found a cheap source of power from small coal, discovered a method of recovering nickel from low-grade ores. This led to the finding, acquisition and development of mines in Canada, the world's present chief source, the ores coming almost totally from the Sudbury district of Ontario. Brunner Mond, together with Novel Industries, United Alkali Co. Ltd. (an amalgamation of forty-eight works) and British Dyestuffs Corporation Ltd., were knit together in December 1926 to form Imperial Chemical Industries Ltd.

Mond Nickel Co. Ltd. was established in 1914 to exploit the mine that adjoined Inco's properties on the Sudbury range. The interests of both companies were fused in 1928. Change of name to its present form was made in February 1961, and the company is a subsidiary of Anglo Canadian Mining & Refining Co. Ltd., which owns the 9 million shares issued out of the 11 million authorised to compose the capital of £5 million. Anglo-Canadian is itself a wholly-owned subsidiary of Inco.

Among the extensive properties and plants owned by International Nickel Mond in the United Kingdom are a refining works in South Wales and a precious metals refinery in a London industrial area, a number of rolling mills in various parts of Britain, as well as the entire share capital of Henry Wiggin & Co. Ltd., manufacturers of nickel and nickel alloys and other products. Two interesting items in Nickel Mond's treasury are the entire capital of Clydach Estates Ltd. and Mond Nickel (Retirement System) Trustees Ltd. This is the United Kingdom end of Inco, which has appointed its delegate board and consolidates the U.K. accounts with its own.

In order to keep its plants working to fullest capacity Inco has arrangements with associates for the treatment of their

194

products. Hence certain nickel concentrates in excess of its own treatment facilities are worked for Sherritt Gordon Mines, and there is an agreement with Texas Gulf Sulphur Co., covering the operation of a pilot plant to investigate processes for the recovery of elemental sulphur. These agreements issue out of certain common holdings that give identity of interest to apparently competitive concerns, tied up with oil and its allied financial groups.

The controlling interests in Inco are not apparent as there is no obvious United States parent, although American capital from most of the leading financial groups predominates, and Inco owns the entire capital stock of The International Nickel Co. Inc. which owns the operating assets located in the United States, and of Whitehead Metal Products Co. Inc., American distributors of non-ferrous metals. Laurence Rockefeller is on the United States Inco board. The Canadian company's chairman is H. S. Wingate, a director of the American banking house of J. P. Morgan & Co. and of the Canadian Pacific Railway. William C. Bolenius, an Inco director, also sits on directorates of various Bell Telephone companies, as well as on that of the Guaranty Trust Co. of New York, Morgan-controlled. Another Inco director, R. S. McLaughlin, is a director of General Motors and on the board of the Toronto-Dominion Bank, which links with du Pont interests. Du Pont itself is under heavy Morgan influence. Donald Hamilton McLaughlin is President of the American Trust Co., which has three interlocking directorates with Morgan banks and insurance companies. He also presides over the board of Homestake Mining Co., linked through its holdings in Idarado Mining Co., with Newmont Mining Co. within the Morgan sphere of influence. Cerro de Pasco, another of D. H. McLaughlin's directorships, owns a number of companies operating mining and oil properties in Peru. Newmont Mining has a substantial interest in Cerro de Pasco.

Theodore Giles Montague, another American on Inco's board, is chairman of the Borden Co., a trustee of the Bank of New York and a director of American Sugar Refining Co. All three of these companies is within the family control of the

195

Rockefellers. John Fairfield Thompson also reflects U.S. interests on the Inco board. Another trustee of the Bank of New York, he represents the same interests on Inco's American distributing organisation, Whitehead Metal Products Co., and points the link with Texas Gulf Sulphur, under Morgan and Standard Oil (Rockefeller) domination. J. F. Thompson reveals the African interests of these groups by his directorships on American Metal Climax, and its British associates, Amalgamated Metal Corporation and Henry Gardner & Co. Ltd., who are also connected with French tin and nickel interests. These are some of the giant combinations involving tin, aluminium and nickel, which are draining away the mineral resources of Africa.

14. Union Minière du Haut Katanga

THERE is perhaps hardly an industrial organisation in the world that has been so widely publicised over the past five years as Union Minière, because of the ducks and drakes it has played with the establishment of Congo independence and unification. This great mining company has been since Congo's independence the bone of contention between the Congolese government and the secessionist Katanga Province. Principally owned by small shareholders, its control rested with Belgian and British financiers.

The largest block of stock in the company, 18·14 per cent of the 1,242,000 shares, which formerly belonged to the Belgian colonial administration, passed at independence to the Congolese government and was held in trust by the Belgian government for a time, pending the settlement of political problems. In November 1964, Moise Tshombe who had by then returned from exile to become Congolese Prime Minister, published a decree which had the effect of transferring control of Union Minière from Belgian banking and other interests to the Congolese government without compensation. The decree gave the Congolese government the entire portfolio of 315,675 shares in Union Minière held by the Comité Special du Katanga, a concession-granting concern, two-thirds of which is owned by the Congolese government and one-third by Belgian interests.

The Belgian government considered that 123,725 of these

shares belonged to the Compagnie du Katanga which is an off-shoot of the Société Générale de Belgique. The effect of the decree was to reduce the voting strength in Union Minière of the Société Générale and its associate, Tanganyika Concessions Ltd. from 40 per cent to less than 29 per cent, while the Congolese government's votes were raised from nearly 24 per cent to nearly 36 per cent. This meant that in any policy dispute the Belgians would have to rally the support of small shareholders comprising about 36 per cent.

For weeks the Belgian government and the Congolese government talked of arranging meetings to discuss the situation. Each had a trump card. The Belgian government held the entire portfolio in trust, while the Congolese government's strength lay in the expiration of Union Minière's lease in 1990.

On 28 January 1965, Tshombe arrived in Brussels for talks with the Belgian Foreign Minister, M. Spaak. He asked for the immediate handing over of the portfolio shares valued at £120 million. These included 21 per cent of the voting rights in Union Minière. The Belgians, on the other hand, demanded compensation for Belgian property damaged in the Congo troubles, and for chartered companies who lost mineral concessions under the November decree. They also insisted that the agreement should cover the interest payable on defaulted Congo bonds.

After days of hard bargaining, Tshombe scored what appeared to be a great triumph. He secured the £120 million portfolio of shares, and also received a cheque from Union Minière for £660,000 representing royalties and dividends on the Congo's 210,450 shares in Union Minière, which gave it 24 per cent of the voting rights in the company. With this diplomatic victory he returned to Leopoldville, his hand strengthened to deal with the continuing political and military problems of the country. Since then he has had cause to wonder just how much of a victory he achieved.

In my address to the Ghana National Assembly on 22 March 1965, I gave details of the Congo situation:

'In the five years preceding independence, the net outflow

198

of capital to Belgium alone was four hundred and sixty-four million pounds.

When Lumumba assumed power, so much capital was taken out of the Congo that there was a national deficit of forty million pounds.

Tshombe is now told the Congo has an external debt of nine hundred million dollars. This is a completely arbitrary figure—it amounts to open exploitation based on naked colonialism. Nine hundred million dollars ($900,000,000) is supposed to be owed to United States and Belgian monopolies after they have raped the Congo of sums of £2,500 million, £464 million, and £40 million. Imagine what this would have meant to the prosperity and well-being of the Congo.

But the tragic-comedy continues. . . . To prop up Tshombe, the monopolies decided that of this invented debt of $900 million, only $250 million has to be paid. How generous, indeed!

Bonds valued in 1959 at £267 million, representing wealth extracted from the Congo, are to be returned to the Congo after ratification by both parliaments. But the monopolies have decided that the value of the bonds is now only £107 million. So the profit to these monopolies is a net £160 million.

The monopolies further announced a fraudulent programme to liquidate so-called Congolese external debts of £100 million. Upon announcing this, they declare Congo is to be responsible for a further internal debt of £200 million.

In plain words, they are depriving the Congolese people of another £100 million. And they call this generosity!

We learn that the monopolies have declared a further burden for the suffering people of the Congo: an internal debt of £200 million on which the Congo must pay additional compensation of £12·5 million to Belgian private interests.

Beyond this, a joint Congolese-Belgian organisation has been formed. It is withdrawing old bonds and replacing them with forty-year issues valued at £100 million. These will pay interest at 3½ per cent per annum.

Note this: as the old bonds are worthless, the new organisation must pay all interest on the old bonds from 1960–65 to the monopolies and EACH HOLDER OF THE WORTHLESS OLD BONDS must be given a new bond for every old one. In short, the organisation is a device to take more, to enrich the monopolies further and to defraud the suffering people of the Congo.

Tshombe has promised not to nationalise investments valued at £150 million and to retain 8,000 Belgians in the Congo. He has set up an Investment Bank to manage all portfolios. The value is placed at £240 million. It is controlled by Belgians.

In one year, Union Minière's profits were £27 million. But although the national production in Congo increased 60 per cent between 1950 and 1957, African buying power decreased by 13 per cent. . . . The Congolese were taxed 280 million francs to pay for European civil servants, 440 million francs for special funds of Belgium, 1,329 million francs for the army. They were even taxed for the Brussels Exhibition.

Despite political independence, the Congo remains a victim of imperialism and neo-colonialism . . . (but) the economic and financial control of the Congo by foreign interests is not limited to the Congo alone. The developing countries of Africa are all subject to this unhealthy influence in one way or another.'

If this quotation appears to contain much detail, the newly independent peoples and their leaders have no more urgent task today than to burn into their consciousness exactly such detail. For it is such material that makes up the hard reality of this world in which we are trying to live, and in which Africa is emerging to find its place.

The full significance of the part played by Union Minière in Congolese affairs can only be understood if an examination is made of the interests involved in this powerful company. Nearly all the large enterprises engaged in exploiting the manifold riches of the Congo come within its immediate embrace or have indirect relations with it. They do not, however, complete the extent of the company's engagements. Its connections with leading insurance, financial and industrial houses in Europe and the United States are shown in the following list, as well as its connections with the Rhodesian copperbelt:

Compagnie Foncière du Katanga.
Société Générales des Forces Hydro-electriques—SOGEFOR.
Société Générale Africaine d'Electricité—SOGELEC.
Société Générale Industrielle et Chimique de Jadotville—SOGECHIM.
Société Métallurgique du Katanga—METALKAT.
Minoteries du Katanga.
Société de Recherche Minière du Sud-Katanga—SUDKAT.
Ciments Métallurgiques de Jadotville—C.M.J.
Charbonnages de la Luena.
Compagnie des Chemins de Fer Katanga-Dilolo-Leopoldville—K.D.L.
Société Africaine d'Explosifs—AFRIDEX.
Compagnie Maritime Congolaise.
Société d'Exploitation des Mines du Sud-Katanga—MINSUDKAT.
Société d'Elevage d la Luilu ELVALUILU.
Compagnie d'Assurances d Outremer.
Société de Recherches et d'Exploitation des Bauxites du Congo—BAUXICONGO.
Exploitation Forestière au Kasai.
Centre d'Information du Cobalt.
Société Générale Métallurgique de Hoboken.
Société Anonyme Belge d'Exploitation de la Navigation Aeriénne—SABENA.
Société Générale d'Enterprises Immobilière—S.E.I.
Compagnie Belge pour l'Industrie de l'Aluminium—COBEAL.
Foraky.
Compagnie Belge d'Assurances Maritimes—BELGAMAR.
Société Auxiliaire de la Royale Union Coloniale Belge—S.A.R.U.C.
Wankie Colliery Co. Ltd.
Belgian-American Bank & Trust Co., New York.
Belgian-American Banking Corporation, New York.

Compagnie Générale d'Electrolyse du Palais S.A., Paris.
Trefileries et Laminoire du Havre S.A., Paris.
Société Belge pour l'Industries Nucleaire—BELCO
NUCLEAIRE.

Tanganyika Concessions is one parent of Union Minière du
Haut Katanga. The other was the Katanga (Belgian) Special
Committee. Union Minière was formed between them for the
stated purpose of bringing together the interests of both
organisations in the mineral discoveries Tanganyika Concessions had made under a concession granted to it by the
Committee in the Katanga province of the Congo. The concession, which has until 11 March 1990 to run, covers an area
of 7,700 square miles, containing rich copper as well as zinc,
cobalt, cadmium, germanium, radium, gold, silver, iron ores
and limestone deposits. Included is a tin area of some 5,400
square miles.

Ores mined are processed at a number of plants, passing
through smelting and concentration stages. Hydro-electrical
energy is supplied from four main power plants, one of which
was installed by a subsidiary of Union Minière, the Société
Générale des Forces Hydro-electriques. Three others belong
to Union Minière itself. These three plants are connected to a
distribution network, part of which is devoted to supplying
electrical power to the Northern Rhodesian copperbelt at the
rate of 600 million kw. per year. Part of this network is owned
by the Société Générale Africaine d'Electricité—SOGELEC—
in which Union Minière has a substantial interest. The company's plants at Elizabethville, Jadotville, Kolwezi and Kpushi
consumed 75 million kw. in 1962, during which year certain
damages caused to the installations in December 1961 were
completely repaired.

Most of the concerns in which Union Minière is interested
are supported by the Société Générale de Belgique. Many also
have connections with Anglo American Corporation either
direct or by way of Tanganyika Concessions and Union
Minière and their subsidiaries. Société Générale has a direct
holding of 57,538 shares out of the 1,242,000 shares of no
nominal value that constitute the authorised and issued capital

of frs. 8,000,000,000 of Union Minière. Other principal shareholders are the Katanga Special Committee and Tanganyika Concessions. Royalty on the concession is paid to the Katanga Committee by way of a sum equivalent to 10 per cent of any dividend distributed over and above a total of frs. 93,150,000 in any year. Tanganyika Concessions, by agreement with the Committee, shares in this special benefit to the extent of 40 per cent. Originally incorporated in the Congo, the company took its seat of administration and all its funds to Belgium during 1960, when the Congo was achieving independence and needed the support of those who, over the years, had drawn such heavy tribute from it.

Société Générale's patronage hangs closely over Union Minière. Attached to the Katanga Special Committee is the Compagnie du Katanga. The Katanga Company is within the group of the Compagnie du Congo pour le Commerce et l'Industrie—C.C.C.I.—constituted in 1886 when Leopold II was creating his personal empire in the Congo. It was on the initiative of one of Leopold's swashbucklers, Captain Thys, that C.C.C.I., according to the chairman of the Société Générale, became the first Belgian enterprise established in the heart of Africa. His name is attached to the repair station of the first railway from Matadi to Leopoldville. Thysville is now an important link in the railway system, and C.C.C.I., in the words of Société Générale's chairman, has since its inception been connected directly or through its affiliates, with all sectors of economic activity in the Congo by the creation of transport enterprises, agricultural industries, cement works, construction and building concerns, property companies, food industries, as well as commercial firms. The company has, affirmed the chairman, 'contributed to endow the Congo with an equipage which places the country in the first ranks of the black African states'.

Several of these interlinked enterprises are included in the list of Union Minière's interests, which frequently join those of Société Générale. Thus Société Générale Métallurgique de Hoboken, a company in which Société Générale owns 50,000 shares of no par value, processes certain semi-finished products from the Union Minière mines for the market in finished metals of high purity and individual specification. In conjunction with the Fansteel Metallurgical Corporation of Chicago, Hoboken created a joint subsidiary, Fansteel-Hoboken, in December 1962, with a capital of 360 million francs. This new company will produce refractory metals, notably tantalum, columbium, tungsten and molybdenum, in various marketable forms.

Wankie Colliery Co. Ltd. represents Union Minière's participation in Southern Rhodesia's coal mines. While its shareholding is not unimportant, Anglo American Corporation predominates and acts as the company's secretary and consulting engineers. Capitalised at £6,000,000, of which £5,277,810 is paid up, the company owns coal-mining rights over 42,000 acres and surface rights over about 29,000 acres of land in the Wankie district of Southern Rhodesia. The means by which the mining interests dominate the government of the 'settler colonies' are many, but the manner in which land is given away by the administration and then leased back from the buyers or lessees exhibits some of the most unashamed and open gerrymandering possible. Thus Wankie Colliery obtained on a long-term lease by agreement with the Rhodesian government surface rights to 26,000 acres of land additional to the above-mentioned stretches, in return for which Wankie has graciously leased some 4,000 acres of surface rights in its original landholdings to the government.

A directorial link, M. van Weyenbergh, associated Wankie Colliery with Société Métallurgique du Katanga — METALKAT—a subsidiary of Union Minière, founded in Belgium in 1948 in conjunction with S.A. des Mines de Fonderies de Zinc de la Vieille-Montagne, to construct at Kolwezi a plant capable of producing 50,000 tons of electrolytic zinc annually from concentrates provided by Union Minière's Prince Leopold mine. The Metalkat plant produces zinc, cadmium and refined copper. With a capital of frs. 750,000,000 represented by 150,000 shares of no par value, the company made a net profit of frs. 160,831,393 in 1961, after providing for various liabilities, among which

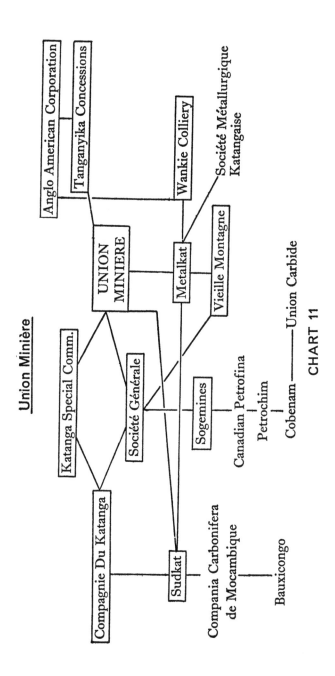

Union Minière

CHART 11

dividends accounted for frs. 120,000,000 (almost three-quarters of net profit) and directors' percentages frs. 7,857,517.

Union Minière's partner in Metalkat, Vieille-Montagne, is one of the big European mining concerns producing zinc, lead and silver. A Belgian company, founded in 1837, it has silver-lead-zinc properties in Belgium, France, Algeria, Tunis, Germany and Sweden and metallurgical works in Belgium, France and Germany. Of the 405,000 shares of no par value constituting its capital of frs. 1,000,000,000 Société Générale owns 40,756. Its accounts for the year ended 31 December 1961 showed a net profit of frs. 143,287,506, after various provisions, of which the largest was for re-equipment, amounting to frs. 100,000,000. Dividends took frs. 101,250,000 and taxes thereon frs. 27,700,000. Directors' percentages took frs. 14,327,760. Legal reserves seem to account for considerable sums which these large companies set aside. This item was credited with frs. 100,000,000 in Vieille-Montagne's 1961 accounts.

The Compagnie du Katanga, like Union Minière, attached to the Katanga Special Committee, joined Union Minière in creating in the Congo in 1932 the Société de Rocherche Minière du Sud-Katanga—SUDKAT. Both Compagnie du Katanga and Union Minière had interests in a large area adjacent to the latter's properties which they decided to combine. With Congolese independence, control of Sudkat as well as its funds were transferred to Belgium. Copper deposits at Musoshi and Lubembe and zinc-lead-sulphur ore bodies at Kengere and Lombe owned by Sudkat were transferred to the Société d'Exploitation des Mines du Sud-Katanga — MINSUDKAT—formed in the Congo in June 1955, with a capital of Congolese frs. 50,000,000.

Sudkat holds interests in the Companhia Carbonifera de Mocambique, concerned with coal mining, as well as in Bauxicongo and Metalkat. Metalkat created a local company in 1962, the Société Métallurgique Katangaise, with a capital of 600 million francs represented by 150,000 shares, to which it transferred its Katanga installations. The zinc ingots produced are being processed by Metalkat.

One of Sudkat's most important investments is in Sogemines Ltd. This company, though registered in Montreal and operating in Canada, is so intimately connected with the Société Générale that it has on its board six of the Société's directors, two of whom are also on the Union Minière directorate. Société Générale's investment in Sogemines covers 259,250 preferred shares of $10 each and 1,281,250 ordinary shares of $1 each, representing over one-fifth of the Canadian company's issued capital. A wholly owned subsidiary, Sogemines Development Co. Ltd., is carrying out exploration work in various parts of Canada and holds minority interests in other mining enterprises. Sogemines Ltd. is an investment and holding company participating in mining, oil and industrial ventures. L. C. and F. W. Park in *The Anatomy of Big Business*, graphically make the point that its 'relationships between Canadian and Belgian capital are based on the alliances that operate both in Belgium or the Congo and in Canada'. (p. 157.)

Sogemines' parent, Société Générale, devotes considerable space in its annual report to the former's operations. The most important concern in which they are interested is Canadian Petrofina Ltd. In 1961, Canadian Petrofina made the record profit of $5,516,926. Petrofina is a Belgian oil company with international associations, especially in the new African States, both inside and outside the oil industry. Its connections with Société Générale are not limited to shareholdings and directorial interlocking. Associations are maintained with several leading banks, including the Banque Belge, the Banque de l'Union Français, the Credit Foncier de Belgique, the Banque de Paris et des Pays Bas, and a number of insurance companies.

Under the impetus of Société Générale and certain associates, a subsidiary of Petrofina, Société Chimique des Derives du Petrols—PETROCHIN—underwent a financial reorganisation during 1962, when certain assets were passed to it, principally by Petrofina. Société Générale used the opportunity to make a participation of 29 million francs to the company's capital, 'in which several other enterprises within its group equally own interests'. Société Générale's shareholding is 58,000 shares of no par value. Cobenam, a joint venture of Petrochim and

Union Carbide, brings together the banking interests of Société Générale with those interested in the great American chemical corporation, the Continental Insurance Co. and the Hanover Bank, which is involved with Anglo American Corporation and the banking consortia now engaging themselves in ventures in the new African States. There is some Rockefeller influence in the Hanover Bank, and it is linked by financial interchanges with the American Fore group of New York, a principal fire and casualty insurance company.

Union Carbide & Carbon manufactures enriched uranium, and through the influence of its direct backers, Hanover Bank, and indirect associations with the Rockefeller-Mellon group, has become the major contractor to the government-owned atomic energy plants at Oak Ridge, Tennessee, and Paducah, Kentucky. For this purpose a separate division was formed, Union Carbide Nuclear Company, uranium and vanadium mines being worked in Colorado, and a tungsten mine and mill in California. Union Carbide's range of interests in the chemical sphere is wide, it having a very large synthetic materials sector. A Canadian subsidiary of Union Carbide is Shawinigan Chemicals, which it half owns in company with Monsanto Chemical Co. and Canadian Rosins & Chemicals Ltd. An affiliate, B. A.-Shawinigan Ltd., is owned by British American Oil, connected with the Bank of Montreal and Mellon. Shawinigan Chemicals has several subsidiaries which are equally controlled with U.S. companies. Société Générale has its own nuclear concern, Société Belge pour l'Industrie Nucleaire—BELGO NUCLEAIRE—in which we have noted Union Minière's interest.

This is only a single short strand of the tangled web that relates predominant banking interests in Europe and America to industrial undertakings in Africa and other parts of the world. It gives only the barest indication of the elastic character of these interests.

The incursions of Société Générale into the oil world are not confined to Petrofina and its associates. Petrobelge, another company carrying out prospecting in the north of Belgium in association with the Société Campincise de

Recherches et d'Exploitations Minerales, has an affiliate operating in Venezuela, Petrobelge de Venezuela. Petrobelge is linked with Petrofina and the Bureau de Recherches et de Participations Minières Marocain in prospecting in Morocco, the first stages of which will be completed in 1963. Italy is another scene of Petrobelge's activities, where in collaboration with the Italian company, Ausonia Mineraria, and the French organisation, Société Française de Participations Petrolières—PETROBAR—it is investigating hydrocarbons in the concessions obtained by Ausonia. In addition, Petrobelge has associated itself with an Italian-French-German consortium in a venture prospecting seismic regions on the Adriatic coast. Both Petrobelge and Petrofina have got together with the Spanish company, Ciepsa, to prospect for hydrocarbons within a concession owned by Ciepsa.

Direct links with Belgium's military programme and, accordingly, with that of NATO, are closely operated through the Poudreries Réunies de Belgique, whose capital was increased during 1962 from 203,900,000 francs to 266,700,000 francs. At the beginning of the year it absorbed the Fabrique Nationale de Produits Chimiques et d'Explosifs at Boncelles, Belgium, whose purchase included a participation in the capital of S.A. d'Arendonk. The acquisition of the latter's selling organisation has added to the scope of the company's civil activities. These Belgian concerns are linked with the Société Africaine d'Explosifs—AFRIDEX—in which Union Minière has interests. The military and nuclear interpenetration gives a special emphasis to the uranium output of the Union Minière complex, which in the post-war years upheld the Belgian economy and helped it to refurbish its industrial equipment. Out of the Congo came the spoils that provided for the further exploitation of the territory and the high productive ratio the lately devastated war-ridden and Nazi-occupied country attained so swiftly. Even before the second world war, uranium was already making the Shinkolobwe mine a very important asset to Union Minière and the Belgian government. As one writer puts it, 'The Union Minière achieved a certain notoriety in the 'twenties and 'thirties by

209

obliging would-be purchasers of radium to pay $70,000 a gram, until competition from the Canadian Eldorado company forced the price down to a mere $20,000 a gram, a level at which both companies were able to make a profit' (*Anatomy of Big Business*, p. 156). According to the calculation of experts, Union Minière's profits were estimated to be three billion francs a year, $60 million in terms of American currency, and over £20 million in sterling.

In spite of the disturbed situation in Katanga and the protests of the company that their business had been seriously impeded, Union Minière's balance sheet for the year ended 31 December 1960 showed a net profit of frs. 2,365,280,563. Dividends absorbed no less than frs. 1,863,000,000, rather more than half the net profits, carrying a dividend tax which went to the Belgian government of frs. 381,578,313. Emoluments to directors, auditors and staff fund (for Europeans) absorbed frs. 84,609,333, while Permanent Committee members received frs. 7,111,567.

Eldorado Mining & Refining Ltd. is by no means independent of the big business and financial interests which have Canada's industry in their grip, and whose associations with Africa and other less developed areas of the world are interwoven. A former private secretary to an ex-minister sits on its board, which is linked with Canadian Aluminium, whose directorate includes a former Governor-General of Canada. As we go along we shall see how these interlockings of international finance and exalted public figures and 'the people's representatatives' create an oligarchy of power pursuing and achieving their special interests, which have no relation whatsoever to 'the public good', with which they are made to appear synonymous. We shall find that the Royal Bank of Canada, represented on Eldorado's board by W. J. Bennett, has connections with Société Générale and Union Minière through interlockings via Sogemines and prominent insurance and banking groups.

Wankie Colliery Co. Ltd., for instance, gives us M. van Weyenbergh, a director of Union Minière, Metalkat and Société Générale, several of whose directorial colleagues sit on Sogemines, whose chairman, W. H. Howard, besides being a vice-president of the Royal Bank and chairman of the Montreal Trust, is linked with the Rothermere newspaper group in Great Britain and is a director of Algoma Steel Corporation Ltd., which owns four coal mines in West Virginia and limestone and dolomite deposits in Michigan State. Algoma supplied the steel for the construction of a $20 million plant at Sault Ste Marie, Ontario, for the Mannesman Tube Co., a subsidiary of the Mannesman steel company, which is a prominent member of the Ruhr industry of Western Germany. Mannesman is said to be fast increasing its penetration into Canadian industry. Its board includes representatives of the Deutsche Bank and Dresdner Bank, both of which are much in evidence in the consortia engaged in Africa and connected prominently with Anglo American Corporation. Chairman of Mannesmann since 1934 is W. Zanger, 'a former member of the Nazi party and of the S.S.; he was one of the group of big German industrialists who financed the Nazi rise to power and provided the armaments for the Nazi war machine. In the days of the Nazi invasion of the Soviet Union, Mannesmann opened short-lived affiliates in Kiev and Dniepropetrovsk' (*Anatomy of Big Business*, pp. 109–110).

These are the forces that link with the South African, Rhodesian, Congo, Angolan and Mozambique mining magnates and industrialists, and we see them now entering the development projects of many of the new African States, hiding their identity behind government and international agencies, whose real character is at once exposed when their affiliations are carefully examined. They are the real directors of neo-colonialism.

15. Economic pressures in the Congo Republic

On 30 June 1960, when the Congo became independent, there began what will undoubtedly be regarded by historians as the most stormy and complex chapter in that country's, and for that matter Africa's, history. Within a few weeks there was a breakdown of law and order when soldiers of the Force Publique, disappointed because independence did not bring immediate improvement in their position, seized arms, arrested white officers and N.C.O.s and finally broke up into rioting bands. It was at this point that Moise Tshombe, with the help of Belgian advisers, began the proceedings which led to the secession of Katanga Province. The newly independent Republic of the Congo was crippled by disorder and unrest.

The story of the United Nations intervention and Lumumba's murder are well known, and so also are the political events which have followed. Less publicised, for obvious reasons, have been the involved economic aspects of the whole Congo tragedy. Yet these are in many ways the more significant and certainly the more sinister since they are dominated by foreign interests whose main concern has always been for their own private gain.

There was not much American investment in the Congo before 1960. What there was, was largely indirect, through Tanganyika Concessions and Union Minière and the Anglo American holdings of the Oppenheimer group, and came mainly from the Rockefeller group. This group also had participations in the important textile company, Filatures et

212

Tissages Africains, created in 1946 by the Cotton Union and the Société Générale. The Rockefeller family holds 60,000 shares, of which 3,000 are in the hands of Nelson Rockefeller and 26,438 belong to Laurence Rockefeller, who also has minority interests in two other companies of the Société Générale's group: Cie Générale d'Automobiles et d'Aviation au Congo and Les Ciments du Congo. He owns about 14 per cent of the capital of the company for the manufacture in the Congo of metal boxes and all other articles from enamelled sheets, and the same share in the Congo company for the production and trade in pineapples, ANACONGO. In 1952 both Laurence and David Rockefeller participated in acquiring about 30 per cent of Syndicat pour l'Étude Géologique et Minière de la Cuvette Congolaise. All petroleum products used in the Congo continue to be imported from abroad and the giant Rockefeller trust, l'Esso-Standard, created a distribution subsidiary in the Congo in 1956, l'Esso Congo Belge, rechristened Esso Central Africa in 1960. Another subsidiary, the Socony Vacuum Petrol Company and Texas Petroleum, have minority participations in the Société Congolaise d'Entre Posage des Produits de Petrole.

There are some American plywood companies there, such as United States Plywood Corporation, with Agrifor and Korinacongo, and in the Syndicat du Papier. Pluswood Industries has an agreement with Cominière, who have together formed the Société Congolaise Belgo-Americaine pour la Transformation du Bois du Congo—SOCOBELAM. Olin Mathieson Industries, which have interests in the Pouderies Réunies de Belgique, have participated with Union Minière and several other groups of the Société Générale in creating the Société Africaine d'Explosifs—AFRIDEX. Olin Mathieson have a fifth of the capital. Others investing there include the Industrial and Investing Corporation, New York, Armco Steel, Bell Telephone, General Motors and Otis Elevators.

Since 1960 the Bank of America has acquired 20 per cent in the Lambert Bank group's Socobanque; Ford has founded Ford Motors (Congo); Union Carbide has taken a dominant participation in Somilu, created in 1960 to exploit a pyrochlore

213

mine. This mineral contains niobium, a rare metal used in making special steels. David Rockefeller made a tour to the Congo in 1959, for 'information', after which his group took up 1,030 out of 26,000 shares in Société de Recherches et d'Exploitation de Bauxites au Congo—BAUXICONGO. In June 1960 he announced that he would take up about eight per cent of the 65 millions of capital in the Cie du Congo pour le Commerce et l'Industrie and C.C.C.I. Dillon Read & Co. and J. H. Whitney & Co., bankers of New York, have created an investment company to examine the possibilities of American investment in the Congo. This is the American Eurafrican Fund.

Interesting as this American penetration into the Congo is, of more immediate concern is the continuing Belgian domination of so much of the Congo's economy. In *Les Trusts au Congo* by Pierre Joye and Rosine Lewin, a clear picture of the events immediately preceding and following independence is given.

According to their account, the independent State of the Congo, under Leopold II, owned a large part of the capital of the original companies, also of the 'chartered companies' created at the time, and of private enterprises. After the Belgian Government took over the administration of the Congo, these participations were increased in a number of ways: by direct intervention in the creation of new organisms of a 'para-statal' nature; by the arrogation of certain rights as recompense for the concessions they gave; by exercise of right to subscribe to the increase of the capital of companies in which the Congo State already owned shares.

As a result the Belgian Congo held a considerable portfolio of investments which, at the most moderate estimate, were valued at about 40 million francs. In addition it possessed various prerogatives, such as voting rights and the right to nominate representatives to administrative boards, in a whole series of enterprises in which it did not hold capital participations. This portfolio comprised participations and rights in:

1 Enterprises of a 'para-statal' character, such as the Banque Centrale du Congo Belge; the Société de Credit au Colonat;

the Caisse d'Epargne du Congo Belge; the Offices des Cites Africaines O.C.A., OTRACO; the Regie de Distribution d'Eau et d'Electricité Regideso, etc.

2 The chartered companies: Comité Special du Katanga (C.S.K.) Comité National du Kivu (C.N.Ki.); Cie des Chemins de Fer des Grands Lacs.

3 Investment companies like Unatra; Cie du Katanga, etc.

4 Mining companies like Forminière; Mines d'or de Kilo-Moto, etc.

5 Transport enterprises like Cicicongo; Transport en Commun de Leopoldville-Chemin de Fer K.D.L.; Sabena, etc.

6 Production and distribution; undertakings like electrical power, such as Forces de l'Est and Forces du Bas-Congo.

7 Private enterprises in which the Congo held only minority interests.

The possession of this important portfolio permitted the public authorities, in principle, to exercise a considerable influence in the Congo economy and even to control completely certain important sectors. Moreover, official statements justified these participations, declaring that they allowed the State to exercise its role of 'guardian of the public interest and tutor of the natives'.

The example of the C.S.K. is significant in this respect. Leopold II had controlled this semi-public organism by reserving to the State the right to nominate four out of the six members of its administration. But after the taking over of the Congo by Belgium the C.S.K. was, during fifty years, the docile instrument of the Union Minière, although it had every opportunity to control the great Katanga trust. C.S.K. was by far the biggest shareholder of Union Minière, and the statutes elaborated in 1906 officially conferred on it important rights in Union Minière, notably that of designating the administrative council and a certain number of directors. C.S.K. never used these rights, but on the contrary confided its representation to the most obvious leaders of private capital. The hold of the trusts on the Congo administration was total, the more so since the big companies were able to ensure considerable material advantages to the representatives of the State who passed into their service.

Before June 1960 the trusts speeded uptheir manoeuvres to prevent the Congolese people from coming into possession of their patrimony. At the time of the Round Table Conference, the financial press was emphatically insisting on the Belgian government obtaining guarantees from the future Congo Republic. 'In the very first place, it is necessary to shelter the enterprises from eventual nationalisation.' The Congolese nationalist parties were, however, unanimous in opposing the maintenance by the Belgian financial groups of an economic protectorate over the Congo after 30 June 1960.

Consequently, they insisted that the Congo portfolio should be transferred integrally and without conditions to the young Republic, which would be able to make use of the rights arising from it to name its own representatives on the 'para-statal' organisms and, if such should be the case, in the private Congolese companies. It was this which frightened Belgian financial circles; the prospect of seeing the Congo Republic making use of the incontestable rights that the possession of the Congolese portfolio would confer upon it.

To avert this, Raymond Scheyven vainly tried the manoeuvre which was quickly recognised by the Congolese leaders: he proposed to answer the financial needs of the Congo by creating a 'mixed investment company', to which the Congo would confer the management of its portfolio, Belgium on its side bringing an annual contribution of one billion francs. If this attempt failed, the Belgian government was all the happier in the case of the chartered companies, whose dissolution *in extremis* it would decree a few days before 30 June. It also decided to dissolve C.S.K. and C.N.Ki. before Congo acceded to independence.

On the occasion of the Round Table Conference, Scheyven parleyed with certain Congolese delegates, whom he tried to persuade that it would be better if the Belgian government itself proceeded with this measure before 30 June. He made them believe that it was preferable because, if the Congolese government did it afterwards, this could create a bad impression abroad, giving rise to the belief that they had something against the private companies.

The manoeuvre was clever. It was easier to convince the Congolese delegates, since most of them showed an understandable distrust towards the chartered companies. They had only too often had occasion to declare that the companies played the game of the big trusts. As to these, certain Congolese parties had called for the dissolution of the companies and the transfer of their rights to the Congolese State.

The Belgian officials charged with giving technical enlightenment to the participants at the Round Table Conference were openly careful to indicate that the Congo Republic could repay the colonialists for their part, by using in the interests of the Congolese people the prerogatives in the companies which would devolve upon the State.

A hurried decree of 27 June 1960, three days before the proclamation of independence, sanctioned the dissolution of the C.S.K. and the division of its assets between the Congo and the Cie du Katanga. At a stroke the Congo Republic lost the possibility of utilising the powerful instruments of command which it would have disposed of in taking over the direction of the C.S.K. and the prerogatives of the Union Minière were preserved.

Through the intermediary C.S.K., which would have in fact become a Congolese para-statal organism, the Congo Republic would in effect have obtained the statutory right to designate the president of the Katanga trust and a certain number of other directors on its board. And the Congolese government could even have pre-empted its views in the general meetings of the Union Minière, through the C.S.K., which was the biggest shareholder of the company.

The dissolution of the C.S.K. not only lost to the Congo Republic the possibility of benefiting from the prerogatives of this organism. The convention of 27 June 1960 accorded considerable additional advantages to the Cie du Katanga, which received full ownership of a third of the lands improved by the C.S.K. (allotment zones), its real estate and bankings, as well as

217

the right to a third of the rents which were expected in the future from the mineral concessions allocated by C.S.K.

If the ground rights and mineral rights not already conceded revert to the Congo, this restitution of rights over the Congolese land and mineral patrimony will not be effected without compensation, since the convention stipulates that the Congo Republic must pay in compensation a forfeiture indemnity of 100 million to the Cie du Katanga.

The C.N.Ki. was formed for a period which will expire on 31 December 2011. Here again, it would have been sufficient if the Congolese government utilised the rights conferred on it by statute to exercise a preponderant influence in this 'para-state' organism. The Belgian authorities, however, concluded with the officials of the C.N.Ki. a convention which decided that the Belgian Congo would withdraw purely and simply as a concession partner and renounce at the same time all its rights in the association.

A decree issued on 30 May 1960 approved this convention and, by a stroke, C.N.Ki. ceased to be a semi-official organism. On 21 June 1960 its shareholders decided, in addition, to transform it into a common stock company called the Société Belgo-Africaine du Kivu—SOBAKI. This company reserved the right to exploit for its own private profit exclusively the mines of C.N.Ki. as well as the integral property of the portfolio which this organism had constituted. If the public authorities take over the administration of the crown lands, the convention provides that the shareholders of Sobaki shall receive in compensation 'a just indemnity'.

To give an appearance of legality to these conventions, the representatives of the Belgian government declared that they acted 'in accordance with the wishes expressed by the economic, financial and social conference which took place in Brussels in the months of April and May 1960'. In reality, in pronouncing the dissolution of the C.S.K. and the C.N.Ki. the Belgian authorities wanted, above all, to place before the new Congolese State an accomplished fact.

In order to show how indispensable the financial support of Belgium was, the Belgian companies had, in fact, taken care

218

to make massive withdrawals of capital at the same time as they pushed to the maximum the export of Congolese products, and on the other hand, limited to the extreme their imports. The Congolese trade balance resulting from the action gave an exceptionally high surplus in 1959 (13,417 million francs), which did nothing to save the Congo from very great financial difficulties. In fact, a heavy proportion of the sums anticipated from the sale of Congolese products were not returned to the colony, and more than seven billions of private capital left the Congo in the course of the exercise.

These manoeuvres have cost the young African State sad convulsions and have brought it to the edge of chaos. And they have done nothing to resolve the essential problem for the future of the Congo: how to recover from under-development.

16. Monetary zones and foreign banks

THE U.N. Economic Commission for Africa's Standing Committee for Trade has recently described the African continent as 'riddled with different trade regimes and payments systems supplemented in most cases by specific economic ties with countries or groupings of countries outside Africa'.* One of the most effective ways in which Britain and France have retained economic ties with former colonial territories is through action to ensure that the new States remained in the monetary zones centred on London and Paris.

There are seven major currency groups in Africa, the French franc zone, the sterling area, the Belgian franc area, the Spanish peseta and the Portuguese escudo areas, the South African rand area, and the countries like the United Arab Republic and the Congo (Leopoldville), with separate currency units. By far the greater part of Africa's trade comes within the sterling area and the French franc zones of Africa.

The sterling area has been somewhat looser than the franc bloc. For example, Nigeria and Ghana have established their own currencies and their own central banks, though they continue for the most part to keep their international reserves in the form of sterling. When I opened the Bank of Ghana at the end of July 1959, I spoke of the decisive part played by a central bank in the economic life of a country: 'Our political independence will be meaningless unless we use it so as to

* *Background Paper on the Establishment of an African Common Market,* 13 October 1963.

obtain economic and financial self government and independence. In order to obtain this it is of absolute and paramount importance that a central bank should be set up by the Government.' In setting up the Bank of Ghana we obtained assistance from the Bank of England, but our bank has always followed a policy designed to secure our economic independence and to foster the general development of the country. The Bank of Ghana, like other banks, set up in a similar way, has no claim on foreign exchange reserves of England, but has complete control over its own foreign exchange earnings.

The East African Currency Board is the main multinational monetary institution in the sterling area. It embraces Kenya, Tanzania* and Uganda in Africa, and Aden outside the region, with a currency freely convertible at a fixed rate to the pound sterling. The member countries of the Currency Board have no control over domestic money supplies. In the long run these are controlled by export and import levels and foreign investment flows, and in the short, by lending policies of the London banks. Under this arrangement nationally directed growth often leads to a shortage of currency which hinders expansion.

In Britain the names of the 'Big Five' banks are household words. These banks with their immense resources are closely linked with big industrialists to form a small and specially powerful group with world-wide interests. In 1951 the 147 directors of the Big Five banks held between them 1,008 directorships of which 299 were in other financial institutions such as other banks, insurance companies and investment trusts. Many of the biggest companies have directors on the boards of more than one of the big banks. 'The more the interlocking takes place, the less one can say "this one is a financier, and that one is an industrialist". There emerges a group of finance capitalists dominating both finance and industry.'†

The dangers, therefore, of too close ties with foreign banks are apparent. Yet the large participations of foreign banks in African banks may be seen from the following:

* Tanzania has announced plans for its own currency.

† *Monopoly: A Study of British Monopoly Capitalism* by Sam Aaronovitch, p. 54.

Republic of Congo: Crédit Congolais is a subsidiary of Barclay's Bank D.C.O. through its affiliate in Antwerp, the Banque de Commerce; Banque Internationale pour le Commerce et l'Industrie du Congo is a subsidiary of B.N.C.I., Paris, through B.N.C.I. (Afrique); Banque Commerciale Congolaise is a subsidiary of Crédit Lyonnais; Société Générale de Banques au Congo is made up of Bayerische Vereinsbank (5%), Société Générale de Paris (51%), Banco Nazionale del Lavoro, Banque de l'Union Parisienne and Bankers International Corporation (Morgan Guaranty).

Congo (Leopoldville): Banque Internationale pour le Commerce is a subsidiary of B.N.C.I.; Société Congolaise de Banque is also a subsidiary of B.N.C.I.; Banque Belge d'Afrique (Banque de Bruxelles and Brufina); Banque Centrale du Congo Belge et du Ruanda-Urundi (Société Générale de Belgique); Banque du Congo Belge (Société Générale de Belgique and Compagnie du Congo pour le Commerce et l'Industrie); Banque Belgo-Congolaise (Société Générale de Belgique and C.C.C.I.).

Cameroun: Société Camerounaise de Banque (Deutsche Bank (5%) and Crédit Lyonnais); Banque Internationale pour le Commerce et l'Industrie (B.I.C.I. du Cameroun is a subsidiary of B.N.C.I.); Société Générale de Banques en Cameroun is made up of Bayerische Vereinsbank (5%), Société Générale de Paris (51%), Banque de l'Union Parisienne, Banco Nazionale del Lavoro, and Bankers International Corporation (Morgan Guaranty).

Gabon: Union Gabonaise de Banque (Deutsche Bank (10%) and Credit Lyonnais).

Liberia: Bank of Monrovia is owned 100 per cent by First National City Bank of New York (Morgan); Liberian Trading & Development Bank [Mediobanca (60%) and Bankers International Corporation (Morgan)].

Libya: The Sahara Bank (Tripoli) [Bank of America International N.Y., Bank of America, California, Banco de Sicilia, Palerno (Bank of America Associate)].

Central Africa: Union Bancaire en Afrique Centrale is owned by Société Générale de Paris and Crédit Lyonnais.

Nigeria: Barclays Bank D.C.O.; Bank of West Africa; Philip Hill (Nigeria) Ltd. is made up of Philip Hill (40%), Banca Commerciale Italiana (30%), and Crédit Lyonnais (30%); United Bank for Africa [B.N.C.I., Rotterdamsche Bank, Banco Nazionale del Lavoro, and Bankers Trust Corporation (Morgan)]; Nigerian Industrial Development Bank (Chase International Corporation, Bank of America, Northwest International Bank, Irving International Finance Corporation, Bank of Tokyo, Instituto Mobiliare Italiano and Commerzbank have together taken up shares to the value of £480,000; Société Financière pour les Pays d'Outremer is made up of International Finance Corporation (£490,000), Bank of Nigeria (£490,000), Nigerian private investors (£20,000) and the Investment Company of Nigeria (£500,000). A government loan brings total funds up to £4½ million.

Ruanda Burundi: Banque de Ruanda Urundi is a subsidiary of B.N.C.I.

Sudan: Nilein Bank (Banque des Deux Nils) is a subsidiary of Crédit Lyonnais.

Ivory Coast: Société Générale de Banques en Côte d'Ivoire is made up of Bayerische Vereinsbank, Société Générale de Paris, Banque de l'Union Parisienne, Banco Nazionale del Lavoro, and Bankers International Corporation (Morgan Guaranty); Banque Ivoirienne de Crédit is a subsidiary of Crédit Lyonnais; B.I.C.I. du Côte d'Ivoire is a subsidiary of B.N.C.I. and Société Ivoirienne de Banque is made up of Deutsche Bank (16%), Crédit Lyonnais (42%), International Banking Corporation (16%), Banca Commerciale Italiana (16%), and Ivory Coast Government (10%).

Dahomey: Société Dahomienne de Banque is a subsidiary of Crédit Lyonnais.

Mali: Banque Malienne de Crédit et de Dépôts is a subsidiary of Crédit Lyonnais.

Morocco: Banque Franco-Suisse pour le Maroc is made up of Swiss Bank Corporation (50%) and Crédit Commercial de France (50%); Banque Nationale pour le Developpement Economique is made up of Deutsche Bank, Banco Nazionale del Lavoro, and Commerzbank;

Caisse Marocaine des Marchés is part-owned by Crédit Foncier de France; Banque Fonçière du Maroc is part owned by Crédit du Nord; Banque Commerciale du Maroc is made up of Cie Industrielle et Commercial (C.I.C.), Credit Lyonnais du Maroc, Union Africaine et Financière Maroc, and Union Européenne Industrielle et Financière.

Tchad: Banque Tchadienne de Crédit et de Dépôts (Government of Tchad and Crédit Lyonnais).

Tunisia: Union Bancaire pour le Commerce et l'Industrie (B.N.C.I. and Banco di Roma); Banque de Tunisie (C.I.C.); Union Internationale de Banque (Société Tunisienne de Banques, Banca Commerciale Italiana, Commerzbank, and Bank of America); Banque d'Escompte et de Crédit à l'Industrie en Tunisie (B.E.I.T.) is made up of Banque Industrielle pour l'Afrique du Nord (Banque de l'Indochine, 5%), International Banking Corporation (Morgan Guaranty), and Comptoir National d'Escompte de Paris.

Madagascar: Banque Malgache d'Escompte et de Crédit (Malagasy Government and Comptoir National d'Escompte de Paris).

South Africa: In addition to Barclays D.C.O., Crédit Lyonnais, and other big U.K. and French banks, there are French Bank of South Africa (Banque de l'Indochine), First National City Bank of New York (S.A.) Ltd., Banque Commerciale Africaine (C.I.C., 12,631 shares) and the Standard Bank.

In addition, there are a number of other banks functioning throughout Africa, such as the British Bank of the Middle East, which operates in Tunisia and Morocco and Libya, and National and Grindlays Bank, with branches and agencies in the Somali Republic. A recently established bank is the Merchant Bank of Central Africa, which is a creation of the Rothschild Banking group. The Banque Lambert has a participation as well as Mediobanca.

Reports of important French banks for their financial year 1963-4 indicate the way in which they are adapting themselves to the new conditions of independent States without losing any of their former influence. The following report of the Comptoir

National d'Escompte de Paris appeared in *Le Monde*, 16 June 1964:

'We have asserted in a new form our policy in Africa. We opened in April, as we indicated last year, the Banque d'Escompte et de Crédit à l'Industrie en Tunisie (B.E.I.T.) which we have founded in Tunis with the Banque Industrielle de l'Afrique du Nord (B.I.A.N.) and the Morgan Guaranty International Banking Corporation; this new establishment has taken over our local branches and those of the B.I.A.N. We also decided to create, with the Malagasy Government, the Banque Malgache d'Escompte et de Crédit (B.A.M.E.S.) to which we have since ceded our agencies in Madagascar, and which is presided over by a Malagasy personality, administered by a joint board and managed by our representative. We hope to give to this traditional sector of our influence a new drive and to emphasise thereby the position which we have held in Madagascar since 1885. In Algeria we are retaining only an agency in Algiers, where in spite of the circumstances we have maintained some activity.'

Three days earlier, on 13 June 1964, *Le Monde* contained a report of the activities of Credit Lyonnais:

'In Morocco we have during the month of February 1963, with the help of the Banque Marocaine du Commerce Extérieur, proceeded to transform our agencies into a company under Moroccan law. The B.M.C.E.E. has taken up an important participation in the registered capital of six million dirhams of the new company, which functions under the registered title of Crédit Lyonnais-Maroc.

In Tunisia, where our agencies have obtained satisfactory results, the conversations taken up with the Société Tunisienne de Banque, the Banca Commerciale Italiana, the Commerzbank A.G. and the Bank of America have ended in the creation of the Union Internationale de Banques, with a capital of 700,000 dinars, which has taken over with effect from 2 January 1964 the working of our agencies.

With the association of the Republic of Chad there was created in February 1963 the Banque Tchadienne de Crédit et de Dépôts, with a capital of 100 million francs CFA. These two participations help to complete our representation in black Africa, where our establishment is now interested in eleven banking companies.'

The French have maintained close monetary ties with the countries of former French West Africa and French Equatorial Africa. The Banque Centrale des Etats de l'Afrique de l'Ouest (B.C.E.A.O.) controls the currencies of Mauritania, Senegal, Ivory Coast, Upper Volta, Dahomey and Niger. The currency issued by the bank is still called the CFA franc, but now, instead of 'Colonies Francaises d'Afrique', the initials mean 'Communauté Financière Africaine'. National monetary commissions have been set up in the various States, and there is a limited degree of African representation on the administrative council.

The same does not apply to the Banque Centrale des Etats de l'Afrique Equatoriale et du Cameroun (B.C.E.A.C.) which is concerned with the Congo (Brazzaville), Gabon, the Central African Republic, Chad and Cameroun. The national monetary commissions have the same powers as those in former French West Africa, but central bank administrators sit on them, and the administrative council is composed of Frenchmen.

As a research group of the Department of Economics in the University of Ghana has pointed out, 'the most significant feature of these currency blocs is that the foreign exchange reserves of the franc zone countries are still pooled in France itself. They are estimated individually for each member, but cannot be drawn upon beyond a certain margin of credit governed in each case by a bilateral agreement with the French government. Local monetary policy, exchange control and duty policy . . . must operate within the framework of this central allocation by the French.'

Certain former French colonies, Tunisia, Morocco, Algeria, Mali and Guinea have, since independence, established their own banks and currencies, but they have pegged their currencies to the franc.

The existence of separate monetary zones is having a harmful effect on the growth of trade in Africa. It is leading to illegal trade and revenue losses in many countries and makes an African Common Market difficult. Like the old, artificial political boundaries which are a relic of the colonial period, the various monetary zones help to emphasise differences when the independent African States should all be working for unified economic development. They perpetuate links with former colonial powers and strengthen the forces of neo-colonialism.

A significant step forward in continental economic co-operation was taken in September 1964, when the African Development Bank was founded. Its headquarters are at Abidjan, Ivory Coast, and its membership is limited to independent African governments. All powers of the Bank rest in the Board of Governors, each Governor being a representative of a member state. The aim of the Bank is to accelerate the economic development and social progress of its member countries, and to accomplish this, the Bank is author-ised to promote the investment of public and private capital in Africa.

While foreign private investment must be encouraged, it must be carefully regulated so that it is directed to important growth sectors without leaving control of such sectors in foreign hands. Here again, we see the need for unified plan-ning. With the support of a Union government and a continental code to govern foreign investment the African Development Bank would be able to accelerate the stimulus it is already giving to the economic development of the continent.

17. New industries: the effects on primary producing countries

THE second world war, fought as it was on an almost global scale, called for scientific and inventive genius in unprecedented measure, all towards one end: that of destruction. The need for vast quantities of equipment and the supply services that were ancillary to the purpose of wiping out people and cities, animated, as peace never did, governmental support for investigation and research into faster and more rational means of mass production. The United States, which became the prime arsenal and provider for its Western allies, was naturally foremost in adjusting its industrial machinery to the new methods at the close of the war. Since then the demands made by the reconstruction of ruined cities and the rebuilding of disjointed economies have accelerated the trend. The policy of containment, military adventures such as Vietnam, Cyprus and Korea, cold war stock-piling and the race in rocket assembly and space-ship building have added their quota. Automation and the use of electronics are fast spreading and, as in America, taking hold wherever large-scale production finds it more profitable to replace human labour by push-button thinly-manned mechanisms.

The resulting tremendous bound forward in productive potential has created an increasing demand for the base materials of industry, and there has sprung up a rapidly enlarging assortment of synthetic raw materials, many of them

228

supplementing natural products and often replacing them. This is having an effect upon the market prices of natural primary products, a fact given prominence by the chairman of Union Minière du Haut Katanga at the 1964 shareholders' meeting. The London Metal Exchange, the body which still operates the world prices of metals, is largely under the influence of the leading producers and processors like Union Minière itself, and its associates Rhodesian Selection Trust, Conzinc-Rio Tinto, Amalgamated Metal Corporation, Minerais et Metaux and London Tin Corporation.

Cocoa users, for their part, are constantly threatening the producing countries that they will use synthetic substitutes and rubber-growing countries are up against the increasing use of the artificial product. Just as the high quotations and fluctuations of primary products are influenced by the monopoly producers, so the threat of the use of synthetics is no idle warning, since the controllers of the natural products are also the major producers of the artificial materials. For the same reason, the producers of synthetics will be careful not to compete too vigorously with the natural products. For example, it has been alleged that Dunlop were slow to begin synthetic rubber manufacturing because of their large plantation interests in Malaya.

All four of the American rubber-producing giants, Firestone, B. F. Goodrich, Goodyear and United States Rubber, are engaged in the production of artificial rubber. United States Rubber works 90,000 acres of rubber plantations in Malaya and Indonesia, as well as concessions in Brazil, Venezuela, Colombia and other Latin American countries. Its synthetic rubber and related plants, with the exception of that at Naugatuck, Connecticut, are placed, like those of its textile division, in the southern States of America, where labour is cheaper than in the north. In 1962 there was 'significant expansion' of the company's plastics facilities, under which the production capacity of its 'Kralastic' material was increased. This is described as a 'tough plastic-rubber blend', for which growing uses are being found in automobiles and various appliances, all formerly using rubber.

Goodyear, among the first twenty companies in the United States, has its own rubber plantations in Indonesia, Costa Rica, Brazil and Guatemala. It operates synthetic rubber plants at Houston, Texas and Akron, Ohio. A 30 per cent increase was made in the company's facilities for research in rubber, plastics and other scientific exploration in 1961, for the company has become interested in chemicals and aeronautics.

Firestone is a byword in West Africa where, until the recent advent of iron-ore exploiting companies, it dominated the economy of Liberia. It is still 'King of Rubber' there and, like other rubber giants, gets its rubber also from plantations in the Latin American countries, as well as Ceylon. It has fifty-eight plants throughout the United States, including four for synthetic rubber and one working on what is described as 'U.S. national defence'. Another fifty-three plants are spread around the world, principally in the western hemisphere.

B. F. Goodrich Company runs to the same form but, if anything, has wider plastics interests, since it is a producer of vinyl resins under the trade mark Geon, and among a long list of subsidiaries and other holdings controls British Geon, in collaboration with the Distillers Company, a combine controlling the whisky and gin trade of Great Britain, with over a hundred subsidiary companies engaged in biochemicals, industrial alcohol, plastics, magnesium alloys for jet engines, and many other operations. BTR Industries, which controls among other companies British Tyre & Rubber Company and the International Synthetic Rubber Company, is included in Goodrich's affiliates. Rubber plantations worked by the Goodrich Company are to be found in Liberia as well as in Latin America and Malaya. This company is tied up with A.K.U. (Algemene Kunstzijde Unie) of Holland, in a company that manufactures synthetic rubber for special purposes, and controls the important French rubber manufacturers, Kleber-Colombes. Like Firestone and United States Rubber, it also has companies in Japan.

These and the other main international rubber companies, such as the Italian Pirelli, the German companies, Continental and Phoenix, the French Michelin and Kleger-Colombes, and

230

the British Dunlop, more or less complete the small circle of trusts that dominate the world's production of rubber. They are all engaged in artificial rubber-making and the manufacture of other synthetics. The furious advertising that goes on in every country of the world to push their individual products leaves no doubt about their keen competition for markets, and all of them have factories as well as a multitude of agents and representatives spread across the globe.

This brief review of the rubber monopolies illustrates their inter-relations and their domination of both natural and synthetic rubber throughout the world. It becomes increasingly obvious as we delve deeper into the operations of the industrial monopolies that they have the developing countries at a complete disadvantage.

As providers of novel basic products for old and new industries on a continually extending scale, the highly industrialised countries are the major investors in and concessionaires for the starting materials that are obtained primarily from largely sub-industrialised sources. Among these we include Australia and the more advanced Canada, which are, for all practical purposes, financial colonies of American-dominated Western capital.

Because of the extremely high capital costs involved in discovering and bringing to perfection new products and their uses and in establishing plants and factories for their manufacture and processing, the production of these synthetic materials has become the monopoly of a few mammoth international organisations like Imperial Chemical Industries (I.C.I.), Du Pont de Nemours, Union Carbide, Courtaulds, Snia Viscosa, Montecatini, A.K.U., Unilever, the tripartite group of the former I. G. Farben—Bayer, Hoechst and B.A.S.F. —Dow Chemical, Texas Gulf Sulphur, Lonza and Seichime. The important Japanese offspring of the Mitsui complex, Toyo Rayon Company, is linked to the major American and European giants, Du Pont, I.C.I. and Montecatini by patent arrangements, Du Pont having taken a direct interest in the company during the American occupation of Japan immediately after the war. These giants join forces at certain focal points in the struggle for domination. All the time they carry on a ferocious competi-

231

tion to secure monopoly markets and original source material supplies, not only for synthetics production but for the metallurgical, electronics and nuclear industries that have become part and parcel of their post-war expansion. It is not surprising therefore that even a cursory glance at their interests should reveal involvement in African raw materials' exploitation, even though their financial shufflings may appear superficially to be very far away from such engagements.

When Courtauld's merger with I.C.I. was mooted in 1961 it had 'world-wide repercussions', which is not surprising when its own ramifications are reviewed and I.C.I.'s weight in the industrial and commercial markets of the world is recognised. Representing over 30 per cent of the British chemical industry, I.C.I. does 88 per cent of its turnover overseas in some fifty countries. Its issued capital is several times larger than the budget of most African States, standing at the end of 1962 at £303,393,910, larger even than that of South Africa, the continent's most industrialised country. From chemicals, dyestuffs, paints, pharmaceuticals, fibres, plastics, heavy organic chemicals, explosives and fertilisers this vast organisation created a new holding company in 1962, Imperial Metal Industries Ltd., in order, so runs the company's literature, to achieve a greater concentration of effort on a side of the company's business which is materially different from its main chemical manufacturing activities: namely, its non-ferrous metal interests other than aluminium. In the latter field I.C.I. is linked on a fifty-fifty basis in Imperial Aluminium with Alcoa (Aluminium Company of America), the empire of the Mellon interests.

Imperial Metal Industries has an interest in Extended Surface Tube Company. So has Stewarts & Lloyds, a £60 million company working basic and foundry pig iron up to tubes of all varieties. Through subsidiaries, associated companies and agents throughout the world, Stewarts & Lloyds has a stake in all the international markets. Among these are a 70 per cent interest in Stewarts & Lloyds of South Africa Ltd., which controls six companies operating in South-West Africa, Rhodesia and South Africa itself; and a 13 per cent holding in the major steel conversion project in Zambia, the Rhodesian Iron &

Steel Company, a subsidiary of Rhodesian Anglo American Ltd., which is controlled by Anglo American of South Africa. Stewarts & Lloyds have come up against American monopoly competition in South Africa, where their subsidiary had been negotiating for some months with United States and so-called Brazilian groups for establishing a plant beside its existing one at Vereeniging, near Johannesburg. The Americans and their Brazilian vassals were trying to jump the gun by enforcing a clause which would reduce the Stewarts & Lloyds participation from 51 per cent to 25 per cent in the event that the steel industry in the United Kingdom becomes nationalised or, in the opinion of the two outside partners, is likely to be nationalised.

I.C.I. is assisting the South African Government in building up its chemical and armaments industries through I.C.I. (South Africa) Ltd. and African Explosives & Chemical Industries, in which it partners De Beers. African Explosives will be supplying from its constructing complex at Sasolburg many of the materials for providing polymers to the nylon spinning plant which is being erected by British Nylon Spinners at a cost of £3 million on the site purchased by it in 1963 at Belville, near Cape Town. The Rhodesian subsidiary of African Explosives is behind the proposed £2 million fertiliser plant to be built at Livingstone, Zambia, with the backing of the government, in connection with which the company is constructing another plant at Dorowa, Rhodesia, for the exploitation of phosphate deposits.

Consumption of fuel and power and common minerals has jumped phenomenally since the war and the western capitalist countries as well as Japan have resorted to non-industrialised countries for quickly growing quantities. Before the war the industrialised countries relied largely upon their own reserves of iron ores or on those of other Western sources. Today the giant iron and steel corporations of Europe, America and Japan, in addition to their investments in Canada and Australia, are turning more and more for their base materials to Africa, where cheap labour, tax concessions and supporting government policies have opened up avenues of richer profits from huge,

233

untapped resources. M. D. Banghart, vice-president of New-mont Mining, a leading American holding company with semi-permanent investments in mining and crude oil, has said that American firms could make a greater profit in Africa than from any comparable investment in the United States. Mr Banghart should know intimately what he is talking about, since New-mont Mining is joined in consortia operating the biggest exploitative undertakings in northern and southern Africa, such as the O'Okiep Copper Co., the Tsumeb Corporation, Palabora Mining, Soc. N.A. du Plomb and Soc. des Mines de Zellidja. It has a 12·1 per cent participation in Cyprus Mines, which gives it a vested interest in maintaining Cyprus for the NATO cause. The fact that United States miners earn an average of $2.70 an hour against the less than 10 cents average paid to African miners in South Africa makes it obvious how such super-profits are achieved. No wonder Newmont's original investment in Tsumeb multiplied twenty times in value in the space of three years.

The African countries are faced with the need to turn sub-sistence economies into organisms that will generate viable and improved conditions of living for their populations. However, many African governments, instead of getting together in united action which would stimulate maximum capital accumu-lation and the construction of a solid over-all African economy, are granting concessions for the working of mineral, agricultural and forestry resources whose purpose is the drawing off of output to sustain and enlarge the industries and economies of the imperialist countries. Not one of the investing syndicates has any intention of founding in any one of these countries an integrated industrial complex that would give impetus to genuine economic growth. Nor are the returns on the export of primary products from mining, agriculture and forestry likely to provide to any important extent the looked-for capital for investing in industrial foundation.

Returns to source countries on exports of primary products are niggardly by comparison with the profits made by the monopoly concessionaires, who are both sellers and processors. A fair example to take in this connection might be Union

Minière. In Katanga it operates over 34,000 square kilometres of concessions, on which it works three copper mines, one copper and zinc mine, five copper and cobalt mines, an iron mine and a limestone quarry. All of these are linked by road and railways owned by the company. First stage concentrates of copper, cobalt and zinc are milled at six plants. The company owns four electricity generating plants which work the foundry at Lubumbashi and the electrolysis plants at Jadotville-Shituru and Kolwezi-Luilu for the refining of copper and cobalt, of which it produced 295,236 tons and 9,683 tons respectively in 1962. The bulk of the copper and cobalt, however, go in concentrate form to the electrolytic refinery of its associate, Ste Générale Métallurgique de Hoboken, Brussels, which also treats the radium residues and uranium metals from Katanga, as well as refining the germanium also coming from the Union Minière production. The zinc is sent forward from Katanga in the form of raw concentrate.

The Katanga output is shipped through the Congo by the Cie des Chemins de Fer Katanga-Dilolo-Leopoldville, and overseas by the Cie Maritime Congolaise. Insurance is covered by the Cie Congolaise d'Assurances, the Cie Belge d'Assurances Maritimes or Ste Auxiliaire de la Royale Union Coloniale Belge. Banking is done through the Ste Belge de Banque, the Banque du Congo Belge, the Belgian-American Banking Corporation. Staff is flown in and out by Sabena. Union Minière has holdings in all of them, and many others as well.

It is the habit of these great monopolies—and we must remember that Union Minière is the world's third producer of copper and its first of cobalt—to fix prices to suit their ideas of profit, subject to certain swings on the world markets, which frequently they operate and rig. Production at less than full capacity and the holding back of supplies are tactics that are often used. Most copper producers have, for the past three years, been operating at no more than 85 per cent capacity, but are now returning gradually to fuller output. Following the strike at Mufulira during 1963, Rhodesian Selection Trust ran its plant at full capacity in order to replenish its stocks, but restricted its sales to 85 per cent. At the end of 1963 there was

235

estimated to be some 300,000 tons a year of idle mine capacity throughout the world as a result of the voluntary restriction of output. Stocks accumulated outside the United States, in order to support prices, were put at 130,000 to 150,000 tons. The price had been stabilised at around £234 a ton for 1962/63. Demand for copper having risen, stocks were exhausted by mid-January 1964 and the price rose on the London Metal Exchange. Rhodesian producers, however, stepped up their price to £236, and from the remarks made by Union Minière's chairman it would appear that the Exchange was forced into line, even though the producers were reducing their output cutback to 10 per cent. Despite the strike, and reduced output, turnover and net profits of Rhodesian Selection Trust were higher in 1963 than in 1962 and considerably above those of 1960, when prices were higher. Turnover in 1960 was £31,019,000; in 1962, £46,298,000; and in 1963, £50,931,000. Profits after tax were £7,600,000 for 1960; £7,735,000 for 1962; and £8,273,000 for 1963. This was the result of the offloading of stocks.

We constantly read about the high prices that are earned for copper, tin, zinc and so forth. What is little understood is that these are the prices for the commodities on the industrial market in their processed forms. The metals leave the countries of their origin mainly in their primary condition of ores or concentrates and sometimes in the first stage transformation, which fetch merely token returns to these countries. The returns are even more paltry when measured against the values that are added the moment the materials are placed on board the transportation carrier at the point of exit; the carrier usually, as we have seen in the case of Union Minière, being related directly or indirectly with the actual producer. The many more surpluses that accrue in the course of transit from producing country to the foreign transformation centres and through the subsequent stages of conversion fall to the concessionary combines and the shipping, transport, banking, insurance, manufacturing and selling organisations with which, in most cases, they are linked. As Victor Perlo dramatically summarises in *American Imperialism*, 'weak countries, without adequate industry to build ships and airplanes, must pay tolls to the imperialist transportation monopolies for the goods they import and export. Countries without adequate financial resources must pay fees to the centres of finance capital for the use of banking facilities and for insurance' (p. 62).

Amounts remaining behind in the producing countries in the form of wages are sadly fractional. Over 50 per cent of the Congo's national income went regularly to European residents and foreign firms. The rest remained to be distributed over the various sectors of the economy. It is not surprising that the territory's 14 million inhabitants live in the extremest poverty. In Gabon one-third of the income goes to the non-African population. Two-fifths of Liberia's total income accrues to foreign firms (U.N. Report E/CN.14/246, 7 January 1964). And when independent African countries attempt to establish a certain rectification by levelling taxes on company profits, they draw resentment that is echoed in dire warnings in the imperialist press that they will stifle foreign investment if they continue such encroachments upon expatriate rights.

'Ashanti hit by Ghana tax,' shouted a paragraph headline in a London City journal dated 28 January 1964, and set forth figures to show that Ghana Government taxation had cut Ashanti Goldfields 1962/63 profits from £1,111,162 to £609,142. Nevertheless the company was still able to declare a total dividend of 37½ per cent, a fall obviously from the 50 per cent and over that had been kept up for several previous years, but still a whacking return on an original capital of £250,000 which had been built up to its present £3 million from reserves out of past and current profits. That the company was able to pay the dividend is proof of the nicely cushioned reserves that have been accumulated over a period of operations, in addition to what has been drawn back into capital.

Diamonds are bringing some extra revenue to the West African countries out of new selling arrangements which are taking some of the profit that formerly went to CAST (Consolidated African Selection Trust) and its De Beers' principals. Ghana has its own diamond market and a government marketing board which takes the commission which used to go to middlemen acting for De Beers. In Sierra Leone CAST profits were higher, but a service fee paid to the government board 'under protest' and higher production costs cut them somewhat. Nevertheless, CAST was able to declare a final dividend that left the total dividend for the year 1962/63 unchanged at 3s. 6d. on a 5s. share (70 per cent), of which there were 18,198,654 issued and paid up out of 20 million authorised. This issued capital, amounting to £4,549,663 10s. was achieved in less than twenty years out of reserves made from an original capital of £250,000. Furthermore, stocks of diamonds held by the group at the end of the working year had an estimated value of £6 million.

Further profits are forced out of Africa in the form of the inflated cost of finished goods, equipment and services she is forced to buy from the monopoly sources that extract the prime materials. This is the big squeeze in which Africa is caught, one that grew tighter from the eve of the first world war. It was estimated by United Nations experts that the dependent countries had to pay $2.5 to $3 billion more for their imports of manufactured goods in 1947 than they would have had to pay if price ratios were the same as in 1913. For the period from 1950 to 1961, according to the Food and Agricultural Organisation of the U.N., the index of returns for primary materials fell from 97 to 91 (70 for cocoa, coffee and tea), while that for manufactured goods rose from 86 to 110. For steel, which is an indispensable commodity on an increasing scale for developing countries, it reaches the very much higher figure of 134. In terms of exchange as between primary producing countries and the exporters of manufactured goods, there has been a decline in ten years from 113 to 82, to the disadvantage of the former. The value of Ghana's exports in 1962 was the same as that for exports in 1961, but the volume had increased by about six per cent. The value of imports in 1962 was reduced by 16 per cent but the volume fell by only 14 per cent. In the Congo Republic (Brazzaville), while 1962 saw an increase of 77 per cent in exports over 1961, and imports declined by 15 per cent, the value of the exports hardly covered half the value of the imports (E/CN.14/239, Part A, December 1963).

18. The mechanisms of neo-colonialism

In order to halt foreign interference in the affairs of developing countries it is necessary to study, understand, expose and actively combat neo-colonialism in whatever guise it may appear. For the methods of neo-colonialists are subtle and varied. They operate not only in the economic field, but also in the political, religious, ideological and cultural spheres.

Faced with the militant peoples of the ex-colonial territories in Asia, Africa, the Caribbean and Latin America, imperialism simply switches tactics. Without a qualm it dispenses with its flags, and even with certain of its more hated expatriate officials. This means, so it claims, that it is 'giving' independence to its former subjects, to be followed by 'aid' for their development. Under cover of such phrases, however, it devises innumerable ways to accomplish objectives formerly achieved by naked colonialism. It is this sum total of these modern attempts to perpetuate colonialism while at the same time talking about 'freedom', which has come to be known as *neo-colonialism*.

Foremost among the neo-colonialists is the United States, which has long exercised its power in Latin America. Fumblingly at first she turned towards Europe, and then with more certainty after world war two when most countries of that continent were indebted to her. Since then, with methodical thoroughness and touching attention to detail, the Pentagon set about consolidating its ascendancy, evidence of which can be seen all around the world.

Who really rules in such places as Great Britain, West Germany, Japan, Spain, Portugal or Italy? If General de Gaulle is 'defecting' from U.S. monopoly control, what interpretation can be placed on his 'experiments' in the Sahara desert, his paratroopers in Gabon, or his trips to Cambodia and Latin America?

Lurking behind such questions are the extended tentacles of the Wall Street octopus. And its suction cups and muscular strength are provided by a phenomenon dubbed 'The Invisible Government', arising from Wall Street's connection with the Pentagon and various intelligence services. I quote:

'The Invisible Government . . . is a loose amorphous grouping of individuals and agencies drawn from many parts of the visible government. It is not limited to the Central Intelligence Agency, although the CIA is at its heart. Nor is it confined to the nine other agencies which comprise what is known as the intelligence community: the National Security Council, the Defense Intelligence Agency, the National Security Agency, Army Intelligence, Navy Intelligence and Research, the Atomic Energy Commission and the Federal Bureau of Investigation.

The Invisible Government includes also many other units and agencies, as well as individuals, that appear outwardly to be a normal part of the conventional government. It even encompasses business firms and institutions that are seemingly private.

To an extent that is only beginning to be perceived, this shadow government is shaping the lives of 190,000,000 Americans. An informed citizen might come to suspect that the foreign policy of the United States often works publicly in one direction and secretly through the Invisible Government in just the opposite direction.

This Invisible Government is a relatively new institution. It came into being as a result of two related factors: the rise of the United States after World War II to a position of pre-eminent world power, and the challenge to that power by Soviet Communism. . . .

By 1964 the intelligence network had grown into a massive hidden apparatus, secretly employing about 200,000 persons and spending billions of dollars a year.'*

Here, from the very citadel of neo-colonialism, is a description of the apparatus which now directs all other Western intelligence set-ups either by persuasion or by force. Results were achieved in Algeria during the April 1961 plot of anti-de Gaulle generals; as also in Guatemala, Iraq, Iran, Suez and the famous U-2 spy intrusion of Soviet air space which wrecked the approaching Summit, then in West Germany and again in East Germany in the riots of 1953, in Hungary's abortive crisis of 1959, Poland's of September 1956, and in Korea, Burma, Formosa, Laos, Cambodia and South Vietnam; they are evident in the trouble in Congo (Leopoldville) which began with Lumumba's murder, and continues till now; in events in Cuba, Turkey, Cyprus, Greece, and in other places too numerous to catalogue completely.

And with what aim have these innumerable incidents occurred? The general objective has been mentioned: to achieve colonialism in fact while preaching independence.

On the economic front, a strong factor favouring Western monopolies and acting against the developing world is international capital's control of the world market, as well as of the prices of commodities bought and sold there. From 1951 to 1961, without taking oil into consideration, the general level of prices for primary products fell by 33·1 per cent, while prices of manufactured goods rose 3·5 per cent (within which, machinery and equipment prices rose 31·3 per cent). In that same decade this caused a loss to the Asian, African and Latin American countries, using 1951 prices as a basis, of some $41,400 million. In the same period, while the volume of exports from these countries rose, their earnings in foreign exchange from such exports decreased.

Another technique of neo-colonialism is the use of high rates of interest. Figures from the World Bank for 1962 showed that

* *The Invisible Government*, David Wise and Thomas B. Ross, Random House, New York, 1964.

241

seventy-one Asian, African and Latin American countries owed foreign debts of some $27,000 million, on which they paid in interest and service charges some $5,000 million. Since then, such foreign debts have been estimated as more than £30,000 million in these areas. In 1961, the interest rates on almost three-quarters of the loans offered by the major imperialist powers amounted to more than five per cent, in some cases up to seven or eight per cent, while the call-in periods of such loans have been burdensomely short.

While capital worth $30,000 million was exported to some fifty-six developing countries between 1956 and 1962, it is estimated that interest and profit alone extracted on this sum from the debtor countries amounted to more than £15,000 million. This method of penetration by economic aid recently soared into prominence when a number of countries began rejecting it. Ceylon, Indonesia and Cambodia are among those who turned it down. Such 'aid' is estimated on the annual average to have amounted to $2,600 million between 1951 and 1955; $4,007 million between 1956 and 1959, and $6,000 million between 1960 and 1962. But the average sums taken out of the aided countries by such donors in a sample year, 1961, are estimated to amount to $5,000 million in profits, $1,000 million in interest, and $5,800 million from non-equivalent exchange, or a total of $11,800 million extracted against $6,000 million put in. Thus, 'aid' turns out to be another means of exploitation, a modern method of capital export under a more cosmetic name.

Still another neo-colonialist trap on the economic front has come to be known as 'multilateral aid' through international organisations: the International Monetary Fund, the International Bank for Reconstruction and Development (known as the World Bank), the International Finance Corporation and the International Development Association are examples, all, significantly, having U.S. capital as their major backing. These agencies have the habit of forcing would-be borrowers to submit to various offensive conditions, such as supplying information about their economies, submitting their policy and plans to review by the World Bank and accepting agency

supervision of their use of loans. As for the alleged development, between 1960 and mid-1963 the International Development Association promised a total of $500 million to
applicants, out of which only $70 million were actually
received.

In more recent years, as pointed out by Monitor in *The
Times*, 1 July 1965, there has been a substantial increase in
communist technical and economic aid activities in developing
countries. During 1964 the total amount of assistance offered
was approximately £600 million. This was almost a third of
the total communist aid given during the previous decade. The
Middle East received about 40 per cent of the total, Asia 36 per
cent, Africa 22 per cent and Latin America the rest.

Increased Chinese activity was responsible to some extent
for the larger amount of aid offered in 1964, though China
contributed only a quarter of the total aid committed; the
Soviet Union provided a half, and the East European countries
a quarter.

Although aid from socialist countries still falls far short of
that offered from the west, it is often more impressive, since
it is swift and flexible, and interest rates on communist loans
are only about two per cent compared with five to six per cent
charged on loans from western countries.

Nor is the whole story of 'aid' contained in figures, for there
are conditions which hedge it around: the conclusion of commerce and navigation treaties; agreements for economic
co-operation; the right to meddle in internal finances, including
currency and foreign exchange, to lower trade barriers in
favour of the donor country's goods and capital; to protect
the interests of private investments; determination of how the
funds are to be used; forcing the recipient to set up counterpart
funds; to supply raw materials to the donor; and use of such
funds—a majority of it, in fact—to buy goods from the donor
nation. These conditions apply to industry, commerce, agriculture, shipping and insurance, apart from others which are
political and military.

So-called 'invisible trade' furnishes the Western monopolies
with yet another means of economic penetration. Over 90 per

cent of world ocean shipping is controlled by the imperialist countries. They control shipping rates and, between 1951 and 1961, they increased them some five times in a total rise of about 60 per cent, the upward trend continuing. Thus, net annual freight expenses incurred by Asia, Africa and Latin America amount to no less than an estimated $1,600 million. This is over and above all other profits and interest payments. As for insurance payments, in 1961 alone these amounted to an unfavourable balance in Asia, Africa and Latin America of some additional $370 million.

Having waded through all this, however, we have begun to understand only the *basic* methods of neo-colonialism. The full extent of its inventiveness is far from exhausted.

In the labour field, for example, imperialism operates through labour arms like the Social Democratic parties of Europe led by the British Labour Party, and through such instruments as the International Confederation of Free Trade Unions (ICFTU), now apparently being superseded by the New York Africa-American Labour Centre (AALC) under AFL-CIO chief George Meany and the well-known CIA man in labour's top echelons, Irving Brown.

In 1945, out of the euphoria of anti-fascist victory, the World Federation of Trade Unions (WFTU) had been formed, including all world labour except the U.S. American Federation of Labor (AFL). By 1949, however, led by the British Trade Union Congress (TUC), a number of pro-imperialist labour bodies in the West broke away from the WFTU over the issue of anti-colonialist liberation, and set up the ICFTU.

For ten years it continued under British TUC leadership. Its record in Africa, Asia and Latin America could gratify only the big international monopolies which were extracting super-profits from those areas.

In 1959, at Brussels, the United States AFL-CIO union centre fought for and won control of the ICFTU Executive Board. From then on a flood of typewriters, mimeograph machines, cars, supplies, buildings, salaries and, so it is still averred, outright bribes for labour leaders in various parts of the developing world rapidly linked ICFTU in the minds

244

of the rank and file with the CIA. To such an extent did its prestige suffer under these American bosses that, in 1964, the AFL-CIO brains felt it necessary to establish a fresh outfit. They set up the AALC in New York right across the river from the United Nations.

'As a steadfast champion of national independence, democracy and social justice', unblushingly stated the April 1965 Bulletin put out by this Centre, 'the AFL-CIO will strengthen its efforts to assist the advancement of the economic conditions of the African peoples. Toward this end, steps have been taken to expand assistance to the African free trade unions by organising the African-American Labour Centre. Such assistance will help African labour play a vital role in the economic and democratic upbuilding of their countries.'

The March issue of this Bulletin, however, gave the game away: 'In mobilising capital resources for investment in Workers Education, Vocational Training, Co-operatives, Health Clinics and Housing, the Centre will work with both private and public institutions. It will also *encourage labour-management co-operation to expand American capital investment in the African nations.*' The italics are mine. Could anything be plainer?

Following a pattern previously set by the ICFTU, it has already started classes: one for drivers and mechanics in Nigeria, one in tailoring in Kenya. Labour scholarships are being offered to Africans who want to study trade unionism in—of all places—Austria, ostensibly by the Austrian unions. Elsewhere, labour, organised into political parties of which the British Labour Party is a leading and typical example, has shown a similar aptitude for encouraging 'Labour-management co-operation to expand . . . capital investment in African nations.'

But as the struggle sharpens, even these measures of neo-colonialism are proving too mild. So Africa, Asia and Latin America have begun to experience a round of coups d'état or would-be coups, together with a series of political assassinations which have destroyed in their political primes some of the newly emerging nations' best leaders. To ensure success in these endeavours, the imperialists have made widespread and wily use of ideological and cultural weapons in the form of intrigues, manoeuvres and slander campaigns.

Some of these methods used by neo-colonialists to slip past our guard must now be examined. The first is retention by the departing colonialists of various kinds of privileges which infringe on our sovereignty: that of setting up military bases or stationing troops in former colonies and the supplying of 'advisers' of one sort or another. Sometimes a number of 'rights' are demanded: land concessions, prospecting rights for minerals and/or oil; the 'right' to collect customs, to carry out administration, to issue paper money; to be exempt from customs duties and/or taxes for expatriate enterprises; and, above all, the 'right' to provide 'aid'. Also demanded and granted are privileges in the cultural field; that Western information services be exclusive; and that those from socialist countries be excluded.

Even the cinema stories of fabulous Hollywood are loaded. One has only to listen to the cheers of an African audience as Hollywood's heroes slaughter red Indians or Asiatics to understand the effectiveness of this weapon. For, in the developing continents, where the colonialist heritage has left a vast majority still illiterate, even the smallest child gets the message contained in the blood and thunder stories emanating from California. And along with murder and the Wild West goes an incessant barrage of anti-socialist propaganda, in which the trade union man, the revolutionary, or the man of dark skin is generally cast as the villain, while the policeman, the gum-shoe, the Federal agent—in a word, the CIA-type spy—is ever the hero. Here, truly, is the ideological under-belly of those political murders which so often use local people as their instruments.

While Hollywood takes care of fiction, the enormous monopoly press, together with the outflow of slick, clever, expensive magazines, attends to what it chooses to call 'news'. Within separate countries, one or two news agencies control the news handouts, so that a deadly uniformity is achieved, regardless of the number of separate newspapers or magazines; while internationally, the financial preponderance of the United

States is felt more and more through its foreign correspondents and offices abroad, as well as through its influence over international capitalist journalism. Under this guise, a flood of anti-liberation propaganda emanates from the capital cities of the West, directed against China, Vietnam, Indonesia, Algeria, Ghana and all countries which hack out their own independent path to freedom. Prejudice is rife. For example, wherever there is armed struggle against the forces of reaction, the nationalists are referred to as rebels, terrorists, or frequently 'communist terrorists'!

Perhaps one of the most insidious methods of the neo-colonialists is evangelism. Following the liberation movement there has been a veritable riptide of religious sects, the overwhelming majority of them American. Typical of these are Jehovah's Witnesses who recently created trouble in certain developing countries by busily teaching their citizens not to salute the new national flags. 'Religion' was too thin to smother the outcry that arose against this activity, and a temporary lull followed. But the number of evangelists continues to grow.

Yet even evangelism and the cinema are only two twigs on a much bigger tree. Dating from the end of 1961, the U.S. has actively developed a huge ideological plan for invading the so-called Third World, utilising all its facilities from press and radio to Peace Corps.

During 1962 and 1963 a number of international conferences to this end were held in several places, such as Nicosia in Cyprus, San José in Costa Rica, and Lagos in Nigeria. Participants included the CIA, the U.S. Information Agency (USIA), the Pentagon, the International Development Agency, the Peace Corps and others. Programmes were drawn up which included the systematic use of U.S. citizens abroad in virtual intelligence activities and propaganda work. Methods of recruiting political agents and of forcing 'alliances' with the U.S.A. were worked out. At the centre of its programmes lay the demand for an absolute U.S. monopoly in the field of propaganda, as well as for counteracting any independent efforts by developing states in the realm of information.

The United States sought, and still seeks, with considerable success, to co-ordinate on the basis of its own strategy the propaganda activities of all Western countries. In October 1961, a conference of NATO countries was held in Rome to discuss problems of psychological warfare. It appealed for the organisation of combined ideological operations in Afro-Asian countries by all participants.

In May and June 1962 a seminar was convened by the U.S. in Vienna on ideological warfare. It adopted a secret decision to engage in a propaganda offensive against the developing countries along lines laid down by the U.S.A. It was agreed that NATO propaganda agencies would, in practice if not in the public eye, keep in close contact with U.S. Embassies in their respective countries.

Among instruments of such Western psychological warfare are numbered the intelligence agencies of Western countries headed by those of the United States 'Invisible Government'. But most significant among them all are Moral Re-Armament (MRA), the Peace Corps and the United States Information Agency (USIA).

Moral Re-Armament is an organisation founded in 1938 by the American, Frank Buchman. In the last days before the second world war, it advocated the appeasement of Hitler, often extolling Himmler, the Gestapo chief. In Africa, MRA incursions began at the end of World War II. Against the big anti-colonial upsurge that followed victory in 1945, MRA spent millions advocating collaboration between the forces oppressing the African peoples and those same peoples. It is not without significance that Moise Tshombe and Joseph Kasavubu of Congo (Leopoldville) are both MRA supporters. George Seldes, in his book *One Thousand Americans*, characterised MRA as a fascist organisation 'subsidised by . . . Fascists, and with a long record of collaboration with Fascists the world over. . . .' This description is supported by the active participation in MRA of people like General Carpentier, former commander of NATO land forces, and General Ho Ying-chin, one of Chiang Kai-shek's top generals. To cap this, several newspapers, some of them in the Western world, have claimed that MRA is actually subsidised by the CIA.

When MRA's influence began to fail, some new instrument to cover the ideological arena was desired. It came in the establishment of the American Peace Corps in 1961 by President John Kennedy, with Sargent Shriver, Jr., his brother-in-law, in charge. Shriver, a millionaire who made his pile in land speculation in Chicago, was also known as the friend, confidant and co-worker of the former head of the Central Intelligence Agency, Allen Dulles. These two had worked together in both the Office of Strategic Services, U.S. war-time intelligence agency, and in the CIA.

Shriver's record makes a mockery of President Kennedy's alleged instruction to Shriver to 'keep the CIA out of the Peace Corps'. So does the fact that, although the Peace Corps is advertised as a voluntary organisation, all its members are carefully screened by the U.S. Federal Bureau of Investigation (FBI).

Since its creation in 1961, members of the Peace Corps have been exposed and expelled from many African, Middle Eastern and Asian countries for acts of subversion or prejudice. Indonesia, Tanzania, the Philippines, and even pro-West countries like Turkey and Iran, have complained of its activities.

However, perhaps the chief executor of U.S. psychological warfare is the United States Information Agency (USIA). Even for the wealthiest nation on earth, the U.S. lavishes an unusual amount of men, materials and money on this vehicle for its neo-colonial aims.

The USIA is staffed by some 12,000 persons to the tune of more than $130 million a year. It has more than seventy editorial staffs working on publications abroad. Of its network comprising 110 radio stations, 60 are outside the U.S. Programmes are broadcast for Africa by American stations in Morocco, Eritrea, Liberia, Crete, and Barcelona, Spain, as well as from off-shore stations on American ships. In Africa alone, the USIA transmits about thirty territorial and national radio programmes whose content glorifies the U.S. while attempting to discredit countries with an independent foreign policy.

The USIA boasts more than 120 branches in about 100

countries, 50 of which are in Africa alone. It has 250 centres in foreign countries, each of which is usually associated with a library. It employs about 200 cinemas and 8,000 projectors which draw upon its nearly 300 film libraries.

This agency is directed by a central body which operates in the name of the U.S. President, planning and co-ordinating its activities in close touch with the Pentagon, CIA and other Cold War agencies, including even armed forces intelligence centres.

In developing countries, the USIA actively tries to prevent expansion of national media of information so as itself to capture the market-place of ideas. It spends huge sums for publication and distribution of about sixty newspapers and magazines in Africa, Asia and Latin America.

The American government backs the USIA through direct pressures on developing nations. To ensure its agency a complete monopoly in propaganda, for instance, many agreements for economic co-operation offered by the U.S. include a demand that Americans be granted preferential rights to disseminate information. At the same time, in trying to close the new nations to other sources of information, it employs other pressures. For instance, after agreeing to set up USIA information centres in their countries, both Togo and Congo (Leopoldville) originally hoped to follow a non-aligned path and permit Russian information centres as a balance. But Washington threatened to stop all aid, thereby forcing these two countries to renounce their plan.

Unbiassed studies of the USIA by such authorities as Dr R. Holt of Princeton University, Retired Colonel R. Van de Velde, former intelligence agents Murril Dayer, Wilson Dizard and others, have all called attention to the close ties between this agency and U.S. Intelligence. For example, Deputy Director Donald M. Wilson was a political intelligence agent in the U.S. Army. Assistant Director for Europe, Joseph Philips, was a successful espionage agent in several Eastern European countries.

Some USIA duties further expose its nature as a top intelligence arm of the U.S. imperialists. In the first place, it is expected to analyse the situation in each country, making recommendations to its Embassy, thereby to its Government, about changes that can tip the local balance in U.S. favour. Secondly, it organises networks of monitors for radio broadcasts and telephone conversations, while recruiting informers from government offices. It also hires people to distribute U.S. propaganda. Thirdly, it collects secret information with special reference to defence and economy, as a means of eliminating its international military and economic competitors. Fourthly, it buys its way into local publications to influence their policies, of which Latin America furnishes numerous examples. It has been active in bribing public figures, for example in Kenya and Tunisia. Finally, it finances, directs and often supplies with arms all anti-neutralist forces in the developing countries, witness Tshombe in Congo (Leopoldville) and Pak Hung Ji in South Korea. In a word, with virtually unlimited finances, there seems no bounds to its inventiveness in subversion.

One of the most recent developments in neo-colonialist strategy is the suggested establishment of a Businessmen Corps which will, like the Peace Corps, act in developing countries. In an article on 'U.S. Intelligence and the Monopolies' in *International Affairs* (Moscow, January 1965), V. Chernyavsky writes: 'There can hardly be any doubt that this Corps is a new U.S. intelligence organisation created on the initiative of the American monopolies to use Big Business for espionage'.

It is by no means unusual for U.S. Intelligence to set up its own business firms which are merely thinly disguised espionage centres. For example, according to Chernyavsky, the C.I.A. has set up a firm in Taiwan known as Western Enterprises Inc. Under this cover it sends spies and saboteurs to South China. The New Asia Trading Company, a CIA firm in India, has also helped to camouflage U.S. intelligence agents operating in South-east Asia.

Such is the catalogue of neo-colonialism's activities and methods in our time. Upon reading it, the faint-hearted might come to feel that they must give up in despair before such an array of apparent power and seemingly inexhaustible resources.

251

Fortunately, however, history furnishes innumerable proofs of one of its own major laws: that the budding future is *always* stronger than the withering past. This has been amply demonstrated during every major revolution throughout history.

The American Revolution of 1776 struggled through to victory over a tangle of inefficiency, mismanagement, corruption, outright subversion and counter-revolution the like of which has been repeated to some degree in every subsequent revolution to date.

The Russian Revolution during the period of Intervention, 1917 to 1922, appeared to be dying on its feet. The Chinese Revolution at one time was forced to pull out of its existing bases, lock stock and barrel, and make the unprecedented Long March; yet it triumphed. Imperialist white mercenaries who dropped so confidently out of the skies on Stanleyville after a plane trip from Ascension Island thought that their job would be 'duck soup'. Yet, till now, the nationalist forces of Congo (Leopoldville) continue to fight their way forward. They do not talk of *if* they will win, but only of *when*.

Asia provides a further example of the strength of a people's will to determine their own future. In South Vietnam 'special warfare' is being fought to hold back the tide of revolutionary change. 'Special warfare' is a concept of General Maxwell Taylor and a military extension of the creed of John Foster Dulles: let Asians fight Asians. Briefly, the technique is for the foreign power to supply the money, aircraft, military equipment of all kinds, and the strategic and tactical command from a General Staff down to officer 'advisers', while the troops of the puppet government bear the brunt of the fighting. Yet in spite of bombing raids and the immense build-up of foreign strength in the area, the people of both North and South Vietnam are proving to be unconquerable.

In other parts of Asia, in Cambodia, Laos, Indonesia, and now the Philippines, Thailand and Burma, the peoples of ex-colonial countries have stood firm and are winning battles against the allegedly superior imperialist enemy. In Latin America, despite 'final' punitive expeditions, the growing armed insurrections in Colombia, Venezuela and other countries continue to consolidate gains.

In Africa, we in Ghana have withstood all efforts by imperialism and its agents; Tanzania has nipped subversive plots in the bud, as have Brazzaville, Uganda and Kenya. The struggle rages back and forth. The surging popular forces may still be hampered by colonialist legacies, but nonetheless they advance inexorably.

All these examples prove beyond doubt that neo-colonialism is *not* a sign of imperialism's strength but rather of its last hideous gasp. It testifies to its inability to rule any longer by old methods. Independence is a luxury it can no longer afford to permit its subject peoples, so that even what it claims to have 'given' it now seeks to take away.

This means that neo-colonialism *can* and *will* be defeated. How can this be done?

Thus far, all the methods of neo-colonialists have pointed in one direction, the ancient, accepted one of all minority ruling classes throughout history—*divide and rule*.

Quite obviously, therefore, *unity* is the first requisite for destroying neo-colonialism. Primary and basic is the need for an all-union government on the much divided continent of Africa. Along with that, a strengthening of the Afro-Asian Solidarity Organisation and the spirit of Bandung is already under way. To it, we must seek the adherence on an increasingly formal basis of our Latin American brothers.

Furthermore, all these liberatory forces have, on all major issues and at every possible instance, the support of the growing socialist sector of the world.

Finally, we must encourage and utilise to the full those still all too few yet growing instances of support for liberation and anti-colonialism inside the imperialist world itself.

To carry out such a political programme, we must all back it with national plans designed to strengthen ourselves as independent nations. An external condition for such independent development is neutrality or *political non-alignment*. This has been expressed in two conferences of Non-Aligned Nations during the recent past, the last of which, in Cairo in 1964, clearly and inevitably showed itself at one with the rising forces of liberation and human dignity.

And the preconditions for all this, to which lip service is often paid but activity seldom directed, is to develop ideological clarity among the anti-imperialist, anti-colonialist, pro-liberation masses of our continents. They, and they alone, make, maintain or break revolutions.

With the utmost speed, neo-colonialism must be analysed in clear and simple terms for the full mass understanding by the surging organisations of the African peoples. The All-African Trade Union Federation (AATUF) has already made a start in this direction, while the Pan-African Youth Movement, the women, journalists, farmers and others are not far behind. Bolstered with ideological clarity, these organisations, closely linked with the ruling parties where liberatory forces are in power, will prove that neo-colonialism is the symptom of imperialism's weakness and that it is defeatable. For, when all is said and done, it is the so-called little man, the bent-backed, exploited, malnourished, blood-covered fighter for independence who decides. And he invariably decides for freedom.

Conclusion

In the Introduction I attempted to set out the dilemma now facing the world. The conflict between rich and poor in the second half of the nineteenth century and the first half of the twentieth, which was fought out between the rich and the poor in the developed nations of the world ended in a compromise. Capitalism as a system disappeared from large areas of the world, but where socialism was established it was in its less developed rather than its more developed parts and, in fact, the revolt against capitalism had its greatest successes in those areas where early neo-colonialism had been most actively practised. In the industrially more developed countries, capitalism, far from disappearing, became infinitely stronger. This strength was only achieved by the sacrifice of two principles which had inspired early capitalism, namely the subjugation of the working classes within each individual country and the exclusion of the State from any say in the control of capitalist enterprise.

By abandoning these two principles and substituting for them 'welfare states' based on high working-class living standards and on a State-regulated capitalism at home, the developed countries succeeded in exporting their internal problem and transferring the conflict between rich and poor from the national to the international stage.

Marx had argued that the development of capitalism would produce a crisis within each individual capitalist State because within each State the gap between the 'haves' and the 'have nots'

255

would widen to a point where a conflict was inevitable and that it would be the capitalists who would be defeated. The basis of his argument is not invalidated by the fact that the conflict, which he had predicted as a national one, did not everywhere take place on a national scale but has been transferred instead to the world stage. World capitalism has postponed its crisis but only at the cost of transforming it into an international crisis. The danger is now not civil war within individual States provoked by intolerable conditions within those States, but international war provoked ultimately by the misery of the majority of mankind who daily grow poorer and poorer.

When Africa becomes economically free and politically united, the monopolists will come face to face with their own working class in their own countries, and a new struggle will arise within which the liquidation and collapse of imperialism will be complete.

As this book has attempted to show, in the same way as the internal crisis of capitalism within the developed world arose through the uncontrolled action of national capital, so a greater crisis is being provoked today by similar uncontrolled action of international capitalism in the developing parts of the world. Before the problem can be solved it must at least be understood. It cannot be resolved merely by pretending that neo-colonialism does not exist. It must be realised that the methods at present employed to solve the problem of world poverty are not likely to yield any result other than to extend the crisis.

Speaking in 1951, the then President of the United States, Mr Truman, said, 'The only kind of war we seek is the good old fight against man's ancient enemies . . . poverty, disease, hunger and illiteracy.' Sentiments of a similar nature have been re-echoed by all political leaders in the developed world but the stark fact remains: whatever wars may have been won since 1951, none of them is the war against poverty, disease, hunger and illiteracy. However little other types of war have been deliberately sought, they are the only ones which have been waged. Nothing is gained by assuming that those who express such views are insincere. The position of the leaders of the developed capitalist countries of the world are, in relation to the great neo-colonialist international financial combines, very similar to that which Lord Macaulay described as existing between the directors of the East India Company and their agent, Warren Hastings, who, in the eighteenth century, engaged in the wholesale plunder of India. Macaulay wrote:

'The Directors, it is true, never enjoined or applauded any crime. Far from it. Whoever examines their letters written at the time will find there are many just and humane sentiments, many excellent precepts, in short, an admirable code of political ethics. But each exultation is modified or nullified by a demand for money. . . . We by no means accuse or suspect those who framed these dispatches of hypocrisy. It is probable that, written 15,000 miles from the place where their orders were to be carried into effect, they never perceived the gross inconsistency of which they were guilty. But the inconsistency was at once manifest to their lieutenant in Calcutta. . . . Hastings saw that it was absolutely necessary for him to disregard either the moral discourses or the pecuniary requisitions of his employers. Being forced to disobey them in something, he had to consider what kind of disobedience they would most readily pardon; and he correctly judged that the safest course would be to neglect the sermons and to find the rupees.'

Today the need both to maintain a welfare state, i.e. a parasite State at home, and to support a huge and ever-growing burden of armament costs makes it absolutely essential for developed capitalist countries to secure the maximum return in profit from such parts of the international financial complex as they control. However much private capitalism is exhorted to bring about rapid development and a rising standard of living in the less developed areas of the world, those who manipulate the system realise the inconsistency between doing this and producing at the same time the funds necessary to maintain the sinews of war and the welfare state at home. They know when it comes to the issue they will be excused if they fail to provide for a world-wide rise in the standard of living. They know they will never be forgiven if they betray the system and produce a crisis at home which either destroys the affluent State or interferes with its military preparedness.

Appeals to capitalism to work out a cure for the division of the world into rich and poor are likely to have no better result than the appeals of the Directors of the East India Company to Warren Hastings to ensure social justice in India. Faced with a choice, capitalism, like Hastings, will come down on the side of exploitation.

Is there then no method of avoiding the inevitable world conflict occasioned by an international class war? To accept that world conflict is inevitable is to reject any belief in co-existence or in the policy of non-alignment as practised at present by many of the countries attempting to escape from neo-colonialism. A way out is possible.

To start with, for the first time in human history the potential material resources of the world are so great that there is no need for there to be rich and poor. It is only the organisation to deploy these potential resources that is lacking. Effective world pressure can force such a redeployment, but world pressure is not exercised by appeals, however eloquent, or by arguments, however convincing. It is only achieved by deeds. It is necessary to secure a world realignment so that those who are at the moment the helpless victims of a system will be able in the future to exert a counter pressure. Such counter pressures do not lead to war. On the contrary, it is often their absence which constitutes the threat to peace.

A parallel can be drawn with the methods by which direct colonialism was ended. No imperial power has ever granted independence to a colony unless the forces were such that no other course was possible, and there are many instances where independence was only achieved by a war of liberation, but there are many other instances when no such war occurred. The very organisation of the forces of independence within the colony was sufficient to convince the imperial power that resistance to independence would be impossible or that the political and economic consequences of a colonial war outweighed any advantage to be gained by retaining the colony.

258

In the earlier chapters of this book I have set out the argument for African unity and have explained how this unity would destroy neo-colonialism in Africa. In later chapters I have explained how strong is the world position of those who profit from neo-colonialism. Nevertheless, African unity is something which is within the grasp of the African people. The foreign firms who exploit our resources long ago saw the strength to be gained from acting on a Pan-African scale. By means of interlocking directorships, cross-shareholdings and other devices, groups of apparently different companies have formed, in fact, one enormous capitalist monopoly. The only effective way to challenge this economic empire and to recover possession of our heritage, is for us also to act on a Pan-African basis, through a Union Government.

No one would suggest that if all the peoples of Africa combined to establish their unity their decision could be revoked by the forces of neo-colonialism. On the contrary, faced with a new situation, those who practise neo-colonialism would adjust themselves to this new balance of world forces in exactly the same way as the capitalist world has in the past adjusted itself to any other change in the balance of power.

The danger to world peace springs not from the action of those who seek to end neo-colonialism but from the inaction of those who allow it to continue. To argue that a third world war is not inevitable is one thing, to suppose that it can be avoided by shutting our eyes to the development of a situation likely to produce it is quite another matter.

If world war is not to occur it must be prevented by positive action. This positive action is within the power of the peoples of those areas of the world which now suffer under neo-colonialism but it is only within their power if they act at once, with resolution and in unity.

Bibliography

Aaronovitch, Sam, *Monopoly: a study of British Monopoly Capitalism*, Lawrence & Wishart, London, 1955

African-American Labour Centre (AALC), *Bulletins*, March and April, 1965

Chernyavsky, V., *United States Intelligence and the Monopolies*, International Affairs, Moscow, January, 1965

Clausewitz, *Vom Krieg*, 1832

Cole, Monica Mary, *South Africa*, Methuen, London, 1961

Coston, Henry, *L'Europe des Banquiers*, Collection 'Documents et Témoinages', La Librairie Française, 1963

Courteney, Frederic Charles, *Economic Aid to Under-developed Countries*, Oxford University Press, London, 1961

Department of Economics, *The Economics of African Unity*, University of Ghana, 1964

Dizard, Wilson P., *The Strategy of Truth: the Story of the United States Information Service*, Public Affairs Press, 1961

Dutt, Rajani Palme, *British Colonial Policy and Neo-colonialist Rivalries*, International Affairs, Moscow, April, 1965

Hilferding, Rudolf, *Marx Studien, Volume* 3: *Das Finanz-kapital*, Vienna, 1910

Hobson, J. A., *Imperialism*, London, 1902

Holt, Robert T., and Van de Velde, Robert, W., *Strategic Psychological Operations and American Foreign Policy*, University of Chicago Press, Chicago, 1960

Jeanneney Report, *La Politique de Coopération avec les Pays en Voie de Développement*, 1964

Joye, Pierre, and Lewin, Rosine, *Les Trusts au Congo*, Société Populaire d'Editions, Brussels, 1961

Lenin, *Imperialism: the Highest Stage of Capitalism*, 1916

Macaulay, Thomas Babington, *Warren Hastings*, Edinburgh Review, October, 1841

Machyo, B. Chango, *Aid and Neo-colonialism*, Africania Study Group, 1964

Marx, *Capital*, 1867

Nkrumah, Kwame, *Africa Must Unite*, Heinemann, London, 1963

Park, L. C. and F. W., *The Anatomy of Big Business*, Toronto Progress Books, 1962

Perlo, Victor, *American Imperialism*, International Publishers, New York, 1951

Perlo, Victor, *The Empire of High Finance*, International Publishers, New York, 1957

Report of the United Nations Economic Commission for Africa, *Part 3: Industrial Growth in Africa*, New York, 1963

Reports of the Economic Commission for Africa Industrial Co-ordination Missions to different regions of Africa

Seldes, George, *One Thousand Americans*, Boni & Gaer, New York, 1947

Statistical Abstract of the United States, 1962

United Nations Economic Commission for Africa's Standing Committee for Trade, *Background Paper on the Establishment of an African Common Market*, 13 October 1963

United Nations Report, *E/CN* 14/239, *Part A*, December, 1963

United Nations Report, *E/CN* 14/246, 7 January 1964

United Nations *Statistical Year Book*, 1945, 1959, 1960

Wilson, Harold, *The War on World Poverty: an Appeal to the Conscience of Mankind*, Gollancz, London, 1953

Wise, David, and Ross, Thomas B., *The Invisible Government*, Random House, New York, 1964

Reference is made to the following company reports:

Anglo American Corporation, AGM, 1962
Anglo-Transvaal Consolidated Investment Company, Annual Address, 6 December 1963
Consolidated African Gold Fields of South Africa Corporation, AGM, 30 June 1961
Grangesberg, Annual Report, 18 May 1962
Harmony Gold Mining Co. Ltd., AGM, June, 1961
Rand Selection Corporation Ltd., 71st AGM, 26 February 1963
M. Samuel & Co., AGM, 1963
Société Générale, Report for 1962

Reference *passim* to the following newspapers and periodicals:

The Economist, Europe (France) Outremer (November 1961), *Nouvel Observateur, The Financial Times, Fortune, International Affairs, Le Monde, Modern Government* (March/April, 1962), *New Commonwealth, The Sunday Times, Wall Street Journal, West Africa*

Index

263

265

19

269

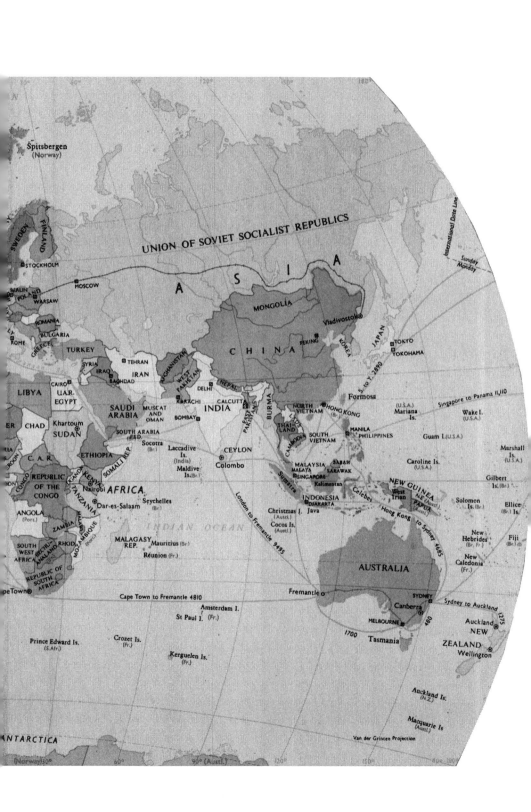